Waking
Immortal Within

*Develop your Spiritual Presence,
Awaken the Inner Master and
Explore Hidden Realities*

By Eric Pepin

*Higher Balance Publishing
Portland, Oregon*

*This book has been transcribed and compiled from live
lectures given by Eric Pepin. Some elements of the live format
have been preserved.*

Published by Higher Balance Institute
515 NW Saltzman Road #726, Portland, Oregon 97229
www.higherbalance.com

ISBN: 978-1-939410-14-6

Library of Congress Control Number: 2014939777
Waking the Immortal Within/ Eric Pepin

Published 2014.

Printed in the United States of America.

Other Books by Eric Pepin

Intro: The Handbook of the Navigator: *What is God, the Psychic Connection to Spiritual Awakening, and the Conscious Universe*

1: Meditation within Eternity: *The Modern Mystics Guide to Gaining Unlimited Spiritual Energy, Accessing Higher Consciousness and Meditation Techniques for Spiritual Growth*

2: Igniting the Sixth Sense: *The Lost Human Sensory that Holds the Key to Spiritual Awakening and Unlocking the Power of the Universe*

3: Silent Awakening: *True Telepathy, Effective Energy Healing and the Journey to Infinite Awareness*

4: Waking the Immortal Within: *Develop your Spiritual Presence, Awaken the Inner Master and Explore Hidden Realities*

5: Coming Soon Summer 2014

6: Coming Soon Fall 2014

7: Coming Soon Winter 2014

Books by Higher Balance

Bending God: A Memoir

To discover more techniques and knowledge from Eric Pepin, and to experience awakening yourself beyond what is discussed in this book, visit:

www.higherbalance.com/experience

ADD TO YOUR EXPERIENCE
READERS ONLY FREE MATERIAL

As a reader you receive special reader-only bonus material you can download for free. You will get new tools and knowledge to enhance all the practices found in the book.

Receive:

Babbler Beater: Eliminating 'Brain Babble' is one of the most important aspects of any meditation. It is the deciding factor to whether you experience hyper-dimensional states of consciousness or simply relax. This sound tool was designed to eliminate babble and assist in training the techniques in this book.

Energy Movements: Apply the techniques on energy movements with ease with simple, instructional videos featuring Eric Pepin. There are 3 videos, which show you how to begin enhancing your sensory and amplifying your field of personal energy.

Higher Balance Method: An entire 3 part, 2 hour, special course led by Eric Pepin on beginner and advanced practices for the meditation technique taught in this book. Called the Higher Balance Method, this extra course gives you entirely new information that continues where *Waking the Immortal Within* leaves off.

Go to *www.wakingtheimmortalwithin.com/readers-only*

"Truth is by nature self-evident.
As soon as you remove the cobwebs
of ignorance that surround it,
It shines clear."

—*Mahatma Gandhi*

EDITORS' NOTE

The knowledge contained between the covers of this book was originally presented to a live audience. The audio was then transcribed by a group of volunteers and those transcriptions were edited by a different group of volunteers. We all felt an enormous drive to get this valuable information "out there." Please keep in mind that none of the volunteers are professionals. We did the very best we could out of love and dedication for The Force, our Guru, and future generations of spiritual seekers, like YOU!

You may come across redundancies throughout this book. This was done intentionally. In order to reach the most listeners or readers, Eric presents his knowledge in several different ways so you can fully grasp the essence of the information. We also understand that some people are visual learners while others prefer audio. If you learn by listening, you can go on line to Higher Balance.com to order the modules separately.

One last thing; these teachings are multi-layered and some of it may not make sense until you reflect and ponder it. In the classroom, Eric is a dynamic, charismatic teacher, full of astounding energy. As students, we understand that Eric shifts multi-dimensionally and teaches on many different levels of understanding. His classes are very powerful.

If you read this book a 2nd or 3rd time you may read something that you swear wasn't there before. This happened frequently to the four of us while editing. As your mind begins to unfold with new revelations, you will grasp deeper layers of the same information. In other words, your understanding will continually evolve and you will grow exponentially.

It is our hope that your achievements surpass your greatest dreams,

Loretta, Viny, Ray, and Diane

Acknowledgements

Effort is the Universal currency. The greatest accomplishments are a direct result of the effort put forth; the greater the effort, the greater the accomplishment. It is with sincere gratitude and appreciation to the following Navigators that I present this book.

Editing team:

Loretta Huinker, lead editor
Viny D'Errico, assistant lead editor
Ray Ross, editor
Diane Pfaff, editor
Justin Schramm, editor
Deborah DeWet, technical assistance

Proofreaders:

Steve Pfaff, Katherine Malone, and Keerin DeWet

Higher Balance staff for their contributions:

Eric Robison, Matthew Robison, Frank Kramer, Jamison Priebe, Thomas Rutledge, and Jesse Borsheim

And to all the Navigators who helped with the original transcription of the audio modules into print for this book.

TABLE OF CONTENTS

INTRODUCTION

IN MY PREVIOUS three books, you've learned the difference between the mind and the brain. You've achieved that level of understanding, which is a pretty incredible feat in and of itself. Not everyone can do that. Most people just don't have the perception to recognize there is a difference between their brain, or who they are physically, and their mind, or who they truly are.

You've reached that level of understanding and you can acknowledge that fine line of separation. It may be subtle now, but as your awareness is heightened and you begin to contemplate the finer details and complexities of your consciousness, the subtlety will transform into a dramatic distinction.

Can you not already feel the difference between who you are when you're at work or with your family and friends, and who you are when you're meditating or doing something spiritual? Many spiritualists understand and acknowledge the difference, but they lack the necessary tools to dissect their own identity. It's not enough to intellectually understand the information; you have to begin to dissect your "ego" self in order to extract your *true-self*. Only then will you be a master of your consciousness and be able to separate who you *really* are from who you *think* you are.

In order to be who you are meant to be and to fulfill your life's purpose, you have to go beyond the brain. After all, the organic brain is very limited to what it can accomplish. It's anchored to this physical world, and it has masked your *true-self* with a multitude of other identities meant for this world, this existence. Without these identities, you can't fully experience this dimension, and with them, you can't experience the spiritual realm.

The solution is to shed the "I's," temporarily, by realizing what they are and how they function. These identities are really just *constructs of your organic brain*, meant to keep you functioning within the confines of the Matrix, the Gaia mind. As a White Cell, you're driven to achieve your highest potential in your journey to the Source, the consciousness of God.

To reach the Source, it's imperative that you first remove yourself from the Matrix. Your brain is a product of the Matrix, as are all of the identities your brain has constructed for you. So, in essence, to reach the higher states of consciousness, you have to remove who and what your brain wants you to be. As a product of the Matrix, your brain wants you to remain here and simply function along with everyone else. It doesn't have the ability to explore the other dimensions. It can't gain entrance ...

But, your mind can.

Now, it's time to journey beyond the limitations of your brain and become who and what you're meant to be.

Good Journeys,
Eric Pepin

PREFACE

The Navigator . . .

I had become fixated on my feet with each step I made, pressing them into the twigs and gravel on the broken steep path I followed. Their rhythm became a respite for my mind that clashed with an occasional reminder of burning calves and lungs as I climbed the steep path upwards.

Sunlight was restricted on this side of the mountain, just cooler temperatures and scattered shadows amongst the trees. I always find that eerily enchanting, but it also allows my mind needed time to unwind its complexities.

And then there it was, the moment I had been waiting for. For me, it is not the view I am searching for but rather what it delivers to me, the moment of emotional shifting. I knew it would last and it could only be felt once at that exact moment or it would be lost.

Allowing my five senses to indulge, I quietly remained in the rear, waiting for what I needed. To be embraced even for a fleeting moment...

My physical aches faded away as my eyes beheld the view and triggered my body's lungs to unconsciously, deeply indulge the air. This is not an ordinary breath, but a magical one, and I knew to catch its rare winds and ride them to the fringes of my soul.

My eyes were witnessing the curtain being pulled,

for the forest trees were parting and giving way to the setting sun's last light. We all know there is no greater moment on Earth than the few moments of golden rays metamorphosing into pastels of red, orange, yellow and then pink. My moment was also gifted with the perfect presence of white bulging clouds creating the coveted Vanilla skies.

All of my genetic ancestry released the endorphins to please my body. I felt the second breath automate and draw in deeply and unconsciously as "I" silently waited on the fringe when it began. At first, it was a steady soft high pitch tone and as I allowed it to move upon me, it immersed me with its thunderous presence.

Looking outward from behind my eyes, I saw what they saw, the setting sun's colors and the trance it evokes on us. But I was searching for something more. The colors of the sky are ever changing, never the same at any moment. They have depth like an ocean but rather a sky. The third breath had begun and automated its draw inward and with that moment I escaped into the Planes of Light.

Existing in two places at one time, even though I knew I couldn't stay, time slowed and I savored it, healed and became whole.

I find these moments ingrained within the architecture of life. When walking by a home and hearing old time tunes playing in the distance, children talking to themselves in play, my dog lying asleep and silently raising his head staring lovingly at me, a grandmother brushing her hair in soft evening lights. When you grow old, I promise you that you will not remember the names of people and places but rather the emotions you felt and that is what you will take with you when you leave.

They can only be felt by the Navigator within your chest and they are meant to heal you on your journey through this place. A gift from God to say, "You are not of this place but home is ever present if you choose to experience it."

You are never alone for God is ever with you. You are loved and needed and have purpose. Try to be mindful and you will learn to read in-between the lines.

When you are lost, your Navigator can always find your way home.

You simply have to choose to do so,

For the Universe – God – would never abandon you.

Eric Pepin

Chapter 1

DISCOVERING THE ONE

YOU ARE NOT who you think you are. That you already know. You are a part of a greater being, but you don't know how to find that other part of yourself. You don't know how that other being thinks because you have a physical body with an organic brain. Your brain takes on many different identities. When you are at work, you have one personality. When you are at home with your family, you have another personality, and when you are out with friends, you have another personality that is separate from the others. These aspects of your personality may be similar to each other or very different. I call each of these individual facets of a person an 'I'.

You have many, many, 'I's, and they all play numerous roles. For instance, you go into a restaurant because you're hungry. That's an 'I'. Your 'I' informs you that it wants to eat – and it wants to eat now! Assume that when you go into the restaurant, the whole place is packed. The hostess tells you that you can either wait for a table or take a seat at the bar. You notice that the chairs at the bar are stiff, metal chairs, but the ones at the tables are soft and welcoming. Your hunger 'I' wants immediate gratification. But you also have a comfort 'I' that wants to wait for a table with comfortable chairs. A higher level 'I' must now intervene to settle the dispute between these two competing 'I's.

'I's can be very simple, or they can build themselves up and become more complex. For example, the 'I' that seeks food might be simple, but the 'I' you maintain at work could be more complex. You use another identity when you are with your family, but when you are with family and coworkers at the same time, a mixed 'I' is created. The 'I's collect energy and grow stronger when you spend more time with them. However, if you choose to not inhabit certain 'I's, they will wither and become weaker.

There are different levels of me as a teacher and how I integrate with the rest of the world. When I am with my students, they know who and what I am. They have seen my different identities and have experienced them during class or from being around me for a period of time. They know there is something more to me than what appears on the outside. I act in certain ways when I am with them: intelligently, foolishly, playfully, and angrily. *These are my 'I's, but they are not who I am.*

These 'I's are aspects of my personality, like jackets that I wear to integrate, blend, and work among you so that I can function and learn. Behind them, you sense in me another being, peering out between the shoulders of these 'I's, looking out at you, always there, but never in front to be seen too easily. When I choose to come forward, my presence is so immense that even the people who are deeply asleep can sense me. But they simply do not know what to make of me.

It is important for you to become aware of your roles. You must begin to distinguish your 'I's. When you are in a state of awareness, you can start identifying your many 'I's. The more time you spend operating from a particular 'I', the more energy it will gain and the stronger it will become. *The goal is not to control your 'I's, but rather to reach a point where you can empower the 'I's to serve your goals.* Your spiritual 'I' serves the goal of awakening. Spending time meditating in pursuit of your personal goals will empower that 'I'. Likewise, the more power you give to an 'I' that is detrimental to your progress, the more it will derail your advancement.

You have to start observing your inner personalities, but you can never remove all of your 'I's because they are required to function in this dimension. You can cut down on the number of identities that you have though, and you can empower the ones that serve a higher purpose.

When you are angry, you can see yourself acting out and *expressing* that anger. There is also another part of you that is *observing* you observing your anger, and it can feel that you are acting out a particular role. That identity or 'I' is the personality that is made from the organic brain; it is running its course. Although it's not really you, it is like an individualized being inside of you. It's like a hologram where part of you is observing you.

By removing the power from the 'I's that no longer serve you, they become weak and come forward less often; it begins the process of your awakening. Death is believed to be a new awakening in many cultures. There is an element of truth to this, but it is not a physical death you are looking for. It is the final 'I' that has to die in order to fully awaken.

Begin now to observe your own 'I's. Remove the energy from them and you will start the awakening process. You cannot stay in that state for very long because you are in the dimension of duality, and it is just not possible. You *can* exist there for great lengths of time when you become good at it. By observing your own I's, you learn that what you thought was you is not really you . . . and you will awaken.

Timing is everything. Everything must follow its own natural course. You cannot force destiny to happen sooner than it should. If you try to rush it, you will fail. If you try to make it happen, you will fail and you will no longer be working with the Force. You will be acting on your own impulses and your own 'I's'. Let's take this it a step further. *What part of you is observing you observing yourself?* How do you know that you are observing yourself? You know this be-cause it is your true-self. It is the *third part of you. There are always three.*

Using an analogy, there are three circles. Imagine a *wide outer circle*, a *second inner circle*, and a *third core circle*. In the outer circle, you have many circles within it. Each one is an 'I', such as: the hiker, worker, cleaner, and the identity that likes to hang out with friends. There are many roles that you play within your consciousness.

In the second inner circle are the 'I's that associate with your close friends, your parents and family. The second circle is more self-reflective, musical, creative, and artistic. It grazes upon both worlds. You can feel the outer more physical world and you can feel the inner core, or a different kind of spirituality.

Your spiritual self, the part of you that you think you are searching for is in the inner core or third circle. This is the part of you that you think is your true-self. But it is still *not* the true 'I,' although you would like it to be. These are the jackets that you wear – your true personality. They are closest to the core of who you are. These identities are the spiritual person, psychic person, in-depth intellectual person, and the person who self-reflects. *Yet there is still something more.*

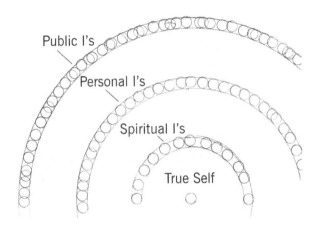

Public I's

Personal I's

Spiritual I's

True Self

Now, I am going to talk about something that you are already aware of. It's a place that you have been to before. You know this place; you desperately seek it out. But you don't know how to maintain your awareness of it for any length of time or how to work within it. I will show you how to get there and remain there more often. Once you remember how to do this, you will maintain it for greater lengths of time. In a moment, I will walk you through an exercise that will help you to shift In-Between so you can recognize that state of being.

When you first clear your mind and go to that place, you may hesitate for a moment. The 'I's know that you are awakening now. They are afraid you are turning on them and that you will lose your identity. It is almost a feeling of suffocation that your body fights. All of a sudden, the body succumbs and relaxes. This is the death that I mentioned earlier. *You have to let yourself die in order to live.* You have to let go of these 'I's that you think you are. It's not that you have to get rid of them; you just have to become aware of them.

Your 'I's will lie to you and withhold information from you. They try to make you forget certain things, and they only let you know what they want you to know. They can be your biggest enemy. *When you begin to have true awareness, you will recognize the truth of what I just said.* Then, you will have more in-depth memories of the things that you've completely forgotten about. You have to empower your 'I's with observation – that is the secret. If you push yourself past observing, trying to study yourself too fast, you will create another 'I'. Don't try too hard! That's how your brain wants to work, but it will be your biggest downfall if you let it – just allow the information to flow. If you try to force yourself to grasp this before you are ready, it will be like grabbing the bull by the horns. You will lose. No matter how certain you are that you will succeed, you won't get there. You *must be fluidic.*

Now, you have the 'me' which is the body – the flesh, and you have the 'I'. The 'I' is your soul – your self-identity. Some of what I teach you may seem to contradict what you have already learned before, but actually it is just a deeper truth, a peeling away of the knowledge. It is like the layers of an onion – you must remove the layers in order to get to the best part. Nothing is the *absolute* truth of what it seems to be, yet there is an element of truth in everything.

If you look at your many 'I's and acknowledge them, you will start to understand what they are. To help you reach an understanding of the 'I's, imagine a room filled with balls. There are empty spaces between the balls because they are curved – they are not squared blocks; think of your 'I's, your personalities, in the same way. There is something that fills the empty spaces in between all of your 'I's; it is your true presence. It is your true self, your true is-ness. *That is what you are trying to find.*

All of your training with meditation has been to control the brain. You're learning to have moments without conscious thinking. You're learning to have non-thought; words are slow, bulky, and cumbersome. You've been learning how to control your thoughts and gather energy at the same time. You don't have to get rid of the old Foundation meditation, but it is time to add a new tool.

Everything I've taught you is a tool that you will learn to use. When the time is right, it will make more sense to you. You already have all the tools you need. You know they work but you don't know how to use them correctly, yet. In this higher state, you will be able to do everything that you ever dreamed possible. But it could take a long time to develop your skills. It might take you hours, weeks, or months. The average person taking another route will spend up to 14 years before they are even able to understand this, so be patient with yourself.

Tone Exercise

Find a quiet place to sit or lie down and begin to relax your body. You are trying to create a level of calmness and peace inside of you before you go any further. Just let everything rest. As you're staring at a spot in the room, focus and stay there. Think about your body – the machine. Think about the weight of your cheeks on your bones. Feel and be aware of your lips on your mouth, the hair on your head, your teeth and your throat. Feel the weight of your shoulders pressed down on the rest of your body by gravity, your spine support-ing the clay mass, the muscle. Be aware of your bones with layers of clay rolled around them for structure and support, the muscles on your bones, the skeletal sticks, the hard, firm, inner core frame, and your kneecaps.

Feel the clothing on your skin, noticing the texture and weight of it. Feel the floor pushing up against your flesh and your buttocks. Become aware of your body; the more aware you become, the more you realize it is not you. The body is a machine, a mechanical you. This machine is made to feel, touch, and take in this envi-ronment. In the process of letting it do that, you have created other personalities on the inside. They are all organic, part of the machine with very complex proper-ties. None of them are truly you. Become aware of your body. Become aware of the machine that it is.

"Doe" is the tonal or vibration of the Earth. When you hear a high pitched ring in your ears, it means your consciousness is shifting. You are shifting like on the musical scale from do (Doe) to re, mi, fa, so, etc. The Doe is what holds you in this earthy state of conscious-ness. It's what makes you act like a Red Cell, a machine that exists in the process of life doing whatever you're told to do. You believe that you have free will but you don't. It's like you are reacting with a purpose, but it's no different than an insect doing its normal errands. It's only more complex.

Now, I want you to listen.

What do you hear?

Somewhere, there's a high pitch ringing. If you fo-cus on it, the pitch will ring true, louder and louder.

The more you listen to it, the more the energy in the room begins to visually change. Your consciousness begins to shift. The moment you start thinking about it, one of your 'I's will take the place of YOU.

Listen to the ringing. Find the high pitch. Focus on it.

Now, breathe in and relax into a normal posture. Reflect on the state of mind you have at this moment. There is a sense of stillness, calmness, clarity in your mind. In the beginning, it is hard to distinguish what that is because it is a new experience and not a sure thing. It's like learning to walk for the first time; you feel unsure of yourself. As you become more aware of the tones, you'll begin to think like I do - without words. Words are slow, heavy, and cumbersome. If you are an energy being, shouldn't your thoughts move faster than the speed of light? What about your awareness, your consciousness? You think slowly because you speak slowly. You think slowly because you are in this physical dimension and you think you are your body. That's why you're stuck here.

A student once said to me, "I realized that everyone I observed seemed to be asleep; as if they were acting like machines in automation."

And I asked him, "Did you feel powerful when you saw this?"

He responded, "Yes, I felt very powerful, like I knew something they didn't know."

So, I said, "That's when you fell back asleep: the moment you felt the power. It was a new identity playing a role."

Utilize the machine. Utilize the body but don't accept it as being YOU. Look around the room. The more you go into a certain state of mind, the more unreal everything seems to you.

When you go into the higher states, you become more aware of things. You obliterate all the other parts of yourself and notice a sense of clarity and understanding. You have no name for what is happening and you can't figure it out, but when your consciousness moves, you understand things you have never understood before. When you solidify again and return to your everyday consciousness from the higher states, the 'I's destroy the knowledge that you brought back. They can't think at that speed. They have to think in this dimension. The 'I's cannot comprehend the vastness of consciousness that you have when you are unencumbered by them, forcing you into a sleep state. There is another part of you that is aware of what you just experienced. That part is suffering, angry, confused, depressed, and in pain. You can feel it but it protects itself. It's like blankets of suffocation weighing you down, telling you, "No, be comforted, relax. It's okay." But in your inner core, you're slowly forgetting what it is that you realized before.

I think without thought. When I start to think as a human, I am encumbered and have to think with the weight of how this dimension works. I am an energy being. My mind is beyond all of this. My mind is as large as the Universe. It is energy. It is static energy. My mind is shrunk, condensed, and compressed when I think as a human being inside of an organic machine. It has no room to move. I think in *words* if I think like a human, and it's slow. For example:

"I have to go to the store." I don't have to say that. I already know.

"I have to use the bathroom." I already know.

"I need to eat." I already know.

You think with slow, methodical thinking. It is often

painstaking for me to adjust from that dimension back to this one. I do adjust, but I don't like it. This is the reason you see my personality conflicted. It is constantly adjusting between who I really am to these three-dimensional frequencies, creating or picking an 'I' to work with you. Most of the time, my 'I' is chosen by my frustration when I come back into this dimension.

When you are in the higher states of consciousness, there are times when you walk or move around and you may not be fully in your true-self because you're still one with your inner core. You're so close to your true-self that it almost feels as if you're there, and you begin to understand things you didn't before. You begin to search for it, to feel and comprehend, and you know it's there. You just can't quite put your finger on it. Then the world intrudes upon you through work, the children, bills, or a phone call from a bill collector. All of a sudden, you're within one of your other 'I's dealing with your problems. You become the panicked 'I,' or the frustrated 'I,' or the 'I' that doesn't want to do anything. These are all identities within your consciousness. These are not you. *The process of true awakening is to recognize them, not to destroy them.* Tag them and identify them. Recognize that they are there. For instance, you are angry and you have enough awareness to see yourself expressing that anger, although you only see it for a moment. Then, you are back with the anger again. If you step back to observe yourself, you will see what you are doing and control that emotion. So, observe your 'I's.

Carlos Castaneda wrote, in one of his books, to observe your hands when you are in the dream state. He said to put your hands out and look at them, then realize that you're dreaming. Look at your hands looking back at you. Imagine that they are you watching you, like in a mirror. Imagine this right now. Just stare out at your hands without moving your eyes around. Keep a fixed stare. You can see them without having to place your eyes directly on them.

Now, see the bridge of your nose, the tip of your nose as if you are looking out from behind your eyes. There's something inside of you that recognized the truth in this. If you let yourself stare, you will see that your hands are like machines. They are tools. They are tentacles, sensory things that take in data and convert it into electricity. When you realize, from inside your mind, that this is your strongest connection to this dimension, it somehow shifts you. It's almost as if these body parts are unreal, but they are real.

In the beginning, the more often you shift into the higher states, the more difficult it will be to accept this dimension. After a while, when in that state, food is no longer appealing because it looks like plastic. Sometimes my consciousness is so intense that I get sick when I look at this dimension. It nauseates me, like I'm on a carnival ride that won't stop. That's because I know it's not real. It's fake, crude. As an energy being that can move freely and unencumbered, the vastness of the universe is my playground. It's difficult to compare that to the small triangular section of space of this dimension.

You must begin by being more aware of that state of mind as often as you can. You will fall asleep. You'll start acting with your "I's," but the point is to catch yourself doing it. See yourself when you have shifted your frequency. Look out from behind your eyes instead of with your eyes looking outward. The more you do this through self-observation, the more you will awaken. Through observation, you become stronger. The true 'I', like in the meditations, becomes stronger. By making yourself aware, you awaken the sleeper. The moment you forget about being aware of your different identities, you fall asleep without even realizing that you fell asleep. Are you aware of the exact moment that you fall asleep at night? No. It's something that happens from one moment to the next. All of a sudden, you are asleep – it happens easily.

When you have shifted your frequency into the higher states, you can look out and see everyone walking, acting, and playing a role. They're all functioning, but they are not truly aware of their consciousness. They are like machines moving around, like insects playing their part. When you see them, you think, "Wow, I'm above all of that now." No, you've just slipped into another 'I'. Do not slip into that 'I'. Simply observe it without making that decision, without judging. Observe, and through your observations, you will evolve. Your inner awareness will begin to have greater depth. You will start to create your intelligence without having to think. You'll have awareness, but not in your current state of mind – It will go way beyond that.

Do you feel the truth in this? Do you feel almost sleepy, yet alert? If you feel that way now, it's from listening to the 'pitch'. Now the real question is, "How well do you understand what I just explained to you? Where do you go from here?" First, you must reflect on everything you have learned before and understand how it all interconnects. There are many different levels of the In-Between states. When you are in that state of mind, there is another realm parallel to this one: *the psychic realm.*

When you are in the higher states, you will look out into the world and see bits and pieces of what I see. You will see the vampires in the world. You will see the energy structures moving through walls. You will see what I call 'the others', the different races of entities amongst us. For the most part, you'll see what you see all the time, but you will become very familiar with the things that are In-Between states, like the psychic world. When you are in your biological self, this world will solidify for you. As you move through other dimensions, you will see the manipulations of other beings, other creatures and energy forms that affect the machines affecting the people.

There are 'others' who are awake in a very different way. They operate for the Darkside. When you have the level of awareness that operates from your true-self, observing your exterior world, in truth you are letting the Force see through you. The Force doesn't work through Red Cells; we instinctively know that. But it can work through you when you become empowered by It. Like tuning in to a particular frequency, the Force will flow through you if you let yourself become clear. You can be a receptor and project that energy out into this dimension. However, it you start to study your 'I's, or you become unaware of your 'I's, they will burden you and you will no longer function in the In-Between state. Maintain a level of fluidity; stay as conscious as you can. You'll get stronger with time.

There are people who have found a level of this awareness through the esoteric arts or other spiritual studies, but they never fully understand them. They reach a certain level, but that's all. There are also people who go much further; they are well aware of their true-self but they've attached their true-self to the

Darkside. This allows the Darkside to exist here in this dimension to function through them. You may wonder how this ties into all the other teachings. It ties in completely.

You know that you have multiple personalities, or multiple 'I's, that you have to remove in order to find the true-self. The 'others' who operate from the Darkside believe that you have merged with multiple alien creatures. They believe that you have different alien personalities that function within you, and only by removing them will you become a 'clear'. There's one major difference that stands out between their way of thinking and ours – we say 'I's and they say they're 'alien entities'. They use lower technology than we do, but the process has a similar result.

However, they focus on removing the light. When you remove the light, it is replaced with an opposite and opposing force. It is the window to this dimension for the Darkside as we tend to be the window for the Light in this dimension. This is why they are so powerful. There are many levels of their followers because it's very difficult to master the Darkside. But no matter how hard they try, there's only a select few that are able to maintain that frequency. Most of them try and end up failing. Nevertheless, they are kept around as useful minions. Some of them are very advanced and have learned to contain and use the abilities of that particular state of consciousness. The longer they can maintain it; they are rewarded with bracelets of achievement for that certain level.

Imagine this: You hold two objects in your hands, and every time you think of something, a nerve jumps. Their goal is to have non-thought, and to show no expression at all. When they ask you a question and you are emotionless, it means you have finally become 'clear'. You've learned to control your mind, which means you've learned to find the true inner-self. If you have movement while doing this, then your brain is thinking and reacting. Emotion makes your muscles retract and expand, which makes the monitor jump. It works the same as a lie detector.

Essentially, they are coming in or going out through a portal. They can be in that state of consciousness, in this dimension, walking around on the surface of the planet, and acting as a receptacle for the Darkside even though they're coming in from a different dimension. We, on the other hand, focus on the Light coming through us. The light is here, the energy is here, but you can't tap the Force until you truly allow it to work through you.

Do you ever wonder why I have chosen this path? If you awaken too soon, the Darkside can take you out too easily. It's better for your 'I's to make you less of a threat in appearance than for you to become too awake, too alert, and too sensitive.

Try these tools in the state of mind that I've suggested. Do the breathing exercises, the energy techniques, the movements, and thought consciousness movement without trying to be an 'I'. Remember, you must be absolutely clear. If you have motives, or control issues, they will prevent you from succeeding. You can only do these things when you have absolute clarity within you. You cannot bend the threads of time while in this reality unless you are absolutely untouchable to them. Then your 'will' shall be your intent. Remember to do it without thought. Do it with a knowing, but not with a series of thoughts that slows you down to this dimension.

You can practice non-thought by observing an object and not *saying* what it is. For this exercise, several objects are shown to you, but you do not say what they are in your head. You should be able to hold absolute silence. So, ask someone to choose several objects and show them to you, one at a time. Then have them ask you what they are, but don't name them (with words) in your head. Just look at the object. If you can't look at them without saying what they are, you're hiding from your own true-self.

Were you successful? If you can be absolutely truthful with yourself, you'll admit that you named at least one object when you thought of it.

Let's say you did something to someone, for whatever reason, and when you reflected on it, you realized that you had an intention to do it. You are utilizing your 'I's, but they lie to you. You accept these lies as the truth because you don't want to take responsibility for your actions. You need to get to a place of absolute clarity.

During the exercise that I asked you to do, you should be able to acknowledge all of the objects without naming what they are in your head. What part of you named them? Which part of you said, "Oh my god, I just said it?" Which part of you acknowledged that you said, "Oh my god?" That's the inner journey, the inner thought that you need to acknowledge.

When you have accomplished this exercise successfully, you will be able to move through time and space and do what you need to do. Until then, it's going to take you a while to sort this all out. The longer you work with my material, the more tools you have to use. You have to start utilizing those tools while you are in the In-Between state of mind. It will give you a much higher purpose, more than you ever thought possible.

When I was at a deli in Los Angeles that is close to the organization that I have been alluding to, I had a run-in with several of the 'others'. They became aware of me at the same time that I became aware of them. They recognized that I have a different kind of technology than they do and wondered how I obtained the level of clarity that I possess. They knew that I am very clear, but not of the same frequency. So they attempted to scan me, go into me, feel me, and experience me. By experiencing me, they would take a part of me with them. They would then incorporate it into themselves, giving them a sense of knowing. They would know who and what I am.

It's like when you look at someone, you *know* who they are. How do you know a person is a pedophile or a criminal? You can feel them. There is something 'about them' that seems different. Well, it's a lot more intense than that. It's more specific, very deep. When they attempted to scan me, I pushed them back. The fact that I pushed them back really blew their minds. They were intimidated by me because I took them all on at once. At that point, they all decided to go into a battle stance in an attempt to dominate me. It's like beings fighting it out, but looking very calm on the surface.

I knew that I had to distract them. Have you ever felt a very sharp pain in your head, so sharp that you had to stop for a second and wait for it to pass? Well, imagine that pain about fifty times more intense. That's what I did. I manipulated the energy and created a very sharp, stabbing pain in their heads, and they felt it. They all knew they better back off so they got up and left. They all looked at me, acknowledging that, for this dimension, they didn't know what to make of me. After they left the restaurant, I got up and left too.

In your clarity, you become aware of an energy field that is called the *matrix*. We know that the matrix exists. We call it "matrix" because of the movie. How do you run the matrix when thinking like a human? How does your crude, antiquated brain run something that's moving at the speed of light, of energy? How do you manipulate it? How do you control it? You're fooling yourselves if you think you can in your current state of mind. Your true higher self is pure energy, so if you go into a clear state of consciousness, it can dance around the matrix. The matrix is slow, heavy, and cumbersome. You can control it, overtake it, and manipulate it. At first, you start off with the small things; the things that you say when you are in an 'I'. "Did I make that happen?" It's because your 'I's are so slow, they cannot see the change happening. The 'I' wants to know, "What just happened?" It's that fast. It's that powerful. When you go that deep into your 'I's, time slows down. When you come back, you wonder, "What is going on? Everything feels like it's taking forever."

In order to enter the matrix, you must shift your consciousness. You must shed all of your different 'I's, so you need to self-reflect and become clear. Then you need to learn to move within this clarity.

In the movie 'Dune', there's a place the *Bene Gesserits* cannot go. They can reach the psychic state of consciousness and comprehend it, but there's a place they cannot go. That higher place is achieved in this state of mind, but it's very difficult to maintain. The reason the *Bene Gesserits* can't do it is because they think with their emotions, and emotion holds them in this dimension. This place is identified by very strong personalities and it is more in-depth.

Everyone has emotions, but between our two sexes, women usually feel them more intensely. It is more difficult for women to free themselves from them. When you remove your I's, you still have emotions, but they are not as bulky as before, so you can go to this higher place and exist. But the moment you think about existing there, you pop back out because you are acknowledging it through one of your 'I's, through your organic body.

When you look at the world and observe the *sleepers*, you cannot judge them. The moment you have the thought, "My god, they are asleep – look at them," you're speaking words in your head. That means one of your 'I's has come forward. It's important to realize that it will happen very quickly. Don't get angry at yourself. Acknowledge the being inside of you that said, "You're slipping away." Notice when it tells you. It doesn't say it in words, you just simply know. That's because it's coming from a higher place. It doesn't need to tell you with words. It makes you aware.

When you are in this higher place, you will feel the people around you. You should not let this encapsulate or crystallize you. You will see very ugly people, feel their intention, and know things about them. Their intention, their 'I', is so strong that you can sense it, yet there is another level even higher than that. There are others who are walking around in a higher state of consciousness who will become aware of you just as quickly as you became aware of them. You can get into a level of psychic warfare with them. Most of those who are that powerful will not engage with you because it is not time for this to happen yet. It's not time to wrestle for the control of the vibration of the Earth yet. It's as if each side is amassing teams, strategizing and structuralizing. Once in a while, there might be a little foot battle to see who will challenge the other to study their reaction.

I recall one of the stories of Krishnamurti. He and several of his students were in a car one day and, as they were driving, they were talking about awareness – how aware they are and how they are evolving. Krishnamurti said, "Didn't you guys feel that?" And they replied, "Feel what?" He thought to himself, "They're all speaking about awareness, yet we just ran over a goat." So keep this analogy in mind as a good example of being aware of your surroundings.

You must begin to go through all of your teachings. You must go through the information you have learned and start to integrate it now. It will make you ... I don't want to use the word 'powerful,' but I must use words that you can understand because this is how I'm conveying it. Don't get hung up on my choice of words because, in this case, my words will be contradictory. I say to you, "They will give you power." Yet I say to you, "To feel powerful is to be denied." This is a very deep truth, and both statements are true. In order to help accelerate your consciousness and communicate this understanding, I have to do it in a way that you, as an organic being, can comprehend until you can reach the 'I' behind it. Then all of the teachings will make absolute sense. You have to ponder, understand, and use them. They are very powerful in their own way.

This brings up a whole new subject. There was a time in my life when I did a lot of miracles. Some of my students have seen me do many large and small ones. Every great Master understands the state of mind it takes to accomplish this; it is how they were able to accomplish everything they did. Although you never knew them personally, you are aware that both Buddha and Krishna had a sense of calmness about them. What kind of calmness do you think that was? Is the In-Between a state of complete calmness, like feeling very relaxed, or is it a much deeper state of calmness with an immense amount of power? The In-Between is like being in the middle of an ocean. There are no waves, there is no movement, and the water is very black. It's expansive everywhere you look. When you begin to realize that the depth of the ocean is extremely vast and wide, you feel its immense power. Well, it is the same thing. Buddha and Krishna were both powerful and aware, yet they also existed in this dimension.

When Lucifer challenged Jesus in the desert, he said, "If you're the son of God, then why don't you create a miracle?" But Jesus didn't do that because of the nature of things in this dimension. If he had created that miracle, he would be changing the will of nature and challenging the forces of God's creation. So, if you try to force your will on something, you are not respecting how things were meant to be. The reason I don't create miracles anymore or interact by creating phenomena is because I am acting out of respect. This is a dimension of duality, so if you take from one thing, it has to come from another. By forcing your will in this dimension, it is like defiling something. It's like violating it. That is the only way that I can explain this to you.

You must have respect for certain things. If there is going to be a confrontation, it should be done at a much higher level, a level that doesn't directly affect the sleepers – the Red Cells – the people who are organically functioning for the path of the planet. That is the biggest reason that Jesus didn't create the miracle when he was tested and why he didn't do the things that Lucifer asked of him. Whenever Jesus spoke to the people, he never fed his ego. He never empowered the 'I' by saying, "I'm aware that everybody else is asleep." The moment you acknowledge and feel the power, you have created another 'I'. Jesus always said, "The will of the Father," or, "My Father." He would never say anything that fed his ego. Jesus always used an outer person, meaning God. That's what kept him clear while dealing with Lucifer. The same thing happened to Buddha, Krishna, and Milarepa.

As you progress in the higher states of consciousness, you're going to have to learn to self-study. The most important thing is to become aware of your environment, your reality, everything around you, its place, and its role. You will become tired of it. You will become nauseated by it and it is going to have certain effects on you, but it will pass. You'll get past it and you will adapt. A part of you will feel tired and you won't want to feel that way. There is a possibility that you will get frequent headaches too, but they will also pass. Being shifted is about expanding your perceptions. You're pushing your brain to digest what you see at the higher frequencies, at a higher speed than what you are used to. The brain will adapt. It's capable, but you're going to have to learn to think on a higher level. Consciousness is something that is around you, not just working inside of you.

You should not go into a shifted state of mind to just sit and stare. You must be able to function and move around; let your mind be there. It's a challenge, but if you make yourself do it, it'll happen. You'll find that other people will pick up on you. Red Cells will also pick up on you and perhaps stare at you; they won't know what is happening exactly, but something about you is affecting them and seems different.

They're used to their connected electrical field. When you're shifted, your electrical field is very different. A Red Cell can feel it, but they are not able to comprehend it. You look like they do and everything feels the same to them. You have two legs, a head, clothing, and shoes, but there's something about you that feels odd to them. But you can't feed into that.

I often use analogies to make things easier to understand: On the Serengeti, the hunters wear a leopard skin to cover themselves so they can walk around unharmed among the leopards. The leopards look at the man wearing the leopard skin and are aware that there is something different about it, but, they eventually accept it. It doesn't feel like much of a threat to them. After a few seconds, they'll just dismiss it.

It's the same way with Red Cells. When you're in a higher state of mind, they will feel the change. They will observe you and think, "I don't know what it is but something is different with you," and then they move on. Others who are a lot more sensitive will pick up on it. They'll try to pretend that they know more about you, that they're more skilled and powerful than you are, but they're not. They're playing a role with one of their other 'I's. They're going to assume that you have some different quality or mysticism about you. The more you play into it, the more you will enforce this 'role playing.' You're inviting it and you don't want to get caught up in all that drama. You want to move in the highest possible frequencies and become aware of everything around you. Eventually, you will achieve a very stealthy mode. You'll get to a level where you can walk among the people, and they won't recognize that anything is different.

There are a few different spiritualist groups that you should be familiar with because they will notice you. One group of people who might pick up on you is the *Fourth Way* people; they practice Gurdjieff's teachings. Another group is the Hindus, but they are unique in their own way. They understand and remember the different identities of God. They see Krishna and their deities as different aspects of the consciousness of God. So, there are some groups who do relate to these teachings, very few, but none of them will be as refined, or as advanced as you if you can achieve a stealth mode.

The group who likes to think of themselves as 'clear' will also pick up on you. When they pick up on you, they will want to know how you got to this level. They are the only group that you should really be concerned about because they are very controlling. They work from the *Darkside* and they see you as a threat; not because they have a reason to, but because you're different from them. They believe their technology is far superior to yours. They believe their way is the only way. They have been taught that if you have some level of awareness and are not one of them, you are not 'clear'. You are being remotely controlled by an alien race that's out to dominate the Earth. So, they've been trained to think of you as the enemy. It's not about seeing you with a higher consciousness. They are not yet aware of the difference, but they are getting close. They believe that all the rest of the people in the world are either aliens, or asleep.

A *Fourth Way* person will respect you. So, again, to establish the point I am trying to make, the problem with *Fourth Way* people is that they don't believe in a higher purpose. The *Fourth Way* people are always neutral – they don't acknowledge either the Force or the Darkside. They believe in the middle path; that in the end – neither one really matters. They see the planet as an organism, but don't like the idea of the body of God. So, in their state of consciousness everything is a form of neutrality. To them, evil doesn't exist, except on the level of altruism. They say that evil is the suppression of life. Discussions with them will be fairly intense; however, as you progress, you will see the flaws in that path. You'd have to be evolved enough to recognize them. They don't choose either/or but they do choose awareness. They just don't choose to act on it. For them, it's all about personal power. They'll say that they prefer to be neutral, but I think that is a selfish way to act. If it's not going to help the Universe, then what is the point?

I remember seeing a movie about elves sometime in the past, in which they say that the magic moves through them. The elves are a part of that force of energy; whereas, humans learn about the magic and learn to control the energy by using objects, but don't actually become it. It is basically the same thing. The Fourth Way people learn to control the energy, but they don't really learn to let it move through them. Many of the Fourth Way people are brilliant and their technology is excellent. So it's ironic that some are into symbolism, tarot cards, and things of that nature. They're like the Chinese Buddhists. There is some worthiness in their belief system, but their knowledge was defiled with the stigma of superstition. Gurdjieff's followers have a great understanding, yet they have faltered because of their earlier beliefs; whatever has been interjected into them.

Ouspensky is acknowledged as one of Gurdjieff's most brilliant students, but at the end of his life when he was dying, he said to give up the path. He said, "It doesn't work. You will fail." Then he was convinced by his daughter to recant those words, which he did, and eventually he passed. He realized that the Fourth Way was flawed. I believe the flaw was they did not choose one side or the other. They chose to function within the Universe, to understand that the Universe functions as an organism, but not to acknowledge a greater purpose for everything. That is what they fail to see.

Not to change the subject, but is there any reason to go back to meditating with music, or should we meditate while listening to the tones, the high-pitched ringing?

Yes, meditate to music. Although the meditation music is not as beneficial as earlier on because when you become more evolved, you have to charge your body so that you can make your higher awareness work with that frequency. But, the more tonalized your physical body is with this dimension, the more solidified it will be. You are trying to reach the higher levels, at this point.

Could I meditate on the chakras while listening to the tones rather than listening to music?

Absolutely, that is the next step. Use the tones or pitches but focus on the chakra points. Do not use the music that you usually listen to. Work with your chakras by listening to the pitches. The pitches will also get louder. Sometimes the pitch gets so loud; it's like speakers at a rock concert. At other times, you could be lying down resting when all of a sudden, you will unconsciously hop in on the sound and it will shift you that quick. Have you ever experienced anything like that?

I did, but I didn't know what to do with it.

So, you work with it. It's trying to find you, to shift you, but it's not working for you yet. That's because you're not aware of what's going on. You should meditate to it. For instance, if you listen to the sound of a *tingsha*, it will sound loud at first, and then slowly fade away. The tones are like the sound from a tingsha. They are very similar, yet they're actually the opposite! That's how this world of duality works. So with a tingsha, you're going from loud to soft. When the sound becomes very subtle, you will recognize it. I'm utilizing this to remind you that, in this dimension, you need to tune into the frequency to shift, to let it work on your brain. When you're in that higher frequency, it will shift you. It's designed to build your structural consciousness to work with a higher level of consciousness. That's really what the tones are for.

If you focus on it, it will become so loud that you won't be able to hear anything else. It means that you've moved inward with your energy, and then outward. It's like turning yourself inside out. Your whole sensory has moved to a higher dimension. The more you can turn inside out, the more you can operate with it. You will see everything externally, through your eyes, but eventually you're going to see the other reality that is here, the other dimension that you only get an occasional glimpse of.

Tibetan Tingsha Cymbals

I have a question about your death experience and your T's. What did you do to occupy your different identities, or your mind?

I have an inner core of 'I's that is so well developed that I had to throw everything but the kitchen sink at it to keep them busy so that I could have a conversation with my higher-self. My 'I's are still attached to this world, in this dimension. And even though I operate from them, they had become so intensely powerful, they made a stand at that moment, and they turned on me. But in the end, they still aren't you. *You must always remember that.* I let them flow with it because I hadn't really expected to find anything. I went in with an attitude of not really working with my higher-self. Through self-observation, I discovered that I was using one of my higher, more intellectual spiritual selves. It had to battle all of those 'I's to get to my true, higher-self. Then the conversation took place, but on a very fast, dimensional level.

You can't attempt to label it, or try to figure it out because you won't be able to. If you try to come up with an answer, you've used something else to figure it out. That will make it less than what it could have been. By the simple act of putting it in a box, you missed the whole experience. It goes far beyond how you think, but it's still you. It's still useful. It's still powerful. You just need time to understand it.

When you are in the higher states of consciousness, is it correct to say you move freely without thinking about it?

Correct. You move in an energy world. You can see the outer world and you can also see the energy. As soon as you close your eyes, it's like going into a whole different world, but it is very similar. What are some of the things you comprehend in the higher states? Things move quickly, don't they? Conscious thought moves quickly because it's energy.

In the higher states, are you free from having to ask a question because you are unencumbered by the 'I's?

Correct. You wonder what that strange feeling is. It's because you don't have any of your 'I's attached to you. They will try to pop up, but you won't really feel a desire for food, sex, or anything else. You won't feel anything, *yet you do*. You'll find that you do feel something. And if you do, you will feel yourself coming right back into yourself. That's when you say, "I want to come back," or, "I can't deal with this." That's an 'I' panicking. All of a sudden, you lose it and you can move again, and you start to understand. Without asking the question, "What is God?" you understand. Without asking the question in the same way you would normally think it, or hear it, or feel it, you just *know*. You don't say, "I want to feel what they're thinking in their mind." You simply know. You can bring yourself into the higher states now when you're ready, without my help. I can take you there very quickly, but you can do it now on your own. You already know the way. Your search for it will be so intense, so be careful not to miss it.

Don't let your frustration take over. Don't let it mislead you. That's the animal; that's the 'I'. Simply let yourself flow; your intent will get you there. When you let your rational brain take over, you lose. It can't possibly navigate you through the air when it was made to drive on the ground!

Is it like non-thought? You can't make yourself experience something when you know you have to stop thinking?

Absolutely. So now, get on the floor and let's do another exercise. Let your body relax. Release your anxiety; breathe it out. Let your thoughts move out. They cause stress, don't they? Release the Babbler. Breathe out.

Do this with your eyes open. When you close your eyes, it's too much of a habit to revert back into your old way of meditating. Right now, you need to experience this fully. Later on, you will fuse the two together.

Look down at your chest. Never look somebody in the eye or look straight forward. Think of your body. Feel the weight of your body. Feel the different parts of your body; the clothing you are wearing, and become aware of the body as much as you can.

Now begin to listen to the tones.

Sometimes you'll hear the tones much stronger in one ear versus the other ear. Try to focus on the weaker side until both sides match; you'll find the pitch gets really loud in the center of your head.

The Tone Technique

Listen.

Listen to your interior.

Listen for the Tone in your ears.

Focus your intention on it and it will manifest. At first you may hear only one sound. Sometimes it takes a little while to arrive. Once you hear it, pay attention for more than one tone. You will notice something that sounds like one or many tones fluctuating in and out, up and down. Observe this.

How many tones are there? Can you count them?

Try to focus and isolate one of the tones. (Initially, it

may be difficult to focus a single tone because of the way they fluctuate. Don't let your focus get away. As you practice, you will be able to tame these tones at will.)

Once you can hear the tone well, see if you can notice two tones; one for each ear or side of your head. Listen to one of the tones on the right side followed by listening to one on the left. Switch back and forth. (This can be difficult at first as each side may try to get your attention while you are listening to the other.)

Listen to both right and left tones together. Bring each side into the center. Allow them to merge or synchronize together into one tone. If there is still fluctuation, it is okay; with practice, you gain more control.

Now, bring a tone or range of tones into focus and make the pitch increase in octaves or intensity. Now, make it decrease in octaves. It is very important to experiment with raising and lowering the octaves of the tone.

Have you noticed the energy in the room change?

At first your results may seem ungraceful. (The way the tones leap and stumble around). The purpose of this is to introduce and exercise a new and elusive mode of thinking. You can raise or lower the tone at will.

The goal is to become more and more skilled in how high you can raise the octave of the tone.

About The Tone Technique

It is very important to maintain your concentration as you increase the tone octave as high as you can. When holding a high tone, don't think about what you're doing or you will lose it; it will fall back down to a low tone. When you lose concentration, it fails.

Reflect on the internal movements of the exercise. Once you can take the pitch to a certain level, you must shift or change your consciousness to move it higher. The Foundation meditation is very important here because you must build energy and maintain non-thought to be able to shift your consciousness in this way.

You must learn to think differently if you want to master this technique. Having expectations will limit your understanding and box you in. If you limit yourself to thinking with your organic brain, you will not go far. For instance, using verbal thoughts; words are cumbersome and slow. You must use your mind to understand and *feel* what the organic brain cannot.

Listening to the Tone is a technique and a meditation. You are concentrating and exercising the mind with the intent of acquiring mental agility. This builds concentration, projection, control of mind, and alternative perception. Your awareness will significantly increase with this exercise; the awareness of your surroundings, and your 'Innerverse.'

You will most likely discover there is something hidden within this technique that you will not understand until you consistently work at it. Do not become fixated on it; the answer will not come in the way you may expect.

Keep in mind that certain sounds are dimensional.

The Tone technique is about having no barriers and experiencing something pure and unexpected. Practice and you will discover amazing things. To master this technique, do it once a day.

Chapter 2

MASTERING THE MECHANISM

YOU ARE NOW dedicating yourself toward your path of inner development and self-consciousness, so it is important for me to point something out to you. Gurdjieff was referred to as the source of the *Fourth Way* people, as I mentioned in the last chapter. No one seems to realize, however, that this knowledge came to Gurdjieff during the time he travelled to the Arabian countries with a group of people. He met the Sufis and Sikhs who in turn trained him; they were the source of his knowledge. As a student, he was no more exceptional than anyone else.

Gurdjieff put his own twist on what he learned and he tried to give it out to his students who, in turn, ended up fighting with each other. They all wanted to be teachers and thought they knew it all. Eventually, they broke off from the Fourth Way and started their own schools of thought, but without their truest source of knowledge, the most enlightened person, Gurdjieff. Never having achieved enlightenment, they lost the quality of the knowledge and ultimately failed. I am trying *not* to make the same mistakes.

Most of their teachings came from an ancient source of knowledge; a certain amount of truth is incorporated into most things. *There is a level of octaves that can be achieved through the tones; the higher the octave, the higher level of consciousness.* Red cells probably are at level one, meaning they have achieved a minor level of consciousness. An intellectual Red Cell may achieve up to level three. Therefore, a person who is diligent enough to reach the higher octaves may achieve a level four, five or six, with level six exponentially higher than five. The meter can go infinitely higher, and if you are a level seven or more, that is considered to be the state of enlightenment. It would be safe to presume that the majority of Higher Balance students are somewhere between levels three to five. How you move up that ladder will be determined by your dedication to this work. Dedication equals effort, and effort takes energy.

There is an energy that you get from the cosmos when you sleep at night. It accumulates because your 'I's are temporarily out of the picture. They are at rest, so you are in a deep stasis. The Universe feeds you this energy, as it feeds all things. When you wake up in the morning, you don't necessarily *awaken*, as in spiritually awaken. You go into another kind of sleep state which provides an accumulation of fuel or energy. When you go through life acting upon your emotions of depression, self-pity, anger, frustration, and all of the things most of us feel, you lose this fuel. It is consumed by your `I`s which ignite these feelings. Use your `I`s, but be aware of them, and sap that source of energy from them.

By providing this energy, the Universe assists you. It is trying to help the *Middle Pillar*. The *Middle Pillar* is something that you are not familiar with right now, but it is your *true-self.* Underneath all of the I's, there is the

Middle Pillar. It is who you truly are and who you are seeking. It is correct to say that you are not who you think you are. The name that you go by is not who you are. Your name is one of the `I`s created from your childhood, social structures, parents and various other things that you have accumulated through time. These 'I's have adapted to be who you think you are. The *Middle Pillar* is crying out desperately to you, and it is why you are here now reading this book. Why you even bother to read it is because somehow you got the *Middle Pillar* to awaken. Or perhaps you met me, and with my strong influence, it is able to reach that pillar to give it energy, to help it gain some ground in a deafening battle that you are not even aware of. It's the battle of awakening.

You are pursuing the awakening of the Middle Pillar. You do not know who that Middle Pillar is. Seldom do you even come close to awakening. Seldom do you even begin to realize that it is there before you fall back into a flood of I's. The Middle Pillar needs as much of the cosmic energy as it can accumulate to begin this battle, in order to awaken, and for your consciousness to rise to a higher level. If you choose to burn up the energy that you collect at night, you will remain an 'I'. You will remain a Red Cell.

It is almost impossible to contain all of that cosmic energy. It takes great effort to do so during the day because it's very easy to fall back into your `I`s. No matter how good you get, you will fall back. Even I fall back occasionally, although not as often and not in the same way that you do. I have a higher consciousness. Sometimes I have to use that energy so that I can communicate with the rest of the world because they cannot become too conscious of me. It is too much of a vexation for them; they don't understand this power. I use a little of my fuel to create personalities, but I am highly efficient at it. I can take a small amount of energy and get so much out of it, whereas your bodies exhaust this fuel too quickly.

I am now trying to give you some ideas to ponder so that you can use constructional thinking as a means to free yourself. This fuel, this energy that you collect from the cosmos, must be utilized to its greatest effect. When you meditate, work in silence, or listen to the tones, the tone is your support system. It helps you to remember. It helps you keep balanced in spite of all the chaos around you. It is your pole to hang onto when the wind is strong. If you choose to think of it, and be conscious of it, it will help center you amongst all the whirling `I`s. The more you listen to the tones, the more they will help you gain control of your 'I's in a way that the brain cannot understand.

As you meditate, you use the cosmic energy that you've accumulated from the night before in order to awaken. Listening to the tones enables this cosmic energy to begin building its structure. It's awakening inside of you. The energy that you accumulate is like an adhesive. Much like Prana, it is the material that you need to build your causal body, and to build your other energy bodies as well.

What do I mean by this? You have a physical body, but you did not always have this physical body. You started off as an organism about the size of a seed. That seed could not understand this dimension. So, it grew and grew *until eventually it could be placed into this dimension.* It still consisted of energy, but now it also had an organic body. This organic body was made from organic things that are also made of energy, such as:

fruits, vegetables, meats, grains, and berries. These things were once matter from the Earth. In this formula, there was also sunlight - energy. It was all organically recreated. You cannot destroy energy; you can only recreate it. Therefore, your body was created, in part, from these fruits, and also from the sun. The energy in your body comes largely from the sun as photons of electricity or photons of **energy**.

You build your body with energy from the inside. For this example, I will make the assumption that we are talking about a Red Cell without a soul. Rest assured that the people in my life do have souls; even the children around me have souls. They are too close to somebody like me. We must look at Red Cells for our source of study.

If you choose to seek this knowledge, you must not become defensive about the people in your life; whether they are parents, friends, or relatives. You must be impartial when seeking the truth. If you start to find yourself becoming too emotionally involved, you must stop your learning, extract yourself from this, and continue to function as before. You must not get too personal. You must be impartial, even with your own self-study, or you will end up losing all of the progress you have achieved thus far.

Now, as a human being, the body was created and the brain evolved from a small brain to a much larger brain. The brain is much like a television; it uses your senses to capture signals from this dimension and then converts them into a format that you can comprehend. As an energy being, you cannot see, hear, smell, taste, or touch so you could not experience or understand this dimension. You would pass through this dimension as if it did not even exist. You harness this dimension with a body that collectively gathers data and turns it into energy. The energy then becomes part of your energy consciousness. The brain can only work on levels of biochemical thinking, which is a crude level of non-energy, but a close second. It thinks with chemicals from little bits of electricity in the brain.

The energy that you collect at night acts as an adhesive. There is 'food' or Prana in the air; hundreds of different forms of energy, and when you breathe you can only accumulate the ones that you are working hard to collect. The Prana is so fine that it is not even visual.

What do giant whales, the greatest creatures in the ocean, feed on? They feed on plankton, of course. Plankton is tiny microorganisms that are hardly visible to the human eye. Whales open their mouths and the plankton flow in and accumulate within their body. Energy works in a similar way, flowing in and accumulating within the body.

There is another energy that you haven't learned about yet: You must build a second body made of energy, which is the creation of the soul. As you build this body, it begins to have new capabilities. You build this body so you can use the brain to translate this dimension into energy. The energy is then collected to create the second body.

Now you are accelerating the building of that body within years, rather than lifetimes. You create a body by using this adhesive, this main core energy, Prana, or the energy accumulated at night, which is basically also a form of Prana. When you meditate or listen to the tones, you pull in this energy. By doing this, you begin the manufacturing of a second body within you. As it begins to develop, you start to have the ability to grasp that which you could not understand before. You could say that you are building a different kind of brain, a dimensional brain, in the same structure of space as your physical brain.

There are a million other dimensions moving through this dimension. The other dimensions are moving at such a high rate of frequency that they do not seem real to us. This dimension is like a car moving at twenty miles per hour. If we are all moving at twenty miles per hour, it is easy to relate to this dimension. Your second energy body can relate to the other dimensions.

Your second energy body is the beginning of the first soul, the rudimentary soul, which you've probably already achieved through your struggles, battles, and your intellectual and spiritual conversations. The first soul is also the most basic of dimensional souls. Now, you must begin to generate the third body. This is where you begin, for you must also build other bodies of energy. It will elevate you to the higher octaves, and also determines what level of human you are in this world. Do you see how this all makes sense now?

You must meditate. You must work on creating a solid structure because if you begin to build a third body which is more ethereal, you will have a soul that is like water. To create this third body with the ability to see at forty miles per hour in order to move beyond this dimension, you must now build something that can move even faster.

If you don't feed your body, it will starve. What are the symptoms of starving? Weakness and low energy, and as a result you will not be able to think as clearly nor will you concentrate as well. You need to have all of your faculties to explore this dimension effectively. If you don't feed all of your other energy bodies, what do you think will happen?

You will starve and die?

Absolutely. When you begin something new, you must always follow through or you will not achieve your intended results. It is imperative that you pay attention to this. You must find a little bit of time in your day to feed your soul so that it can move on at the end of this life. Now you're probably thinking, "Between eating regular food and feeding all my other bodies, it will take a lot of my time." The human body only needs one cupful of food a day for nourishment; we consume a lot more food than we need to survive. Feeding your energy bodies to keep them healthy really does not require much energy. You need to learn to work with them, think with them, and utilize that dimensional brain.

It's important that you ponder the knowledge that I give to you. Without it, you are not using your dimensional brain and you cannot excel. You cannot progress beyond just an 'ordinary human' unless you make the choice to do so. You must realize, internally, that you have to put aside a certain amount of time each day to nurture and work on yourself. You must be willing to do this.

As a parent, you make your child go to school. Do they want to go to school? Most children would rather stay at home. You make them go because you know that their education is very important for them to succeed in this life. Yet, when it comes time for you to learn, you are like children again. How eager are you to do your homework? How long does it take for you to get around to it? If you had a child, wouldn't you be chastising them?

You want to work on yourself, but you say it with words that have little emphasis, "I want to work on myself. I want to awaken. I'm here now." It is easy to be here. It's easy to show up, but are you using your mind? Are you using the dimensional thinking that you've applied and worked so hard for? Will you achieve a higher frequency while living in this dimension? It's not just going to happen. You have to work on yourself. It's very rewarding and gratifying.

You are looking for great peace in your soul, your spirit, to complete you. It will come when you can truly understand this knowledge. This world dominates your thinking, your brain, and your mind. It dominates all of the other potential dimensions within you because it's the only one that you choose to feed and interact with. You don't interact with the other dimensions because either you simply do not know how or you are not willing to put forth the effort. You'd rather put your efforts into menial tasks.

It is a choice that you make in order to awaken. It is a choice that you must realize within yourself. When you've made that choice, you need to pursue it extensively with great enthusiasm. But if you decide this is not for you, you need not put forth the effort. When you're ready to apply yourself, you can approach it again. But then you will have to start all over.

People will bypass you. Some of my newer students who work with me are passing my older students because the older ones have not applied themselves. They boast that they have the knowledge, but their egos rule. The newer students, with time and much effort, have already caught up to them . . . I remember hearing about Arnold Schwarzenegger's comments on Sylvester Stallone. Schwarzenegger said, jokingly, that he remembers being at the top of his profession, being famous, but always hearing optimistic comments about Sylvester Stallone. It's like he could hear Stallone's footsteps pounding in the distance, coming up from behind him like this presence was already there.

Your level of effort determines the distance. If you want to heighten your octave, then it will take some work. If you want to excel, it takes more work. If you don't want to do that, people will bypass you. You cannot deny one's octave. It is as real as this entire planet. It is by your efforts that you will surpass others.

Now, let's talk about the tones. I want to hear something from everyone. I want to hear about your experience. What have you learned about the tones?

I hear three distinct pitches. It's difficult for me to hold onto the tones when my eyes are closed later in the day or at night. When I found the tones, I felt a pressure in my ears, my nose, and behind my eyes at my sinus point, a big pressure.

Let's take a look at what you said first. Three tones, that's wonderful because some people only hear one tone. To hear three is like three out of a hundred thousand tones. Most people don't hear anything at all.

Now, the reason for the sinus pressure is because, indirectly, you're becoming more aware of your body. Certain things about your body have become more apparent to you. The tones work for you at night instead of during the day because of the lesser amount of obstructive sounds around you. You pay more attention to the obstructions. Some people do better during the day with tones because they're used to dealing with them and focusing on them. When it's quiet, they reach out to the more subtle tones that they hear, and that's where they focus their attention. But this works the opposite way for other people.

Having your eyes open means you're associating with everything that you're seeing, which means you've seen everything repetitively. This is a way to bring you into a form of a relaxed trance; there's nothing for you to babble about. When you shut your eyes, your mind is looking for something to think about. Your mind is bored. It's like a child that needs stimulation. Some people work better with the tones when their eyes are open; others work best with their eyes closed. You must experiment to find what works for you, but whatever way you choose, stick with it. Don't switch in the middle of your meditation. But it makes no difference in the end. Sometimes you'll close your eyes so that you can focus on a particular technique. Other times, you'll choose the opposite. It may work better for you to have your eyes open because you are trained in meditation to have your eyes shut. Perhaps by having your eyes open, it'll teach you to walk, move, and interact with life in a slow, simple way. It allows you to hold that state of consciousness longer.

As I was practicing awareness of my body, I found that I was more successful hearing the tones. However, in the beginning while observing my body, I started feeling sick and didn't know what to do. I felt somewhat distracted.

The reason that you felt sick is because it was the first time you really thought about your body. You are used to externalizing your senses, touching and feeling everything that's around or outside of you. You don't usually feel what's inside of you, or even think about it.

Consciously think about your body rather than thinking about what you're feeling, touching, or doing. It'll help you to observe how simple the brain is. You said that you felt sick when you thought about your body. When do you usually think about feeling your body?

When you're sick?

Yes, that is true. This is what I want to teach you about instinctual `I`s. Right away, the body makes you feel ill because it assumes that's the feeling you should experience. It's been trained to feel that way. You said that when you started to feel the body the second time, you were able to get past that expectation and found the tones easier, that the sound suddenly came to you. What do I always tell you to do when you begin an exercise?

Be aware of your body.

Be aware of your body. Be aware of yourself. When I tell you to be conscious I'm saying, "Think about your body." When you think about your body, it brings you here in the present. All of a sudden, you feel different because you have shifted, and that is the point. You want to be conscious of yourself.

That reminds me of something that happened to me when I was meditating with the tones, thinking about the body. Usually when I meditate, I feel the massive expansiveness of the Universe, like it's massively empty. I feel the vastness of the Universe. When I was aware of the body, instead of feeling it outward, I was feeling it inward.

Well, that's because there's a whole inner-universe within you. Are you familiar with a black hole? A black hole is a place in space where gravity pulls so much that light cannot get out. The gravity is so strong because matter has been squeezed into a tiny space. The hole is called "black" because it absorbs all the light that hits the horizon, so it reflects nothing. There is also something called a white hole. This hypothetical cosmic body acts in the exact opposite manner of a black hole. Instead of pulling in matter, a white hole expels it like a sort of cosmic exhaust valve, giving off serious amounts of energy. So, somewhere out in the universes, there's an explosion of material expelling outward. You could almost say that it's a Big Bang. In fact, I'm willing to bet that sometime in the future, scientists will discover that our Universe is really just an *out-hole* for some gigantic black hole elsewhere. It's going to take science a long time to get there, but when you do, you heard it here first.

There are micro black holes that are vast, but they are micro in comparison to the Universe. In a way, this is how the Universe breathes and moves its fluids. It sucks in material and blows it out, creating something else within it in a different location. It just moves everything all around. Since it's so vast to us, it seems very slow because we are micro. It's all about time, ratio, and size, but that's a whole different subject matter.

So, within you, you have a micro black hole, but also micro white holes. You are a multidimensional being once you build energy vortexes within you. Once you build a body, you have a doorway that can pull energy outward.

Where does my knowledge come from? Where do I get my energy from? It's not just from the energy around us. *Once I got here in this dimension, I created a device within me to pull the other energies from the Universe in and then out. This way I can push them out of me into this dimension.* That will give you something to ponder!

When you go into yourself as you described, you felt that everything was so vast. *It is really not you that you're going into, but you're going outside of yourself into another dimension.* This is a very complex idea and gives you much to think about. When you meditate, you feel another kind of vastness. How can that be? In a way, it does not make sense to you. But if you were to go into some hyper-dimensional universe, perhaps it would. You could say that there are many universes here. Maybe you are moving into another frequency that goes beyond you. You are turning your energy inward, but it's still projecting outward. This is multi-dimensional thinking for you to make that other brain work.

Are the tones like a wave that you can ride to access these other different universes?

No, that is thinking with the human brain again; you simply experience the tones. Don't try to control, tag, or force the tones because you will be unsuccessful. The organic brain cannot comprehend this, so don't try to understand what you are doing. Simply experience the tones. Then your results will become knowledge to you.

I want to hear more observations about the sound, whether they are simple or not.

When I first began to experience them, I heard a static sound. Then I found the tones. You can come in and experience them, then go to a fine line. Also, you can change the pitch at will. You can make the pitch higher and you can bring in another octave. Then, all of a sudden, you hear all the static around that, too.

Yes, you can hear the tones by willing them. Like a baby taking its first steps, you will learn a new way to experience something that you were not aware of before. You simply are using your organic brain to understand something that wasn't made to be understood. So anything that you come up with is always going to be incorrect. Do you know why? Words are inadequate. As long as you accept that, you can build a new principle for thinking on the unthinkable.

So, I'm controlling the tones because, with intention, I am choosing how much I want to focus on them, which controls the octave of the sound.

You are controlling the octaves through your Middle Pillar, not your `I`s. You strengthen the Middle Pillar when you are exercising it. Only your Middle Pillar can master the octaves. By becoming more aware of the octaves and learning how to work with them without controlling the sound, without identifying them or giving them structures, you are using your mind to do what you want. That is a different kind of thinking.

When you investigate the tones, more will be revealed to you. The more that's revealed to you, the higher the octaves, and the more you will become conscious.

Be aware of where you are right now. Are you thinking about your body? Are you here or did you go too far into your I's? You can see your arms. You can see your hands. Try to remain conscious before you fall asleep again.

I want to hear more information on the tones.

When I picked up the layers of the tones, I realized they're all going on at the same time, but I can still tune into several different octaves. When that happens, I feel a movement within. I've been doing this with my eyes closed and it's as if the space and the darkness that I perceive with my eyes closed doesn't look as if I can move forward into space.

Precisely.

To me, it's like a subtle movement or frequency of dimension based on the sound. I think that's what I meant earlier by, "The sound can take you to other places." When I focus on different octaves, I feel movement and I can go back and forth with each sound, with each octave, higher or lower. It feels like a different place and you can experience it as a different place.

And it is a different place. Do you remember seeing the movie *Dune*? Remember the Navigators, the whale-like creatures? Do you remember what they did?

They folded space.

Right, they folded space. But they didn't fold space by physically traveling to a certain place. Do you understand how it's done now? There are other forms of movement that transcend the word *movement*; that transcend our concepts of movement. How do you think I make storms? How do you think I affect the weather? How do you think I can do the miracles that I can do?

Do you think it's going to be through rudimentary books of magic or simplistic science? That is so juvenile and elementary. There are other kinds of movement. There is no limit to what you can move, but you must learn to move in a different way. When you were a child, you fell down before you learned to walk. But you learned to become mobile with your physical body. The tones will teach you a different kind of movement.

When you were a child, you could not understand that which you were not ready to understand, yet you still learned. You understand this now in the most basic concept. You are learning to move in a different way. Do not become engrossed by this. Do not focus on the power of it. Do not become fixated on it. It does not operate in the same way that you think with your organic brain.

One time, I heard a rumbling sound instead of the higher pitches. It was distinctly four or five octaves below any of the lower sounds I heard before, and then it came from within my body. It was an audible sound.

Right, you could say that certain tones are from this dimension and other tones are from other dimensions. When you move through the tones, they will move you and you can travel through them, as you were saying. In the future, you will make new discoveries that will astound you.

You must follow what I'm saying to you. You cannot do this without help. You must do this with guidance or you will fall asleep, which most of you have done already again. Are you aware of your body? Are you conscious of yourself?

Navigating through those places takes concentration and knowledge of skills. When you learn to do that from this dimension, you will understand how to apply it to others. *The second that you lose your consciousness, you feel movement.* I have now given you a great, great knowledge, but do you fully understand it? There are people who would give up everything for a chance to learn what I just told you.

Is there anything else about the sound?

When I first meditated with this method, I felt a strong need to. So I struggled with that. When I went to sleep, I had difficulty hearing anything. When I woke up, I could hear the tones.

What time of day did you practice this?

I would say about six p.m.

If you were really tired and you just got home from work, what time do you consider to be your resting time? You have an inner clock and you happened to meditate during the time that your body wanted sleep. When you are meditating, you're shutting everything down. When you shut everything down, you go to sleep. When you can't sleep, it's because your mind is restless. When you're lying in bed and you're wondering, "Why can't I go to sleep," you're too busy thinking about other things.

If you use the meditation techniques to silence yourself for brief periods of time, you'll find that you will go right to sleep. When the body rests, it sends a signal to go into the sleep state. Consequently, the body wants to go to sleep. If you meditate after you wake up, you'll do your best meditation. Around midday, do your second meditation. If you have a third meditation, do it later in the day or early evening. You need to think about your routine. Sometimes when you listen to the tones, you realize your body needs more rest than you thought. By thinking about the body first, it establishes a pattern. You just need to work with that.

Let's get back to work on the tones. We wanted to study words. Words really have a very important effect on you. They affect how you think, how you automatically react. Before I begin, what am I going to say?

Are you conscious right now?

That's right. Are you conscious right now? Are you aware of yourself? Are you aware of your body? How quickly did you fall asleep?

The meaning of the words that you use daily is very mechanical because you have an internal recognition of their meaning. In life, all words are taken as the absolute truth, but they can be limited or misleading. Let's break this down a little further. Tell me what the word 'mechanical' means.

Machine-like, automatic, systematic.

Give me some visuals. What could we visualize that would be considered mechanical?

A robot. A locomotive engine. Cars.

Good. How about an erector set? Isn't that considered to be very mechanical? You can also say the gears of a watch are mechanical. Have you ever taken a watch apart to look inside? When I think of something mechanical, I usually think of the gears in a watch. I see the complexity of them, the niches, and all the little wheels turning. There are many of them; some with springs and other miniscule parts. To me, that's the epitome of a mechanical object. That is also what comes to mind when I think of a human as being mechanical. What is the similarity of the two concepts? When I say that the body is mechanical, what am I really saying?

The movement of the body is mechanical?

Movement, exactly. Let's keep this very simple. Let's deal with the basic facts.

The body has its own program. It's limited by its own structure.

You're still thinking from the organic brain. Can you give some analogies? Have you ever seen someone dance like a robot? Wouldn't that be a very limited way of moving mechanically?

It's controlled movement.

Controlled. Are there any other examples of what we do as human beings?

The process of eating, chomping on food without even thinking about what you are doing?

Right. Every time I watch National Geographic, I see a praying mantis eating the arm of some other insect, but there's nothing going on in its mind. It's just chomping on the other insect. Then, when I go into a restaurant, I see the people eating automatically without any thought. Immediately I think, "Doe. Automation." When I think, "Oh, consciousness," I look and everyone else is still munching on their food. This is very mechanical behavior to me. Then when I consciously shift, someone passes me by saying, "Hi, how are you?" It seems very robotic. People are very mechanical. Our feelings and our emotions are automated. The chemicals that flow through our brain create electrical reactions that allow us to interact with this reality.

Let me give you another analogy. Imagine a wooden hand that is made of little pieces of wood that are connected with rubber bands to make it operate. There are strings that attach to all the "joints" of the hand. The hand doesn't move by itself. You have to pull the strings so that it moves. Does it seem like your arm could be like this when you look from a different perspective?

Inside of our bodies, we have muscles that are operated by a wondrous machine called the brain. It's like a push-button electric system. It differs from the analogy of the hand that operates mechanically with strings that are pulled; the body is electrical. But it does operate like a bunch of strings with rubber bands and many other different moving parts, if you really think about it. Well, that's what the human body looks like to me.

The body is very mechanical. When you try to associate it as being mechanical, two things happen. *One*, you are going to freak out. You'll feel sick. You'll start feeling strange and you'll start making weird motions with your body thinking, "What did I just do?" *Two*, you will be aware that this is one of your `I`s. You need to understand what *being mechanical* is if you expect to discover who you really are.

Through self-observation, you begin to free yourself. The more you can understand that the body is like a machine, the more you realize that you can slip out of it. Since you think the body is all that you are and accept it as YOU, you cannot escape from it. When you are aware that the body is like a jacket that you wear, or something that you have a symbiotic relationship with, the faster and more capable you will attain hyper-dimensional thinking. You are not able to reach that level now because you're thinking with your brain and it's not YOU.

The meaning of the words you use daily is mechanical. What do I mean by that?

It means that the words really don't have much substance to them.

Do you remember the very first time you ever ate an orange? Do you remember the taste of it? Do you remember looking at the skin of an orange with little dimples on it? You can remember sinking your fingers into the orange and pulling back the skin. You can feel its fleshiness and texture as you peel the skin back. Can you remember it spraying juice when you took a bite? Do you remember the whole peeling process? The pungent, delicious, sharp, zesty, refreshing smell of that orange! Almost hearing it but not hearing it; seeing the white membrane inside of the orange, almost knowing at some point to peel that back so you can see all the juicy bits of the pulp inside of the orange.

Do you remember that experience? Then why have you forgotten it? Every time you eat an orange now, it is a process of munch, munch, munch. That's what you're doing. You're not conscious of what you're doing. It is work to experience every single thing all the time, but if you put forth just a little bit of effort, how amazing the world would become! We are all like machines. We need to escape from being machines and remember who we are. We need to be conscious, and we need to do that as often as possible. Through consciousness comes a higher evolution of being. We use words without giving them any thought.

For instance,

"Do you want to go to the store?"

"Do you want to do something with your hair?"

We're like machines, but we also have our 'I's. You might be thinking, "No, I don't feel like going to the store." But instead you say, "Sure, I'll go to the store. What do you need?" You have conflicting emotions inside of you – none of those are really you.

When you begin to utilize self-observation, self-study, will the words mean something more to you? How empty are the words in your life? Do you ever think about the meaning of the words when somebody says to you, "I love you?" It's mechanical; don't you think?

Let's take a moment right now to reflect on someone that you care about, knowing the person is probably consciously asleep. Do not judge them; realize they still have work to do on themselves and there's nothing you can do about it. Can you imagine if you looked your loved one in the eye, and just for one moment, chose to be conscious here and now saying, "I really love you." Can you feel the difference in the meaning of the words?

You will fall asleep again. You will forget to put the meaning back into your words, and your words will be like a rudimentary sentiment at the end of the day. This lesson is not just for other people; it is also for you. Maybe your loved ones won't become aware of the emphasis you place on your words because they're asleep, but they will eventually notice. All of a sudden, the phrase won't seem so mechanical anymore. It's the subtle things that we are missing in our awareness. We must escape from being machines if we truly intend to do anything great in this life.

Are there some more examples of words that you use all the time? How about something that you can relate to with the other people in your life? How about talking to your children?

"You guys are being really noisy."

"Why do you get so upset?

"Why did you do that?"

When you say those words, they are automated. Now ask yourself a question, how do your children respond? Usually, they will get quiet for a while and then go back to the way they were acting in the first place.

When your children are being noisy, a better solution is to consciously go into the room, look them in the eye and say to them, "I need you to be quiet right now." Do it with consciousness in your eyes. Explain in a normal voice, in a loving way because they are going to be shocked by your actions. Make it personal because they are consciously asleep. You've got to go out of your way to make them aware of what they are doing.

When I am sitting with my students in a classroom situation, I am conscious. They feel something from me. Everyone feels it, and when they look at me they wonder, "What is `the look` that Eric has?" Do you know what that 'look' is? I'm conscious. You may not have a name for it, but you know there's something very different about me.

There are times when my students look at me and I look back at them, but they don't feel the difference. When I'm conscious, they *know* I'm 'here'. Sometimes my students will come in and carry on a conversation without noticing anything different. At other times I come in and, if they haven't seen me for a while they'll say, "Eric's back. It's him, *that* Eric, *the* Eric." I find it amusing because my students often refer to me as if I were different people.

It's one of my 'I's that I let do whatever. If you saw "the look," it is the real me. When I have to go to work, I have this other 'I' that comes through. I may not know what is going on at the office when I walk in, but everyone thinks it's 'me'. For those of you who are really excited right now by that idea, I'm just joking. I have many 'I's that I use.

So we're working on mechanical words again and you already fell asleep! Everybody fell asleep again. Let's get back to consciousness. Let's get back to what we were doing. What is your example of mechanical words?

"Would you like a cup of tea?"

Can you relate to that one? "Would you like a cup of tea or a cup of coffee?" It's a good one. Someone comes into your house and you automatically ask, "You want a cup of coffee? Do you want something to drink?"

Do you see how automated that question is? Can you imagine coming into someone's house when they are completely conscious? "*Do you want a cup of tea?*" My God, it would be like something out of *Alice in Wonderland*, if you think about it. Somebody comes in and they're ultra-conscious. "Hi. How are you? *It's so nice to see you.*" Can you imagine the difference it would make in your life? It would be very interesting.

Here are a few more automated questions:

"What do you want for dinner?"

"How is the weather?"

"Hello?" (answering the phone)

These are all great examples of automated conversation.

> **At work, somebody said I was being really rude because I don't sit down with the group and say, "Hey, how are you doing?" I walk in and I say, "Hi, how are ya?" and that's it. On other days, I come in and I say, "Hi," and I sit down and do my thing. So my co-worker said, "You don't often ask me, 'How are you doing,'" and I said, "Because I really don't care."**

That sounds rude to most people, but if you think about it, do they really want to *know* how you are doing? What if you really told them how you *really* feel?

Here's another good one:

"How's it going?"

Sometimes, I'll sit there just to mess somebody's day up and respond, "Well, life sucks," and I do that once in a while when I feel like shocking people. Generally, I'll say, "Yeah, everything's fine," and that's a normal response. Don't you feel it when people say, "How's everything going?" and you're like, "Oh, everything's fine." *You can observe yourself saying it.* You're aware of yourself at times going, "Yeah, everything's fine." You never say, "Well, no, things are tough. Life sucks." You never say that.

You can't say that.

I think we all should do that once just to shake things up.

Trying to remain conscious here, I'm thinking about what I'm going to do the next time someone asks me, "What's up?" I'm going to jump up on the counter and say, "I'm kind of frustrated with everything."

Think about that and decide who you will surprise with that response. Look them in the eye and say, "Do you really want to know?" If they're being honest, they'll say, "No, not really," Or "Okay, great." You know what's going to happen? They're going to be shocked. You're going to feel this strange vibe from them, "Wait a minute. You've broken the code!"

We all function mechanically; our responses are purely mechanical. What would happen if somebody turned around and said, "Well, I actually have all of these issues, do you have a minute so I can tell you? Why don't you pull up a seat while you're standing there and let me go over it all with you?"

That is strange because I know what their response is going to be, yet I ask anyway.

Yet you ask it. That's another observation. Did you happen to catch that? I know what they're going to say, but still ask it. How automated are you? Are you being conscious right now?

Next?

The response is always, "I don't care." You know that's going to happen.

Who attacks that phrase? Who attacked that one just the other day, or who's been attacking it every so often? I shock you with that one, don't I? "Why don't you just do something instead of doing the same routine?" I throw out something because I'm conscious. Other times, I think, "There's no point in it. They're asleep again. There are times when I get fed up with that one and I say something to challenge you on it. In any case, it's a very good one.

Next?

"Are you having fun?" I always say it whenever somebody's doing something and they look bored.

In a way, when you say that you're conscious. Do you realize that? That's not truly automated. It's almost being half aware.

Right, but it's automated because I do it every time I see somebody bored.

Right. That's why I call it half automated, but you're doing it because you recognize what the response will be. It's an acknowledgment of a state of consciousness rather than a statement like, "Good-bye, hello, what do you want to do?" You're noticing them in a certain state of consciousness. You're now saying, "Hey, are you having fun?" What is that doing? You're shocking them. That's actually very good, you know.

"Thank you" and "You're welcome" are automated responses. I never give it much thought when I'm actually thanking someone.

Can you imagine spending the whole day consciously thanking people? Wouldn't that be something you could do to practice one day – spend one day saying, "Thank you," consciously.

Next?

"Good Morning."

We're realizing now how mechanical we all are every day. This is a realization and this is good. It's good because you are really starting to notice it. By noticing something, you free yourself. Can we ever be completely free of the `I`s?

No.

Never, but we try to get as much airtime as we can. What do I mean by that? Does anybody know what I mean by airtime?

A radio station broadcasting is referred to as being on the air.

In other words, there's commercial time, there's radio time, and then there's plugging. When you're talking to somebody about something and you say, "By the way, what do you think of my book? It's called *Pepin's Concepts in Getting Media Bites?*" That's airtime;

it's getting your piece of time in. When I say airtime, what I mean is the amount of time you consciously spend in your day before you fall back asleep again. It's the amount of time that you end up just functioning or being mechanical in the day. Every so often you're conscious and you get this little blip in your day. You want to get as much conscious airtime as you can. You have to fight for it. You need to work for it, but you need to be clever about it.

If you're on a radio station and they're interviewing you, they don't want you to talk about a product you're selling. You've got to be clever about how you slip your sales pitch in there. This way you don't have to pay fifty thousand dollars for thirty seconds. You could say the amount of time you spend meditating is your fifty thousand dollar effort versus your media bites, which is your easy effort.

If you had little alarms for every time you see a blue Volkswagen Beetle drive by, you would go, "Oh, trigger consciousness," and then you're conscious. It's like getting that little broadcast in.

As you begin to self-reflect on this, you will go through a period of greater understanding. People may look at you and think something's wrong with you. Something's very different. Most people can't relate to this.

I made a decision to start meditating three times a day every day this week. During lunch, I decided to go out to the park to meditate. People at work told me that I was acting very strange. They started asking, "Are you okay? Is everything okay? You've been acting different lately."

Can you believe that? Most people will not understand why you feel it is important to do what you are doing. They don't get it.

The day I decided I was going to meditate during lunch, all of these people came up to me asking, "How's it going? Let's go get lunch. We really need to go get lunch." So finally I said, "Okay." I went to lunch and everything was fine. The next day I decided, "I'm going to meditate." And it happened again. They kept pushing and pushing. It felt like I was fighting with them, that they knew I wanted that time but they wouldn't give it to me. Finally, I made a decision not to meditate at lunchtime, and nobody asked about lunch.

My boss is normally a very easy going, laid back kind of guy. Nothing really bothers him. On Friday, he told me that he wanted me to work on Sunday and I said, "I can't really work Sunday; it's not a good time for me. I'll work Saturday." For some strange reason, he resisted me. He's like, "Well, no, we need you here on Sunday. We're coming in at 10 a.m. That's just when you're going to do it."

We almost got into an argument. Finally I talked to him and tried to calm myself. I said to him, "Hey, how's it going? I really need this time to do something personal; how about if I work this time instead?" It felt like he was okay with that, but it's just strange how people are reacting to me lately. It feels as if the earth consciousness is consciously trying to keep me in the Doe.

That's a very interesting observation. People are Red Cells, but they are sensitive, too. When they feel something changing, they're aware of it and feel some resistance. It's like a herd of animals doing their own thing; like they're oblivious to their surroundings. But the second something feels different in their environment, all their heads pop and they run.

People are going to feel the significant changes in you that are different from your normal behavior. This is why I've learned to play my characters well. I am loved because I'm like a TV character, so full of life. Think of all my personalities; they are so real. They're *too* real. When you think of me, do you think of some mopey, boring guy who mutters, "Hi, what's up?" No, when you see me, it's like I'm animated and yelling, "What the hell is the matter with you?"

You told me to tell them that I am going through some changes, everything is okay, and that I am aware of the changes. It's not like I was acting any different. I was aware of the changes because I was doing a lot of self-reflection.

It's nice if you use the word "meditation." *Use safe words.* Do you know what safe words are? Things like, "I've been doing a lot of *yoga* lately." "I've been doing a lot of *meditations.*" "I've been going to *drumming circles.*"

When you say meditation, yoga, or familiar terms, in automation they'll respond, "Oh, okay." Somehow they'll accept that there's something going on even if they don't understand it. They'll think that you are just going through a mellow out phase. They'll be able to tag it, and will feel better with that. You need to do that, especially if you're going to work in an atmosphere where you deal with other people.

Do you think people are picking up on the fact that I am conscious of my body movements? Or the way that I move is somehow different?

You know that you need to interact with the people around you. You're being forced to do something that you may not want to do. It's like being told that you have to do a chore. You don't want to do it, but you know you should. It's frustrating and you're resentful about it.

The people around you may gang up on you and cause you to get fired up. They may say, "Who does he think he is? Do you know that he said, '*Thank you*' to me? Thank you!' Ahhh, how could he?" They may turn on you; therefore, you need to learn to work with people.

One day, while I was working at an old job, I was complaining about a person in the office that I didn't like. My boss overheard the conversation and said to me, "Well, Eric, you're not so easy to work with either. The only reason we keep you around is because you get more sales than anyone else." So, you better figure out your self-worth. Either you're going to learn to interact with others or you need to become so valuable to the people you work with that they can't afford to get rid of you. In this case, that's what I decided to do. Can you imagine me in an everyday work place? I would have to shut myself down! I'd go into work, "Hey, how you guys doing? Hey, what's up?" I was just sitting there, thinking, "Oh, my god, talk about suffering with meaningless conversation. This is suffering!" You have no idea what I go through to interact with the world.

For the past week, I've been very isolated in a reclusive sort of way. I get up early every day, but when my family calls at night I'm like, "Okay, yeah, yeah, I love you too, bye-bye," and I cut them off. I can only stand so much time around other people.

You are discovering who you are now, and that's a very interesting process. Often, there are a lot of frustrations, pains, sorrows, joys, and new things to learn about yourself; just like when you were young. If someone gets pulled into doing something and you try to stop it, they get mad at you. They want to continue doing what they're doing while you're saying, "No, we have to do it this way." They get mad at you because you're trying to impose your will on them.

You're going to go through some frustrating times with people in general, maybe not so much with the people who are close to you. You're going to find that when you are working on yourself, at times you're going to want some solitude.

You'll discover that the lower a person's tonal, in terms of spiritual evolution, the more you're going to want to disassociate from them. Some friends may be level ones, or red cells; you may separate yourself from them, but you will replace them with friends of like mind. It may be difficult to be around family members for a time while you are in this place of self-discovery. Level two people can be taxing, so you may tolerate level three's a bit more. These are the people you have grown up with. They know what you're doing but may not accept the changes in you. Some people may react to the new changes and become resistant because it makes you different from them. Their world is changing, and you were a central part of it. When you change and they feel you changing, they're going to try to bring you back into familiar territory.

Are you still conscious?

I became conscious that you were going to ask us if we were conscious!

Since you are becoming sensitive of being conscious, you're starting to realize there's a level of psychic frequency connected with this. When you're conscious, you have psychic awareness that progresses through time. You can implement those abilities easier when you're fully conscious.

Okay, I'm going to initiate a different topic with the word *"meaning,"* and we will discuss its context. First word: *meaning.*

Meaning... something one wishes to convey by language.

Okay. While contemplating these words, you will learn to free yourself by becoming more conscious of their meaning, rather than just using them mechanical-ly. Maybe you can get something out of it.

Our human language is extremely limited. The English language consists of a few words, but those words can have many different meanings. Often, the older cultures have more words to use than the English language does, and there can be translation problems from one language to another. If you speak a second language, you know that it can be very difficult figuring out words, how to express them, or even understand what they mean because there may not be a word similar to it in the English language. Or there may not be a word for it in the other language when you try to translate it. You have to either create a new word or find another word that is similar to get your point across.

Going back to ancient India and Sufism, the language had thousands of years to develop dialects and other ways to emphasize the meaning of words. When it is translated into another language, it loses a lot of its meaning. The next time it is translated into a different language, it loses even more of its original context. The Bible is a perfect example of this. It's the same with the *Fourth Way* teachings. That is a huge loss, but it's important to pay attention to the context of the words that you use in order to maintain the truth.

My mother said something to me when I was young that always stayed with me, "Knowledge is power." The more words you are familiar with, the more often you utilize them, the more intelligent you become.

Your brain tags everything; it's how the brain works as an organizational system. The stronger your vocabulary, the more people will grasp what you are saying. For instance, how do you describe the word *epiphany* in just one word? What other word is there for epiphany?

It's like a realization.

It is a realization. Anyway, what is an epiphany?

**It's like when you say, "I get it!"
You understand all at once.**

Yes, it's when a realization suddenly becomes clear to you. We need another example of an epiphany.

It's different than a realization because a realization comes over time. It's like watching the movie "Contact" when you see the entire Universe and you're in awe of it. It's like the last piece of the puzzle. Everything suddenly clicks.

Yes, but I'll give you an even simpler explanation. For awhile, I had this device; it looked like a piece of metal with a mesh screen on one side and it had a metal clamp. I looked at it and couldn't figure out what it was or its purpose. I kept looking at it and then I put it away. Over time, I would pick it up, puzzle over it, and then I'd put it away again. One day, all of a sudden, I had an epiphany. I realized it was a garlic press. I had never seen one before.

That is an epiphany. It's a realization. I finally understood that it was a garlic press and how it was to be used.

Is it an awakening?

It is a kind of an awakening, but an awakening is more personal and something that happens on the inside rather than on the exterior. By understanding the usage and meaning of the word epiphany, I could say, "I had an epiphany today," and you would understand what I meant. You would think, "Oh, something smacked him in the head and he figured something out." Words are very important. How else would you describe that moment when I figured out how to use the garlic press if you couldn't use the word 'epiphany?' What would you call it?

A realization.

A realization. I had a realization today.

A Revelation.

A revelation is good, but a revelation can mean a lot of different things. It's better to get even closer to the definition of the word, so that you know for sure that the other person completely understands what you mean.

Now, write down the word 'I'. Do you want a really tough exercise to work on? The word is *Friday*. Do you know why I chose this word? It's because *Friday* has the word 'I' in it. On that day of the week, try not to use the word 'I' all day long. Watch how often you use it when you aren't even thinking about it. We are such creatures of habit! You can tell people that you are doing a psychology exercise.

You could just write down the word.

Well, that's one way of not saying it. So how else are you going to say the word 'I' without saying Friday? When you say 'I', it becomes personal and you refer to yourself. If you cannot say the word, watch how automated you become. Watch how you spend the whole day trying to be consciously aware of it. So, on Friday you cannot use the word 'I' all day. Take note of how well you do; you will be very surprised.

You really must make an effort to do this exercise because it will show you how conscious you really are. On Tuesday, the word is 'Hello'. 'Thank you' is Monday. This is a silent kind of work. It's not about externalizing yourself but internalizing yourself. It's about the inside of you. It's what *you* get out of this exercise that matters. It will help you realize how you're thinking now. Take your time. Don't rush and don't try to be egotistical about it: "I achieved it." You only will discover that the tortoise wins the race!

You may work with a friend, comparing notes on how you both did. Have fun with this, and you just might learn something about yourself.

Chapter 3

REVERSE ENGINEERING THE SELF

Prequel

INITIALLY, I SET up a ranking system to gauge the levels of people's consciousness. It is now time to share with you what I have not shared before. The ranking system is a tool that I used years ago to talk to people who were around a level two to give them a gauge of how much they needed to progress spiritually.

We're ingrained with goals throughout our lives; we get red or blue ribbons for first place, we have school grades, and we have awards and position titles at work. Even though the levels of the ranking system are ethereal, it will give you a sense of what you are working toward. Without that, nobody could move forward in consciousness.

When I talk about the seven stages of human beings, I am really talking about the levels of consciousness of an individual. It's a matter of how much you can comprehend. Your consciousness is a frequency, vibration, your tonal.

You are consistently progressing towards a goal of enlightenment that is attained through the knowledge you are capable of understanding, and your ability to activate it. Once you reach level three, the only way you can move to level four or five is to activate that level of knowledge. *The only way to obtain knowledge is by applying, changing, or interacting with reality in ways that are not considered normal in this dimension.* Seven seems to be the mystical number in the universe: Once you reach level seven, the next step is enlightenment.

People need to orient themselves with some sense of direction. How far do you need to go, and in which direction? So, the levels are really a way for students to gauge themselves, to have an idea or a goal that is attainable for them to achieve because, in this three-dimensional world, you think in terms of mile markers. For instance, you walk forward and you measure the distance. You go a mile, but you can also go back to judge how far you have come. Everything in your mind is set by variations of distance, or levels. Therefore, my whole approach to this concept was to give my students an idea of where they were in their progression and an understanding of what they are working towards.

Each level is a stage of perception that depends on the level of your intellect. A level one might be someone who barely understands the Gaia mind. A level two might be someone who understands the Akashic Records and the Doe. At level three, you understand the matrix because your intellect has matured. You see these levels as stages of development and you pass through each one. After level seven, you have reached enlightenment. That means you understand that everything is just an illusion.

The chakra points are something very different than the stages of the human being. They are located on the body; the neural system is affected by them. At the end of the day, everything comes down to consciousness. When you are meditating on your lower chakra, since it is a grounding chakra, it will tune you into earthly matters. The heart chakra is more heartfelt and emotional, but it also offers an additional state of mind to perceive the same information that you just looked at from your lower chakra. You are building a fuel, or energy. You are converting Prana into a sort of lens to see through.

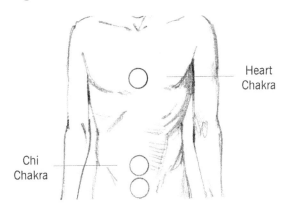

Meditating on your lower chakra is grounding and tunes you into earthly matters. The heart chakra is emotional, but also offers an additional state of mind to perceive through.

I am aware that this ranking system may keep you at the first or second level, or have a crystallizing effect on you. It's difficult to move up through the levels of consciousness when the guard rails are purely made from the lower levels. It can keep you there by default. However, I feel it is a necessary evil to get you to launch past it. But I don't want you to dwell on this concept. I want you to think without having rules and guidelines, to get you to think outside of the box. This system is highly important. It's a way of thinking; I can't get you to level four, five, six, or seven if you continue to use the same guidelines of structure, making everything that you've learned obsolete.

So, comparing the levels to chakras is similar to giving you training wheels for your bike. When do you take the training wheels off? I don't like ranking systems, yet I encourage them based solely on the knowledge of the student. If I don't give my students a sense of direction, they cannot possibly understand where they are going.

It's an enigma. It's like looking at a prism light; when you move it around, the depths and colors change. So, at the end of the day, I need a way to explain the seven levels, the chakra points, the whole perception of a heart chakra person, and crystallization, so I use this ranking system. You've got to keep in mind an expression that I often use, "I am a contradiction, but I'm not a contradiction at all."

You need to have a fundamental structure in order to get out of the organism of the matrix. You have to use it against itself, and that is what I am doing. There is a seven level system, and you must move upward within this system when you reach level three to go any further. Then, you have to scrap it and understand that it has its limitations. It's like having training wheels; at some point you have to give them up or you will never truly understand how to ride the bike. The whole time you thought you were riding the bike, but you really weren't. So this is a duality. It seems like a contradiction, but in my mind it's not.

When you first started out, I had to give you something so that you could find me on the other side. I needed to give you confidence and make you feel safe. As you matured, you started asking questions and looking at reality differently. You evolved to a level three or four. Honestly, though, you don't want me to put levels on this because all I am doing is pushing you back to a level two and I'd be crystallizing you. You've got to take the training wheels off; otherwise, you won't be able to ride up the dirt hill. You are not going to be able to race down the road, or join a relay race if you continue to use those training wheels.

So, let me ask you this: If there are seven levels of human beings and you fit on this scale as one of those seven, how does that make you feel? When you first begin, your thoughts would most likely be, "That's me! That is my identifiable role. That's what I am." But as you evolve, your Navigator knows, for certain, that you do not want to be in any of those categories because of their limitations. But it's necessary, based on what you're able to understand. You have to work towards something. You have to accept the fact that the training wheels are to give you courage and move you into an unknown area. The training wheels give you a sense of competence to progress further. Now, you are being told to let go of those things. You don't want to follow that same old road. You want to move beyond that.

I never liked telling my students that level seven was the limit. When I first introduced the levels to my older students, their mindset was, "Will there ever be an end to this? We want an end. We want to finish!" Well, it's not that simple; the journey isn't going to end all of a sudden. Your goal is to move beyond being human while you deal with life's challenges. As you grow, your thoughts will be very different, more like an enlightened master.

I feel that all spiritual teachings fall short because they have a beginning and an end. I cannot place an ending on your spirituality. I can only leave it open-ended so you can progress further than I have done.

That is my hope. No matter how smart you think you are right now, in five years you will look back and think you knew so little at this point. But you will change and you are going to grow exponentially. Without setting limitations, you now have a sense of direction so that you can reflect back on where you were five years ago, ten years ago, or twenty years ago. You can ask yourself if it made a difference toward your path.

Having a sense of direction is like this: In the middle of the night, you jump into the ocean. You can't see where you are but somehow you have to orient yourself. Are you swimming deeper into the ocean? Are you swimming upward? Are you swimming sideways? By defining a sense of direction, you are orienting yourself. So, using this as an example, are you in your heart? In your chest? In your mind? Where are you now, as a point of reference for where you need to go?

That is what I am doing when I talk to people. I say, "You are more heart chakra. You are more mind chakra." I am trying to give them a sense of direction.

Reverse Engineering the Self

There are seven levels of people on earth. The first type is focused solely on the body center. Their world is shaped around the physical body, and they see life in a certain order. Life for a level one person is very methodical, mechanically structured, and designed.

A level two person's focus is on the heart center, the emotional center. They are very spiritual, new age people. They speak a lot about, earthy, touchy-feely, free love. Level two people want to feel the love. They tell everyone that the universe is about love, and they speak a lot about love from Mother Earth.

Level three is the intellectual type of person. They understand the cosmos and its dynamics. A level three person has an idea of how God's consciousness moves and interacts with the world. They see the planet as a living organism; they see the higher truths, and they can integrate with the dynamics of level one and two. A level three person visualizes things from a much larger perspective because their consciousness, knowledge, and abilities are more refined.

Transitioning from level one to level two isn't as simple as jumping to the next step because each level has about fifty micro levels within it. As you approach level two, you move further up the micro levels of level one, which begin to mirror level two. There are about fifty micro levels within level two, so the same thing happens as level two approaches level three.

Your goal as a spiritual person is to become a level four human being. When you become a level four, you master the previous three levels and you develop a very different perspective of the world. Your spirituality dramatically changes to the extent that you now understand things far beyond what you ever could before. By pushing yourself a little harder, you will reach level four. It is only achieved by putting forth more effort.

There is a level five human being, a level six, and a level seven. Nothing above a level seven can exist on the planet. If it did, it would be extremely unique and rare.

You can learn how to be in a very high place. Then you'll be able to lower your octaves so you can communicate better with others. There are certain times when I communicate with you and you can sense a difference in me. At that moment, I am coming from a much higher place, speaking to you in a way that changes your tonal. As I get deeper into conversation, I project out different octaves of consciousness.

Try to imagine yourself on another level. It will give you an idea of where to start working on yourself to initiate your awakening process. It's important to realize that where you are now will not make you happy. How can you be happy when you have the understanding that it is not far enough or good enough? Without making it to the fourth level, you're in big trouble. It can take years for you to attain the proper state of consciousness to get there.

There are seven levels of the body. You can see similarities between the seven bodies and the seven levels of humanity, especially in the first three. There is a correlation: three and seven are really the secret numbers.

The first body is your flesh. The second body is the electrical energy field that coexists with your flesh. It makes your eyes blink, your mouth move, and your organs function. Your electrical energy is generated by the food you eat. You cannot destroy energy; you can only recreate it.

The third body is the creation of the soul. Most human beings do not have souls. They are biochemical beings who consist of two bodies: the body of flesh and the body of energy. With the standard belief system that most people possess, they do not create a third body. They pacify themselves by believing that they already have a soul. It's generally thought that, without any effort, you are automatically born with one. Like an Acme soul press, *everybody* gets one. This belief provides comfort in their life; but in my opinion, when they're dead, they're dead. Like the atheist's point of view, there is nothing that exists after physical death if you have not created a soul.

I feel sorry for your parents, siblings, and the friends that you've grown to love. I'm not saying that they do not have loving, caring emotions or that they are not beautiful people. On a biochemical level, they all have many wonderful qualities. The bottom line is that you either want to obtain a soul, or you don't. If you want to pacify yourself with the concept that everybody has one, that's your choice. I believe it doesn't work that way. It takes effort, work, and self-reflection to develop a soul.

The soul, much like your brain, your biological intelligence, works on the same principle as, "*I think; therefore I am.*" The soul is created through self-reflection and self-awareness. It is the very beginning of its most subtle creation. Creating the soul doesn't mean it is strong enough yet, and it doesn't mean that you created a third body. You must strengthen the soul through hard work and much effort. When you think about your physical body and realize how mechanical it is, the soul becomes stronger. This process only yields one result - to become aware of something more than just your physical self. By recognizing there is something more, the third body begins its creation, its birth.

Then it begins to stabilize, but it doesn't have a name yet, nor does it have a way of knowing what it is. You have no way of fully understanding it with your biochemical brain. By trying to become aware of it, it begins to form a structure. By learning, studying, and trying to define it by using words, it begins to form some mass on an energetic level. The physical body is like a glass and the water that's inside of it is like the electrical energy in that body. These are two different things, but they are really one that serves one purpose: to give your body nourishment.

The third body is created through a process of distillation. In the same way that you can extract pure water from tap water, there is a third body that is created by separating the water from the minerals; thus, it becomes a third body of water, a very pure one. Creating the third body is the full creation of the soul, and right now you are in a distillation mode. Right now, because you are reading this book and because you are pondering this knowledge, you are distilling and creating your third body. You're doing this because you are obtaining the third level of humanity. It comes from having the mental aptitude to begin to investigate internally.

Let's take a closer look at a level two human. We've looked at level one and we can see how everything is external. There's very little going on internally in a level one human. The second level has too much biochemical emotion. Most of their lives is spent in the surrender state, so they are not capable of accomplishing or attaining another level because they don't have a strong sense of self-discipline. Many people who are in the second level tend to use drugs, particularly marijuana, to help them loosen up. Other addictions, such as alcohol, are often used as well. They have to rely on chemical stimulation to help them *feel* something. They need to force themselves to open up with an outside source, which makes them spiritually lazy.

Therefore, they are like an earth tonal, "mother-love" energy. However, there are some new age people who are on the higher end of the second level, heading into the third. They have successfully surrendered the drugs and have become more complex in their understanding of things. Somehow, they survived instead of crystallizing in level two's mid or lower micro-levels. You should strengthen your ability to become aware of the people who are still at the earth tonal level. Be aware that they are, for the most part, still crystallized. Typically, people don't think that this emotional place is crystallizing or that it hinders their spiritual growth.

The first level feels like solid crystallization. You can feel it if you think about it. The second level doesn't solidify you as much because there is a lot more flexibility in the feeling of love. It is like the Earth energy. The Earth is like a snake that wants to hug you and love you, but it will also bite you the second you retract from it. Its venom numbs you. It makes you feel that things don't matter, that everything is okay, and that life is good. What does marijuana do? What do all recreational drugs do? In a lot of ways, they do the very same thing.

When I say earth, I mean marijuana because it is the prime source of this particular subject. It's an earth substance. I believe there is a correlation; it is not a coincidence that marijuana has been such a popular drug for so long. There is a purpose behind it. Marijuana is extremely dependent on its symbiotic relationship with human beings because its potency level is completely unnatural. Its symbiotic relationship is a way of seducing and keeping people numb and addicted. It becomes cyclical because the addiction creates a demand for more marijuana. This way, it can continue reproducing itself. So, it has mastered many human beings by forcing them into that cycle.

The second level, the level of love energy can be very dangerous. It's hard to get through because you can become suffocated with this energy. You want to flower, but you perpetuate in the one chemical emotion that feels good, so you ultimately cease growing. This is why a lot of users turn to other drugs. There are a lot of people associated with this love energy. You tend to gravitate to a certain area, usually self-gratification. Although gratification can be quite physical, it's also a rather numbing feeling. You want to feel love and be compassionate all the time. These things are all great, but they imply, "If you are not like me, then you can't understand it," and that is not true at all. This kind of love is usually a façade. Under closer scrutiny, most of the people using drugs who proclaim all of this love are very manipulative and selfish people. You have to take a closer look at them. Don't be deceived by what is presented. There are wonderful qualities of love, but for the most part, it's not what it's meant to be because most people are liars; it is human nature.

There's a wide spectrum within the second level human being. By understanding and becoming more aware of the first three levels, you will have greater insight. When you look at people, it will be easier to understand them than before.

Levels one, two, and three are most definitely structured areas. There's not always such a definite point when becoming level two. People will often deviate between both areas as it is a growth process. As you sit reading this material, you get a certain amount of knowledge. Your level rises a bit, but as you get sucked back into everyday life, your level goes back down. When you stop, you drop down a couple more octaves, but you're a little bit more than you were before.

There is a fluctuation that happens consistently. As you build yourself, you move up one level. When you meditate and you have an experience or receive energy, you never really lose it. There is some accumulation; no matter how much you think you forgot or lost, you still gain. Don't think there is a *specific* point that you must reach. This is how human beings think. It's not about whether you are this or you're that. There is room for flexibility. As you build, you are able to sustain yourself for longer periods. Eventually, you keep building until you have a solid enough platform to continuously push yourself higher through your endeavors.

Can different 'I's be on different levels?

Well, this depends on your flexibility; which 'I' is dominating and by how much? The amount of time that you give particular 'I's has a big effect on your total vibration. If you're only thinking about doing trivial things, your everyday 'I's dominate your life. Let's say that there is a change in your life and as a result, you are becoming more spiritual. So, instead of doing trivial chores, what will you be doing most of the time now? You will start going to spiritual meetings and doing spiritual activities. You will buy spiritual objects for your house. Spirituality is constantly occupying more of your time, which in turn dominates your total vibration. Before, your spiritual 'I's were an accumulation of little spurts of spiritual actions. Once you start this process, you start changing your focus. You start progressing. You are always changing.

Would that process affect the level of your other 'I's?

Inevitably, you begin to have less need for them because you recognize how trivial they are, and you create greater ones. Or your `I`s become more complex and they learn. You have changed since you first started reading my books. If you think back to whom you were then, you must've had a lot of powerful `I`s originally. Through study and self-reflection, you've lost a lot of them and new ones have taken their place. It's one of those things that you don't necessarily see or feel. It's something that changes very subtly. You don't know that it is going on. Do you feel the hair on your head growing? Yet it grows. It can make a significant difference in a short period of time.

When we speak of level one, level two, or level three, we use this as a way to quickly reference where people are spiritually. When describing another person, one could say, "I met this person and she's definitely a solid level three." That means she's capable of understanding what we know. We don't have to worry about how much of a debate we're going to get into with her. If you said that she is about a three, that means you're hesitating and she's walking the border between two and three but she hasn't quite put it all together yet.

Everybody starts out on level one and works themselves to level two and level three. Some people just do it faster than others. Sometimes you have assistance from your family. Sometimes people are naturally inclined to excel in this area. As a child, you start off mechanically. You're affected by your introductions to different perspectives and by what the people around you believe. Eventually, you might meet someone powerful enough, like me, who will shock you and bring you up through these levels.

Can you go from level one to level three?

It's absolutely possible to do that with a strong teacher. Sometimes, I think, it's also possible without a strong teacher. At some point, you have to travel to level two in order to get to level three. Naturally, you have the essence of all of these levels within you. You have these centers in other ways: the mind, body, and spirit. You have emotions. You *have* all of these things. But to get from level two to level three, you have to go through a level of emotion. Then, you can make sense of level three. If you didn't, you wouldn't be able to make it far into level three. You would be computer-like. In a way, being computer-like would actually bring you back down to a lower level. You need level two to become electrical; to think without being on the tracks. You can float above those tracks but still understand them. In order to make it to the third level, you need an understanding of both levels one and two.

I've met people that are strong threes and none of the other two levels.

Don't be fooled, they are really strong level ones. In order to get to level three, you must have the support of levels one and two. To get to level two, you still must have the support of level one. You could be all in the mind. You could be brilliant but still be at level one. When you approach level four, it's more of an energy level of thinking that becomes dimensional. I have heard cases of mathematicians who were working with math in their mind. All of a sudden, their reality became hyper-dimensional. They saw the bars and objects moving through the walls. They could see some level of dimension and understand it. But just because they could see it, that does not mean they could *move with it.* That still puts them on a level one. Just because you can *see* it does not mean you can *conceive* it.

So one is not just body, two is not just heart, and three is not just mind?

That's correct, it becomes like a diamond with many facets. When you look through it, you can see all these other dimensions within it. You can't always say that someone is one thing specifically. There are many combinations and intricacies that define the potential or the level of that person.

A mathematician may brilliantly understand the quantum physics of the universe, but that doesn't mean they can move through it. An atheist can be a level three up to a certain point. Instead of taking level two and understanding true emotion, they only understand biochemical emotion. It's a poor substitute, but you can still take an old, beat up car and get to your destination. It's not going to take you to level four. Nor is it going to take you across the country or over the sea. You can figure out certain things on your own, through observation, but you can't totally understand it.

Don't you need some comprehension of the Force or God to move on to the fourth level?

Yes, that's what happens in the third level. Remember, there are different micro levels within level three. When you are in level one, two, or three, there are multiple levels inside of them. *You're looking at the same thing, but from a different perspective.* You're not moving. It's a trick, a hologram.

It's like in Star Trek when the holodeck character, Professor James Moriarty, came to life and said, "I think, therefore I am," and took over the ship. To regain control of the ship, the crew created a fake reality for it, and they projected themselves into the fake hologram to make Moriarty believe it could come out of the original hologram and walk around. Instead, it was really transferred onto a little microchip. Moriarty still travelled around in his own dimension, but that dimension was a whole generated computer program. In a way, intelligent level one people think they're moving ahead, but they can't. They've done all that they can in this life. They have to back up, review, and understand so they can strengthen those other levels in order to actually move up. In truth, they're in the computer chip. And the computer chip is really level one.

They've always been on level one. They think they are at level three; they have the attributes of level three. *However, they're really working on a dimensional level three that's within level one.* Not everything in this world works the way you assume it does. Time is not what you think. Space and dimension are not what you think. You're in a maze. You need someone who can see the entire maze from a distance to give you directions. It is very difficult, and it takes an extreme amount of trust. If you don't have trust and you refuse the help that's been given, you can't be helped, so you're not going to be found.

Let's say that you realize you're in a maze. You know you need help and you must have trust, but you have a shred of doubt and for whatever reason, you don't completely trust the person who's helping you. Think about it logically. What difference does it make? You're going to be lost without that person, so you may as well take a chance and gamble on them. It doesn't take much to figure out that you will not advance if you do not even try.

My advice is to not move so quickly. Take your time. Don't try to understand so much with your brain right now. The *brain* cannot give you the answers you're looking for. It's just a habit that you keep going back to because you don't know how to use anything else.

You are progressing. That's what's important. Don't worry about whether or not you are stagnating. You've made it to where you are now. Have you not made significant progress? Why be concerned with your brain telling you, "Well, you could be stuck going in a loop." You know that you are not. Why concern yourself with your future by panicking about something you haven't even approached yet? You're sabotaging your success. Your enemy is already winning. Your `I`s are preventing you and your logic from winning.

Are you beginning to understand the complexity of this level? You are probably going to forget again. It'll never be the same. Don't you feel a little exhausted right now? It's work. You're pushing your energy. Like a physical workout, you are pushing your energy to make your physical body understand what it just did.

Let's say an absolutely brilliant, genius scientist comes from Russia. Suppose he sits down with some American scientists and they're talking. His English isn't very good and he says to the Americans, "You know a tubular... and what is the word?" After awhile, the Americans are going to say, "Well he's a nice guy, but he's not really that smart." Why do they assume he is not that smart? It's because of his limited command of the English language. If he spoke to the American scientists in Russian, he would be able to communicate all of his thoughts in the language of physics and be able to take them through an intense journey. There are words in other languages that there are simply no words for in English.

I remember a time when I was talking to my mother and I was telling her, "Tell my grandfather such and such." She said, "Well, there is no word for that in German." Then I asked, "What do you mean?" She's said, "There's no word that I know of that would explain that." I said, "Then tell him blah, blah, blah." And she said, "There's no word for that either. I understand in English what you mean, but there is just no way to explain that in German." So we had to keep simplifying it. Finally, she found something that she could work with and offered that to him in hopes that between Austrian and German, there were other words to expand his thinking so he could grasp the concept. My biggest problem when using hyper-dimensional thinking is trying to give concepts to you in human language so that you can understand.

I often use different analogies and really strange words. Or I demonstrate things by throwing my body around. I communicate using sounds and facial expressions to help you understand something that there are no words for. By helping you understand this, you get the big picture. This way, you can construct an energy body so that you will be able to comprehend it. There are just some things in English or other languages that cannot be explained in any other way. We communicate in this dimension through words. It's our way of taking one person's vision from their mind and giving it to another person to explore.

I can't take you where you need to go unless I can find ways to communicate what you need to understand. Your organic brain cannot process the data fast enough. It is like a computer from the 80's.

The brain works on several levels: chemical, low radiation impulses, and electrical. Did you notice that we are at *three* again? When you develop your mind and you are constantly meditating and going into a higher state, you create a hyper-dimensional brain that is still somehow connected to the physical, but it is moving at the speed of light. It's hyper-dimensional. Your physical brain and electrical brain occupy the same amount of space. Both are trying to receive data and work with each other. You can be conscious of this high-speed data, as it is part of you.

When the dimensional brain gains knowledge, it slows down in order for it to become part of the organic brain. The chemical level of your brain is really the slowest. Unfortunately, that's what you use most of the time. It's important that you grasp these concepts. That is what will free you.

The electrical impulses are only about two percent of the brain's capabilities, and the chemical is about eight percent. The knowledge is minimized because it has to now go from hyper-dimensional speed to electrical. The electrical immediately loses at least sixty percent of the data because it can't handle the speed. It's like writing a program and, all of a sudden, it becomes corrupted because you lost some data.

After losing sixty percent, that gives us forty percent to work with. However, that's slowing down to low-radiation which also has a mass loss, leaving us maybe five percent to work with. That five percent has to slow down enough so that it can be interpreted by the chemical level in order for it to write to the organic. The chemical still moves slightly faster than the organic placement of it, which is like putting the data in files and drawers to be used later. After all of this, we're down to probably less than one percent of the original data.

Is that why you only get images or flashes when you analyze an experience later?

Precisely, it's still static electricity. The brain is just incapable of storing it fast enough to keep all the data. By building a second, third, or fourth body, you incorporate that into your physical body and learn to speed up the process.

Humanity started off first with the reptilian part of the brain. The mammalian part of the brain came next, followed by the neo-cortex. These parts process respectively at slow, medium, and then much faster speeds, giving vast capabilities. Once again, there are three.

After that level of completion, humanity developed the frontal lobe. This really generates a lot more thought and ties the brain together. It does not fully develop until you're in your mid-twenties.

From the frontal lobe, humans learned to process data that they were previously incapable of understanding. Humans could still see with their eyes, hear with their ears, and smell things; but they couldn't fully understand that there are layers to the data their senses collected. This evolution of the brain creates a technology, one capable of grasping more of the data or the experiences people are getting. This in turn created a third brain, which is way beyond the capability of animals. All this enabled the brain to work faster and better. *Therefore, it made it seem like things solidified into our reality.*

When you collect energies from breathing and meditation exercises, you create a *fourth brain*. But it doesn't necessarily adhere to the level of the organic brain. If you have the electrical aspect of your brain working at three percent, and low radiation impulses working at another percentage, why can't you use that energy to increase the percentage that you operate at? What would happen if you brought those two energies up to fifty percent capacity? What would happen if they always ran at fifty percent capacity? Wouldn't you be able to hold a greater amount of data because you were thinking in light instead of thinking with chemicals in small bits of energy? Why not think with more energy?

When you meditate and feel electrical charges running through your head, and you feel tingling and different heat sensations, would that be an effect of raising the low radiation and the electrical currents?

No, in those cases, you are just becoming more aware of the chemical reactions.

So you're feeling on a more minute level?

That's correct. Feeling and becoming aware of those sensations begins to separate your energy from your physical body so that you think more with energy. The more you're aware of your body, the less you think with biochemical thoughts from your organic brain. *The chemicals can process data but they can't acknowledge themselves. You need something higher to acknowledge or observe the chemicals. By doing so, you become more of that energy.*

Do you actually feel the chemicals moving in your head, creating electricity?

Yes, you separate from it. No longer can they store themselves. You need something else to store them and that's what you start to think with.

When you receive large amounts of information, what percentage of the data do you actually take in?

In my organic brain, I probably take in about fifty percent. The rest stays hyper-dimensional because I move the knowledge around. It's not a matter of thinking it or knowing it. I receive one hundred percent of the data. I have problems when I try to move it into my organic brain, vocalize the knowledge, and find associations of thinking so that I can explain it. It's like somebody trying to translate a language.

A good translator can translate, but another translator who's listening to them will always say they didn't translate correctly. I always try to give you the best interpretation, but whatever comes out can never be one hundred percent accurate; it's always flawed. In the case of a translator, it's not that they're bad if they don't get it one hundred percent right; they may have a good grasp of a language. They may just be struggling to translate it in a way that you can understand it in your language.

Is the goal to create that fourth body so it can collect more of this data?

Yes, because then you won't need to rely on my explanations as much. If you have that fourth body, I can talk and broadcast to you from hyper-dimensional thinking. Then you can just take the data. Sometimes I do this with my students. In a lot of ways, this is how they made it this far. It's not just from what I've taught them. It's from literally pushing them.

Is that the universal language?

In this dimension only, emotion is the universal language; but it's still crude.

Are the finer levels of emotion biochemical?

These finer emotions are still crude but they'd probably be part of the fifth body rather than biochemical. Through your dreams, you can learn and experience things that you may not be able to in your waking life. If you dream of a yellow bus, does it mean that the dream is only about the yellow bus? No, if it's a yellow school bus, does that mean it is only about school? No, that bus is a symbol that your brain is comfortable working with.

Images and concepts like this are simple blocks that don't shock the brain too much. It's the small details in between the symbols that are really teaching you - the way somebody walked, or the way somebody talked to you when they got off the bus. Or what they said to you when they got off the bus rather than who they were. Or how they looked you in the eye in a certain way that gave you a certain feeling, but everything else about the bus was normal, simply kids getting off the bus.

In between those large symbols are lessons that you resonate with. Sometimes there are more of those types of moments, sometimes less. Sometimes it's fear that gives you those moments. Sometimes it's dealing with an overwhelming situation in your life. Perhaps in your dream, I'm getting off the bus but it looks like a much older person. As you look that person in the eyes, it dawns on you, "That was Eric!" How did you know? It didn't look like me, but it was my eyes, my *presence*. The dream taught you that there are things within people you may not be seeing on the surface. So you've learned something from it.

Is it a bad thing that I had dreams about you but don't remember what happened?

It doesn't matter. You don't necessarily forget hyper-dimensional knowledge. It just needs to solidify and that takes time. There were times in my youth when I received a download of information and then ten years later, I remembered a dream containing a particular training. It would help me to understand how to deal with a current situation. There are things you are learning now that may not be useful to you for another five, ten, or twenty years. You may be looking at something and then recall that you've had some insight about a particular moment or place. Not particularly a déjà vu, but a sense of knowingness, a sense of awareness of it. That's what you have to pay attention to.

Let's get back to discussing the levels of humanity. Some things can prevent you from entering the fourth level. Pettiness, selfishness, and anger will prevent you from moving to the next level. *So will too much love.* Ego, judgment, and comparison will guarantee that you never fully enter the fourth level. You may enter slightly, but you'll never gain any distance within this level. It's like two magnets pushing against each other. As hard as you try to push them together, they will repel and it will take a huge amount of concentration to get them to even touch.

That power of repulsion will eventually overpower you and prevent you from moving forward. Your ego and all of your identities are not welcome in this place. They are incapable of going there because they are still chemical; they are solid. They can't go there. As long you hold onto them and think they are you, you will not be able to enter fully.

I see ego, comparison, and judgment all the time. It's time now to move beyond that. It's time to show you what transcends the word "power." Power is petty and small. Power is inconsequential, insignificant, and meaningless. That's like saying that we're concerned with the dirt that's within the fibers of the carpet from five years ago. Do you really even care?

Ego can be very subtle. Everyone has it and everyone is controlled by it. Ego makes you lie to yourself. Ego makes you think that you're more than what you are. You lie to yourself because you dream of what you will become. Ego guarantees failure because when you decide that your ego isn't completely who you are, you're so disappointed with yourself that you give up. You lie to yourself all the time. *You must transcend that.* You must shed it or you will forever be in battle with it.

Being concerned with who is moving ahead and who is moving behind is fruitless. Those who are moving ahead deserve to move ahead because they've earned it. The people who make it are the people who seek it out in earnest, with honesty and sincerity in their heart. They try to find the highest level of truth within themselves.

You still have a sense of right and wrong; therefore, you can also move beyond that. Selfishness and control over someone succeeding beyond you is pettiness. Pettiness is vile. Most of the time, you don't even know that you're being petty until it consumes you. You may not even know where your pettiness and your ego are coming from. You are simply reacting. But if you really were to observe your ego, you would see the truth of where it's coming from. You must look at your own greed and your own pettiness.

Pettiness is the one thing I do not like seeing in students because it shows me their true colors and that they do not deserve what they have learned so far. A petty person molests life, trying to take what is not theirs through power and manipulation. The truth will always elude them. They are not allowed entrance no matter how powerful they want to be. They become spiteful, angry, and frustrated when they realize that they cannot enter.

This is what creates dark beings. They feel that they're being punished, as if they've been extricated and are unwanted. Their ego creates rage, so they demand, "I have a *right*; you *owe* me; I *suffered* for you." To that, I would respond with a statement like, "I don't owe you anything. If you want to enter, there are rules. If you think you're going to change those rules, you're a foolish person. Go on your way. You're wasting my time."

Pettiness is very unbecoming. Try to remember that when you're being petty. You can stop any time you want. The only reason you don't stop is because you have a feeling that you must continue. You have a feeling that you must follow a role, just like when you go through an anger cycle and observe it. You recognize that you're being petty, but you keep doing it anyway. Why? It's because of your ego. You have to turn around and say, "I'm sorry I am being petty right now." You have to stop it the moment you catch yourself doing it. It's the only way you'll help yourself.

When you make a comment, you better think about what place it's coming from. Is it coming from your true center or is it coming from your center of power, greed, or lust? If it's coming from one of those places, you have to stop yourself as quickly as you can consciously recognize what's going on. What kind of selfish motives are you acting upon?

The movie *Crouching Tiger, Hidden Dragon* is a good example to explain what I mean. I use movies all the time because they're good tools to help you to understand better. There's something very interesting in this movie that you probably have not noticed. How much emotion do the master characters show?

Very little to none.

They have very little emotion. It's as if they have mastered their `I`s. When you look at these masters, don't you admire them? Instinctively, you know the truth! Even the actors in the movie, who really aren't what they're portraying, instinctively know what is expected of a master. How do they know how to present the characters in this manner? They just know because it's within them. They know what the truth looks like, or at least a representation of the truth. Maybe they learned it from other masters, or somebody demonstrated it and they looked at it and realized, "That is a master!"

When we see a Kung-Fu master, or a spiritual master, they speak peacefully and they move and act gracefully. That's true power. They are working from a place of power within themselves. They've learned to control all of their `I`s. It can be faked, but not for long. How much of a master do you want to become? You must begin to eradicate the petty `I`s, the petty ego's, everything petty.

It is a beautiful place in which these masters reside. When you see them gently and quietly talking and moving, they are in that place. The way they present themselves, their is-ness, is magnificent. I hope that all of you can attain this someday. You begin attaining this through self-awareness and by having it shown or pointed out to you. Over time, you will find this and develop it within yourself. You have a choice: you can either come with me or you can fall behind.

Pay attention to your movements, your reactions, and how something is said to you. To be truly of a higher evolution, you must try to attain a level of consciousness in a different way. The fastest way to do this is not by mastering yourself in such a way that you force yourself to attain it. You accomplish it by cutting loose the things that are not really of you, leaving behind your true being. The more `I`s you can get rid of, the more you can resonate purely instead of wasting energy by trying to overpower them. It's all a process of how you think and how you feel.

When somebody criticizes you, or they look at you in a condescending way, don't let this attach to you. It really doesn't matter; those things are trivial. You only have to interact with them in a way that helps you to master yourself. Do not allow your ego to tell you, "You have to be spiritual; you can't relate to them." *Listen without reacting.* You need the symbolic relationship of work and integration with people. Without it, there is no life to breathe into you. It's what will help forge you. It's what will help make you smooth and polished, like the stone beneath the waterfall. It takes time for it to become a perfect, smooth surface.

Don't be affected by the wearing and tearing of people trying to pull you into their negative worlds. You must interact in such a way so they can acknowledge you are a guiding light that they can begin to appreciate, a representation that goes beyond them.

A martial arts master doesn't turn her back on society. You don't see her holing up in the temple and never coming down. She meditates, but talks to the people as well: "I had a great meditation. I worked and discovered this truth and I had a revelation about it. I spent time with my teacher."

Remember where she is telling this tale from. She is out in the world integrating with the people. She may become a teacher. We all would like to become teachers, but do you think she was always one? No, she carried water, milked the cows, and worked with her hands doing rough labor. You have to learn to work with life before you can become a master.

When the master goes out in public, does she think he is untouchable and her knowledge so unattainable that she can't bring herself down a level to speak to the thugs at the restaurant? Do they not respect her? She doesn't isolate herself from them. She integrates with them and the other people in the village. She fulfills her duty as a security person. That's really what she is. Do you think that every day is a Kung-Fu battle? Or every month? How about every year?

There were times during the year that she attended her labors and her needs. But yet she also presented herself, and the people who saw her would think, "She is an amazing person. She's a hero." They did not see her as a master. It didn't matter to her; she didn't care. What did I just say?

She didn't care.

Do you understand the meaning behind this? It did not feed her ego because it was irrelevant. She would not have cared even if they saw her as a shoeshine girl.

You have to learn to work with life before you can become a master.

You have to work and integrate with life. If you don't do that, you're lying to yourself. You are feeding a different kind of ego. You need to operate from that placid place when you integrate with life: talking to co-workers and other people. Set the tempo. Set the level of how you will be perceived. *If you make yourself out to be foolish, you will have the weight of other people's energies projecting at you, enabling you to play this role.* You will create a role for yourself.

It's very important to control the way other people see you because it will have an effect on how well you do with your own training. *How much success you have is based on how other people view you.* This is why most spiritual people leave their family at some point in their lives; their family thinks of them in a certain way. It's also why people leave their job and start a whole new life. The people in their new life don't know much about them. Yet there is some fascination about them.

You don't have to go to those extremes in this day and age. You have everything here and now. Just recognize that you need to control how people see and regard you. You don't want other people to lavish their attention on you.

Don't speak too much. Instead, talk about meaningful things. Go out, function and do what you need to do, but don't babble on about trivialities.

When you look at computer games, you are looking for something that interacts with you. You are subconsciously mimicking those machines in whatever you are doing. You try to create your own humanness in the mirror of a computer. It's obtuse in a way, but you can also learn a great deal from that. It is a mirror of how your mind works. So you are constantly trying to improve it to meet that level of awareness.

Playing computer games really does nothing for you. It is the *same repetitive thing* that you are being ingrained to do. It's the same game over and over again. When you move up a level, the creatures just have a different look. It's the same program but they amp up the power to match your new skill. It's the same fight; it just looks different. It's appealing to your hunter-gatherer instincts from primitive humanity, making you feel like you're getting more points, more money, or more power.

In the end, you're stuck in that dimensional loop where you think you're moving up to level three, but you're really stuck in level two. You're *so* sucked into it because it is really a lower level place that makes you think you're on level three, intellectually. It puts you in this inner world where you feel as if you're progressing, but in the outer world you're not progressing dimensionally.

Self-pity has the same effect; there's no progression. You think you're progressing by working on yourself, but the next week you go right back to where you were and you don't even think about it. You're still depressed and you're still in the same place. You've never progressed from this inner world, so you're still on level two.

If you move to the fourth level, you will be thinking in hyper speed. Your awareness will be in hyper speed. Everything around you appears to slow down. In our reality, it looks amazing. It's that sense of knowing, just like the silence within the person.

The answer that you're looking for is in Aikido. Aikido is performed by blending with the motion of the attacker and redirecting the force of the attack rather than opposing it head-on. This requires very little physical strength, as the aikido practitioner "leads" the attacker's momentum. The aikido practitioner uses the opponent's own force against them. Do you understand about operating from that place as a master? Forget about what Hollywood presents to you. You must find the accuracy behind the truths.

In any kind of martial arts, even the master is still a student to a master of hyper-dimensionality. Since a hyper-dimensional master moves *so quickly*, he does not have to move to strike; it already is done. I assure you that even a master will know that. They wish they could learn the knowledge; but since they work so much from their body center, *they master the body before they become the master.* At some point, because of their mastering, they learn about the two other centers; but by the time they do, it's too late.

In order for you to be able to go into a deeper state, you must know where the `I`s come from. In order to deal with a problem and tackle it, you must not grab the tree by its leaves or the weed by its top and pluck it. You must get to its *roots*. If you understand the source of something, you can comprehend the power of it. If you just try to deal with it on the surface, you can't see what's fueling it from behind.

Where do the `I`s come from? There are really three major `I`s, but there is one that is hidden that we must bring up. There's the body center, the emotional center, the intellectual center, and the instinctual center. The three that we are most concerned with are: body, emotion, and intellect. The fourth, which is a product of these three, is instinct. It doesn't really concern us, so we only want to know about these three. The body center is the lower chakra. The emotional center is the heart chakra. The intellectual center is the mind chakra.

You go into a restaurant because you're hungry. That's an `I`. You're hungry so it's telling you, "I want to eat. Where are we going to eat?" So you start debating in your head where you're going to eat. That's all coming from an `I`. When you go into a restaurant, the whole place is packed. There are a few uncomfortable, metal chairs available, so you take one of those seats. Over in the corner, you see some cushy ones. Some people are just finishing their meal and you know that, eventually, they're going to get up and leave. You'd have to go back in line to get that table, but you don't know how long it's going to take.

So the hunger `I` says, "I want immediate gratification." But the body `I` is saying, "I'm uncomfortable." So those two `I`s are probably coming from the same center: the body. In the intellectual center, you reason by saying, "Well, if I get up and go over there to sit down and make myself comfortable, then I'm not going to get to eat, and I am hungry." That's the intellectual `I`.

All of these `I`s come from various body centers, each with their own set of rules. Each `I` has a list of obligations and responsibilities. The *comfort* `I` is concerned with how you are sitting and the position you're in. It takes care of all these things that have to do with your physicality.

Your emotional center is charged with all your emotions. When you see something, you react, but there's also an internal reaction that decides how you're going to react: whether you're going to be sorry, happy, sad, joyous, or whatever. It comes from that center and it dictates what you're going to experience.

The *intellect* is the one that regulates caution. It looks to see if there's something dangerous or if it's safe. Is this person trustworthy? Is it safe to put my body in this predicament? That's its list of responsibilities. Through these three comes your basic functions and from them come all of the `I`s. Each of these three primary `I`s may have another fifty `I`s within them. They all correspond from those three chakra points.

Are you seeing some interesting truths now? Your body is not who you are. Your mind is not who you are. Certainly, your emotional center is not who you are. So your `I`s pretend that they're you, but they're really not you. They come from primitive humanity. They come from your reptilian brain center. They are the basic survival instincts that every creature has.

A baby has four basic functions: happiness, sorrow, intellect, and instinct. Instinct isn't like, "I had an instinct that something was going to go wrong," or "they were a bad person." That's intellect. Instinct is survival. Instinct makes your heart beat and your organs function. It makes you breathe without thinking about it. Instinct is a sensory inside of you that keeps your body functioning. It keeps your body working, even if you're not paying attention to it.

If you go into a coma, does your body stop functioning? No, it keeps working. It doesn't need you to be there. If you get into a bad car accident, you're put on life support if your body is severely physically damaged. In most cases, it still works, even with half the brain exposed. So instinct is not something you need to study or be concerned about. It has its purpose, but there is something that you must really understand.

Every human being is afraid of death. Since you're afraid of death, you're prevented from achieving enlightenment. This fear prevents you from moving to the fourth level because who you are is associated with your physical death.

Some people are afraid to go into a deep meditation. They get really nervous and stop because they feel themselves separating from their body. They are afraid their body will stop functioning; their heart will stop beating, they will stop breathing, and their body will die. Therefore, they think they really are their body. So they can't go beyond who they are if they are constantly afraid of something happening to their body. How can you reach enlightenment and how can you go beyond who you think you are?

I am discussing this to help liberate you from fruitless thinking. By telling you that the body is instinctual, you know that you can be totally gone and the body will still function without you. So your fear of leaving the body and it shutting down is totally misplaced. *Your fear of dying prevents you from awakening.* Of course, you don't want to die because you need to complete the work on yourself while you're here on Earth in order to attain these other levels. If you cut out too soon, you're going to come back and you may not make it this far next time. Depending on whom you are, your circumstances, and the past lives of your soul, it may still be too much work. So why stop now?

Instinct plays a very important role, even though it's not necessary to pay attention to it. We don't have to worry about controlling our heart, lungs, or anything else. It's a waste of time to train and master it. Let it do its own thing. You *can* affect it. You can learn to work with it. Why put your energy into it when it's difficult enough to master the other things that will ensure your enlightenment? Where do you want to put your energy and your time? You see time as linear. You see yourself young and then old: birth to death. So you've got a certain amount of "time" to work with, to occupy your attention. How do you want to use it?

We know that the `I`s originate from one of our emotional centers. We now have an awareness of their roots. They came from primitive humanity. They are survival instincts. When you get hungry, you know it's time for you to nourish the body.

Scientists say the procreation of cellular life is the meaning of everything. Humanity was never really designed to become intelligent. It was a by-product of protecting the genes and procreating more of our species. That's evolution. We became intelligent by accident.

Think of a lion. It isn't as intelligent as you but it must have an intellectual `I` that's very crude because it knows which animals are the weakest. In its own crude way, it knows which animals to single out. It knows when it's hungry. It could lie on the grass all day. So how does it know when to get up and eat? Is that an intellectual `I`? No, that's its body `I` saying, "It's time to feed me. Do something about it. I am hungry!" The intellectual `I` then takes over. For what reason was it created? To ensure that the cubs are going to grow and survive, their genes must be protected by the senior, the larger, and the stronger lion. So it is the emotional center that comes from that. So we have now created three centers.

Have you ever noticed that if you really study creatures of a lesser intelligence, you can see that their `I`s are very simple? By studying animals, you can see they're very limited in how they express their individual `I`s. Some are even more simplistic than others because they can only function with simple tasks. When my cat shows joy, he just rolls around. He doesn't show joy when he is eating his food. He's just gratifying his sensory for eating. When he wants to gratify his need for pleasure he does that, but he doesn't eat while doing that.

A human can show joy and eat at the same time. By studying animals, you can learn certain things. A cat is very limited in how they express their individual `I`s. His intellectual `I` decides what he's going to do. That intellectual `I` is probably inspired either by his emotional center or his body center. Half the time he looks like he doesn't know what he wants. That's because he doesn't. No `I` has taken over yet! So it's down time instead of airtime. There's just nothing to decide on. *He wants for nothing.*

If you look at other species, you can see the ones that are more advanced and the ones that are less advanced. You can still see the structure of their `I`s. Monkeys are more complex. They have more `I`s or their brain is a little faster so they learn to integrate their `I`s at the same time. They don't appear to be separate but they are separate. They are just multitasking, doing it so quickly that it appears to be one state of consciousness.

You learned to process the motor centers, the `I`s, and the energy centers so you can make them work and integrate them at the same time, but they are still individual. They are just moving so quickly that they look like just one process. If you could *slow* them down, you would see that they are very individual desires showing emotion and joy, yet eating and doing everything at the same time.

The `I`s come from your primitive instincts. It's just more complex machinery for your survival instincts created through evolution. You were never meant to say, "I think; therefore I am," but it began to happen so fast that it started to create a type of consciousness. This integration is what created a sense of individuality. That's what separates you from the animals in the world. Your individuality comes from the speed at which you operate.

Are all these different `I`s creating what seems to be us?

Yes, they create what seems to be you, what you think is you, but it's not.

Will we create a soul by separating the `I`s?

No, separating them is what frees you. It's unencumbering you because all of those `I`s are *slower* than what you think. We cannot move *slowly* enough. But by doing so, we move even *faster!*

A level one person has a body, but no soul. If they came to understand the `I's and they removed them, wouldn't they be conscious?

They wouldn't be able to understand the concept of `I's. I could explain it all day long but I would have to create their energy and expend a great deal of my own energy in order to get them to that level.

Would they create a soul by separating the `I's?

Yes, but it would collapse or they wouldn't be able to separate the `I's. You have to make a soul, too. You probably have a Middle Pillar from past lives. They don't. If they separate the `I's, it creates insanity. By slowing down the `I's, you're taken to that place that the martial arts masters are going. To them, it's slow. This is the only way to describe something that there is no word for.

In essence, by removing your `I's, you're going slower. This is why I say, "You cannot go slowly enough." By slowing down, you can be more aware. Have you ever noticed that when you *really* get into that place of stillness, there is this ultra-sharp awareness about you? Think about it. Why is it that you crave to go to that place? Why do you say, "Eric, you're In-Between now." It appears slow, but I'm moving *fast!*

By becoming aware of the body, by making everything stop for observation, you slow it down. You're slowing the brain so that you can free it up some other way because it isn't going to stop entirely. It has all this momentum and you're slowing down a process that is familiar. It has to go; it has to move! That sets it free to be on this other level; then you are hyper-dimensional.

You're experiencing at the *highest* level, but it goes beyond words and you learn eventually to operate from that place. That's when you're just barely heading into the fourth level. Unless you have training and discipline, you get so frustrated with it you can't do it. It'll break you down because you haven't been working with your teacher. You haven't been practicing right.

I sometimes will push people who are level two or higher. That's a very big push for them. When I push a level two to the brink of four, they feel very tired, weak, and thick. You've got to be very careful if you haven't built a soul. When someone hasn't really fully created it yet, it's unstable.

When you're *shifting*, you're moving *faster* than what the body can handle, so you start sweating. You're moving to a hyper-dimensional level. In fact, there is a very pristine level of energy there. But it takes a certain kind of awareness to even subtly know it's there.

In the movie Crouching Tiger, Hidden Dragon, there are several scenes in which a few of the characters leap into the air and fly a short distance. What's going on there?

This is very similar to anxiety dreaming. In anxiety dreaming, you run, jump in the air, and fly a certain distance. Most of the time you have to kick your feet or you glide. You can only go so far before you have to land again. Sometimes you can hold it and sometimes not. Generally, you can fly only above the treetops in anxiety dreaming. You can't shoot out like Superman. There's some kind of limitation or there's some law of physics that you don't really understand, but you know that you're being affected by it.

How did this come to be?

Anxiety dreaming most likely came into being from primitive humanity. Somewhere along the line, you probably fell or went into water and freaked out because you had no level of control. You couldn't push yourself up for air. You had no way of knowing how to swim, so your hands flailed constantly and there was a tremendous sense of helplessness. That's the anxiety part.

When you feel this anxiety, all that your brain recognizes is the adrenaline that's being released in response to the feeling of helplessness. Your brain puts into sequence different things to help you regulate it. At some point in your life, you most likely went into the water and panicked because you didn't know how to react. It felt very foreign to you. After a while, you learned that you could control it through movements so you learned how to work with it.

That's how it gets incorporated into the dream. You probably had anxiety from your daily life that carried over into your dream state. It comes out as a feeling of helplessness. There's a sense of having no control, but there's also a sense that you do have control. So it's a happy medium. You can only go a certain distance before you have to land again.

Much like swimming in water, you give yourself a push and just move in your dream. You jump and move, but there's something that most people don't realize that they are doing in their dream. If you pay very, very close attention to yourself, without letting your body or your thoughts get distracted, you'll realize that you are holding your breath when you're doing it. Your breath begins to slow when you leap.

If you have to breathe, you have to land. Think of the correlation. Now think of another correlation: breathing is connected to your thinking. *Your thinking in this dimension is what holds you here.* When you hold your breath in meditation, have you ever noticed it's as if you can keep your thoughts a lot quieter or completely quiet? Is there not a correlation?

To fold time and space, we need absolute silence to operate from a higher place. Just by thinking about this, your brain becomes quieter. You can also feel a slight heaviness in your chest. It's as if you're containing and holding your breath in order to propel your mind forward so that you can move without moving. You will find that your breathing and your clarity of mind can move you to a higher place. This makes your mind very quiet and you become very still.

That brings us back now to talking about the Masters. They seem to have very limited `I`s to work from, probably only enough to survive and function in life. They operate from this higher place.

So, your breathing can be used as a tool if you know how to breathe correctly. Most students take twenty years to learn to breathe in such a way that shifts their consciousness. You've just used a wormhole to get to that same level, to learn that kind of breathing. Once you've been there, you should be able to find your way back. So sit and think about that place, breathe shallow, and feel the clarity of your mind. Know that this is the crudest level of the beginning. Yet, it's light years ahead of the normal organic brain.

Focus on the breathing now as one of your tools. Find that place where you're holding your breath, but you're not holding your breath. Take in very slow, shallow breaths. Become comfortable with it and instinctually know that your body will take care of itself. Don't worry about it. Set yourself free but use the breathing to bring you to that state of mind and will yourself to go forward.

In the movie *Dune*, they spoke about folding space. There are beings called Navigators who have used so much *spice* that they've evolved to a point where they can move through space without moving. They can travel without movement. They operate from a big tube-shaped craft and allow all of the spaceships to enter. All this originated from ancient teachings that the author utilized to write the book. So there's a lot more truth to movies than you might think.

The Navigator then projects his mind so that he encompasses the whole ship, as if it was him, and within his own mind he moves across the universe. But he becomes non-existent. By creating your destination in your mind and making it so realistic, it re-fabricates your present reality. Hence, you have moved literally to that place. It's advanced thinking for you. You still have a long way to go.

Chapter 4

THE FIRST SUNRISE

IN MY TEACHINGS, your body is a micro universe. There are 10 trillion cells in your body that adhere to the commands that are sent to them. How do your kidneys, liver, and other organs know how to work? It's because you have millions of secretion glands that do many different things. How does your body know that your skin has to retract when it's cold so that it gets goose bumps? Or how does it know to expand and sweat when you're hot? Do you have to tell the body how to function? No – because you have an inner communication within your inner-universe. There's another part of you that's like a machine. It runs a program that sends signals to instruct the cells of your body to do what they are supposed to do.

In this life, there is one thing for certain that you can count on – you were born and eventually you will die. You were once young and youthful, but you are not as young as you were just thirty seconds ago. You are not as young as you were even five days ago. You are guaranteed to get wrinkles and get older. The organs in your body will eventually deteriorate and cease to function.

Scientists have discovered that a cell can turn over and regenerate itself seven times. That's what keeps you youthful. It directly corresponds to the aging process. If your body could reproduce itself, you would live forever unless you had a life threatening disease or a traumatic injury. For the most part, your body shouldn't age at all. When a cell detonates, it dies and it is replaced by a new one. You keep producing new cells, and that is why you don't age instantly.

I believe it's possible to slow the aging process down to control the health of your body. It's also possible to control the energy of your body. You can become one hundred percent energy or light. Many great teachers and spiritual masters have attained a heightened frequency by consuming so much energy; they can illuminate themselves and emit a certain glow about them. I have demonstrated this at certain times in my own teachings.

You have an entire universe within your body. The question is not, "Why are the organs doing what they are supposed to do?" Rather it's, "How are they being told what to do?" What exactly is being communicated to them? If the body is being told how to work, are the cells then also being told to turn over seven times? Is your body told only to exist for a certain amount of time? Are your organs designed to slowly deteriorate even though they have been repaired? Your body will never be as good as it used to be. It declines over time, but it's not a one hundred percent decline. So there is a little bit of repair work done, but not like when you were young. If something has tweaked the body a little bit, then your body should be as good as new, shouldn't it?

Illnesses in the body, such as cancer, tumors and cataracts don't just appear suddenly. They are created because the cells that repair the damage get confused.

They start building bad structures from the cells that they normally repair.

Let's say a "wall" in the house (body) is your kidney. I am the worker so I fix, smooth, repair and paint it. Then all of a sudden, I get a little disoriented, a little confused, and I decide to make cancer. I can't just make cancer out of nothing. I need building material, so I start smashing down the wall. Then I use that material to build a useless tumor. So the other part of the wall, that I used to build the tumor starts rotting. That means I will have no wall. Eventually the whole ceiling will collapse making the house useless. All the cold air will come into the rest of the house, meaning the destruction of your house, or in this case the death of your body.

Why do the cells get confused? They are receiving erratic electron impulses that misguide their building processes. So the body misses rhythms and it skips beats. Eventually the cells get so confused that they start screwing up what they are doing.

If you start introducing unhealthy materials into your body, your cells will get perplexed. Every time you smoke a cigarette, you're introducing building materials into your body. Your body doesn't know the difference between a toxic substance from smoking or vitamin A, B or C. Your cells are like little children, so they start building with whatever they have available. Then the bad material spreads to the other cells, creating destruction and eventually death. It doesn't work with the mechanism of your body, your inner-universe.

Your body has rewritten the signal by changing the pulses of your inner universe to incorrectly send data through your body to the organs. So your body gets confused, acting like it is drunk. When you stop taking drugs or you stop smoking cigarettes, the cells of your body burn up the toxic material and start to repair the body. There are only so many times the cells can screw up until, eventually, it causes irreparable damage.

The reason the body becomes deteriorated is because of your thoughts. So, it is important to understand how your thoughts are produced. The Universe is a giant living organism that provides low radiation impulses, which are used by the brain. The brain also produces low radiation impulses to tell the kidney how to function and how to work properly. They tell the heart how to beat. It's not just an electrical impulse. It's a low radiation impulse that works with the brain, and tells the rest of your body how to orchestrate itself. It's like a giant inner-universe with a million sounds going on, but it is synchronicity; it's beautiful.

Everything in your body has its own cycle. Just like a woman has a menstruation cycle, men have cycles, too. Externally, you have all these different things, like solar systems, moving around you. But you also have different cycles moving within your body that mimic the whole universe. Everything is repeated over and over. Well, that's science.

You know the brain uses low radiation impulses. But how does the planet know how to live, or the plants, or the universe? The sun and the stars throughout the universe throw off radiation impulses that hit various worlds throughout the cosmos. These worlds react to the radiation, like a giant orchestra affecting this entire living organism. That's how God thinks, but on a much grander scale compared to how the mind works. However, the mind is a micro scale of the galaxy. You want to be able to hear the will of the

Universe so that you can function better and learn how to experience God.

What happens when your body starts to screw up and the cells stop doing what they are supposed to do? What happens when they stop receiving the correct signals and they start acting on their own? What happens when they start creating tumors and disease? The cells need to get the right signal in order to discern what they're supposed to do. So if they get the right signal, you are healthy. If they get the wrong signal or it is temporarily screwed up, the cells start to become erratic. You don't always listen to God. You do whatever you want.

Nature listens to God. *You have to find a way to listen to the vibration of God so that you can correct yourself and become a highly spiritual, immortal being.* Then you can harness this and become one with the energy instead of a screwed up frequency just going to work, doing your job, coming home, having sex, cooking dinner, and getting excited about a movie. You self-reflect very little or not at all. Out of the entire week, you might give one percent of your time to self-reflect on your spirituality, your is-ism, your being-ness of what you are. You don't generally think about that. You simply look like push-button robots going through the motions of life and rewarding yourself for it. You never really reflect on your spirituality.

Some people believe that the secret to tapping into this outer force of energy is to listen to the inner force of energy. You are a miniature copy of the universe. If you listen to your inner-universe, study it, and learn how it works so that you can communicate with it, then all you need to do is turn to the larger version outside of you and communicate with it.

It helps to separate yourself from the physical body in order to have the realization that you are so much more. The Buddhist monks, as well as many other cultures have used Aums for thousands of years because they know something that you may not understand – your body automatically functions. By chanting certain tones and pitches, your body can resonate with the tones. The glands in your throat will reset themselves correctly, initiating the healing process. It's not just a spiritual thing. There's a healing process that goes through your inner-universe.

You can stop it from happening because you have that power. Or you can choose to let it happen. If you analyze it too much or think about what you are doing, you're not allowing it to happen. What are you supposed to feel? Some people simply experience it; they don't *think* about it; they *feel* it. Become whatever it's doing to you. Just let it create you. That's the difference between a human being and plants. You don't let God *make* you. You decide everything for yourself because that's the way you think. You don't listen to God, so you don't experience God. Plants let God do whatever It's doing.

First, learn to let go of a certain part of your is-ism or yourself. What you consider to be yourself isn't really you. When you let your mind go and just do the Aums, they reach a certain point where they uplift you. If you can – let yourself go. It's a very pleasant, relaxed, purifying feeling within you.

When you do Aums, your mind and everything else becomes clearer. Your mind isn't busy thinking meaningless thoughts. It's clear. And when it's clear, you can receive a galactic source of information from the Universe. It's healing you. But there's also an inner secret within all of this that most people aren't aware of. It is maybe one of the most important things that I could point out to you. Your emotions are your enemy, to a certain degree. You may wonder, "What! What do you mean emotion is my enemy?" Emotion does have its place of importance; there's a part of you that's real and there's a part of you that is biochemical.

Emotions are a chemical reaction that the body releases, as a result of the actions committed by the body. If you shout angrily or throw things around, there is a release of adrenaline and excitement that's really *not* you. You are amused and your amusement is a reaction of how you respond. You learned this sociologically since childhood from other children, your parents, and your peers. There is another part of you that is solemn, very ambivalent, or indifferent to your feelings. You have intertwined the chemical self with the electrical self so that you can't tell the difference anymore. It's like mixing oil and vinegar together. For the most part, your emotions are what prevent you from having a spiritual awakening. Your emotions keep you mentally occupied so you cannot self-reflect.

Everybody has been "there." Let me explain what "there" is. "There" is a point where you're feeling exhausted but not tired enough to sleep. There are other people around you, but nobody is talking to you. They are doing their own thing, and there's music playing. You're sitting down, you're tired, and you have no expression on your face. It's a moment when there is nothing going through your mind and you're just zoned out. Is this not a pleasurable feeling?

It feels good to just let your mind not think of anything at all. It's a total shutdown. That is closer to your true-self than anything else you are reacting to right now. Ninety percent of what you react to is biochemical. You are an energy being coexisting in a physical body. You are energy. Your energy is the potential for a soul. If you are dead and you leave your body, what are you? You are energy. Well, this energy is in your physical body coexisting with you. As energy, you can't smell. Nor can you see optically. As energy, you can't hear sounds and you can't taste. As energy, you can't reach out and feel the texture of something. You need a physical machine to collect the data, take the texture, record it into millions of electrons in your brain, and store it as energy. The brain converts it into an experience, similar to how a TV works with a signal. You can't smell, taste, hear, see, or touch. It doesn't appear to be there, yet your body harnesses it and converts it so that you can experience it.

You are energy. You can't even see this dimension. If you wanted to touch something, you would pass right through it. Since you are energy, you need to have a physical body in order to experience this dimension, this structure, and collect data. If you hear, it turns into electricity. If you see or taste, it's turns into electrons because you are an electrical being. You are a soul. So, the brain is a machine and electricity powers it. But it's really YOU pulling the levers, pushing buttons, and moving things so that you can operate this body-machine. So, you coexist, thinking this is who you are. This is *not* who you are. You are something far more than this, but since you can't remember who you are, that part is shut down. So, you interweave the electricity, the machine, and the apparatus. And you believe all of this is one, but the reality is – it is two!

Then the machine starts to take over and dominate who you really are, your soul. It amplifies your feelings and emotions, creating responses that really aren't yours. It mimics learning because you want to learn in this dimension. It becomes so dominant that it suppresses the core of your spirit. So, you forget who and what you are. You only have glimpses of moments through a window when you sit, stare, and feel that moment of something beyond all of this. You don't have a name for it; it's simply a feeling.

It's like going to the restroom. You wake up in the morning, get up, and go to the bathroom. You're sitting there on the toilet listening to the hum of the fan. There is nobody in the room and you just start to space out. You're so relaxed that you let your body go. You let go to a point, but there is a certain part of your mind that is in another place just for a few moments. And it feels good, but it's not laugh out loud good. It's not like what you feel like when you are dancing, but it's still good. It's not the feeling you get if you're high on some kind of drug, but it's good. But it is not because you're going to the bathroom and you feel relieved. A part of you might be relieved, but there's also another part of you paying very special attention – and that is the secret. *You need to have self-observation.* Remember that word.

That's the secret to consciously awakening. That's the secret to discovering where you are hidden so you can remove the identity that you believe is you. Then you can awaken to a higher tonal. When you self-reflect and realize your higher tonal as an energy being, the energy starts to move faster because you have given it some attention. You have a realization. You start to feel and sense things. Then you can clear certain emotions out of your mind. You will find that your spiritual and psychic abilities are enhanced a hundred times.

Have you ever lay down on a bed and heard something playing, but your mind is in a void? It's "out there" and you hear some background music. All of a sudden, it's playing very loud in your head. The sound gets very loud, but it's not coming from anything that you are aware of. It's from somewhere else, but it's in your head. If you think about the sound, it goes away. It just stops. Now maybe it's just me. Maybe I've got this Mozart thing going on in my head, but I am assuming everybody has done this, too.

This is a very rare moment. It's one of the things that you cannot necessarily remember. You are not supposed to remember it or reflect on it for very long. It is a higher consciousness, but you can't reside there if you use the brain at the same time. So the second that you think with your brain, the sound stops.

Then you start playing around with it. You're lying there and you're thinking, "Did I just do what I thought I did?" That's because it sounded really cool. Then you try to recreate it. So you let your mind go and you think. You don't realize you're doing it, but you know that you have to let your mind go because you've already come to the conclusion that if you think about it, it will stop. Then you try to start the music in your head again. When you forget about what you're doing, the music starts again. And it gets really loud, but the second you hear a tone, a movement, or something, it reverts right back to being a very faint tone to nothing at all.

This is part of your inner-universe. *You can do anything within your mind.* You can leave your mind and go into a total hologram universe and make it as real as any room right now if you learn how to enter it. The machine prevents you from crossing over into that realm.

I teach you to meditate because it also teaches you the concept of wax on, wax off from the movie, *The Karate Kid*. In the movie, Mr. Miyagi begins training his student, Daniel, by having him wax his car, sand the floor, and do some painting. Each chore uses a specific movement. Daniel doesn't see the connection until Miyagi reveals that Daniel has been learning defensive blocks through muscle memory by doing these chores. In much the same way, by practicing different things, we learn techniques that can be used to help us spiritually. I often refer to this as wax on, wax off.

The meditation that I teach really transcends this, but it's at the right time and the right place to expose the student to new things so that she/he has other realizations. Otherwise, students are so transfixed with getting the big picture that they never quite get there because they haven't collected enough tools to make it happen. So, inside of this place, your mind is beyond your comprehension.

You can learn to exist as a higher being in a physical body. Strive to exist in this higher level; the place where you can sometimes hear music. It's very crisp and clear, but it turns off when you lose focus. I exist there whenever I go into a spiritual mindset. In fact, there are deeper levels where it moves faster and clearer than water. To me, the human mind is just like muddy water. You can't penetrate it, but it is water. My mind is clear enough to see all the details penetrating through the water. It's like being on a super nootropic cognitive brain enhancer.

I was watching a show recently, Gene Roddenberry's *Earth: Final Conflict*. It's a science fiction television show. They have a brain enhancer that meticulously describes this concept. I am always looking for other ways to describe what I'm experiencing. If I can explain it so you can understand this better, you can mimic it and create it also. So we're taking the knowledge from the higher levels and bringing it down to this dimension. It's a way of transcending this thought.

You will become more aware by doing self-observation exercises. The more that you observe yourself, the more you can elevate the body.

So, let's do a little exercise.

First, move your hand. Don't think about moving it – clear your mind - just become aware of moving it. What do you feel? Do you feel the joint moving in your arm? Do you feel the heaviness when it turns over? Can you also feel your elbow and the weight of it?

That is self-observation. Your hand is an extension of you, but it's not you. If you say the words, "A, B, C, D," from what place do you say it? Do you say it in your head? This is all rooted together.

So, through self-observation, you self-realize ... What are you? Are you a machine?

Let's try something else. Close your eyes for a minute. Now take your tongue and feel the inside of your mouth. Don't just move it around; feel it! Feel the smooth structured teeth in your mouth. Think about these structures that are just about four inches below your brain. Does that really feel like you? Think about it. Nobody really thinks about their teeth. The same way you can't feel your heart, you can't feel your lungs, you can't feel your intestines, and yet they're all there. We only relate to everything outside of us.

If through self-observation you can pay more attention to the structures and the mechanisms of your body, your brain will start to feel the energy moving. Eventually you will get to the point where you learn how the cycles are moving within your own body. When you do that, you have self-realizations. It's like bursts of something coming out of you saying, "I AM."

As long as you think this density is you, then that is what you will be. If you never question it, you will always be a machine, an organism on this planet that simply moves, reacts, and responds in a certain way. There are only so many responses that you can have. You must sit down and do self-observation every day. The more often you pay attention to your self-observation, the more you pay attention to your body and it's organisms, the more your mind will relate to this hidden energy. Remember, it's really about energy.

Let's do another exercise. Put your arm out. Take your hand and without touching the hair on your arm, run your hand so that it just barely touches it. Pay attention to the feeling. This is an abnormal thing for you to do, but you probably did this when you were young. Everyone has probably done it at some point in their lives. You studied your body as well as many other things. When you were younger, you were more spiritual. You were more sensitive to energy, feelings, and senses because you were more aware. You instinctually studied the vessel that you occupied because you were still a spiritual being. You just couldn't recall what you were. The memories hadn't been blocked in your head yet. The machine hadn't taken over for you. So, you felt and explored many different things.

When you turn inward, you explore. This raises your sensitivity and increases it. So, through self-observation, you raise your consciousness. You also become more sensitive to the people around you. Your sense of smell is intensified because of your awareness.

Your sense of hearing is intensified. All your senses are intensified in that state of mind.

You should make it a practice to do these things as often as you can because then you will reside in a higher state more often. The one thing that you do in life is experience, so if your senses are more acute, you will sense more and experience more of life.

I believe in science but I also believe in spirituality. I think that science and spirituality is the same thing; it's just a matter of fully understanding this concept. Science is baffled by this. They now believe that one of the reasons why people can recall past lives is because it's recorded from multiple generations of your ancestor's DNA. When your ancestors spoke, the gene recorded this vast information, which is the equivalent of the entire Smithsonian Institute. Scientists believe that's the reason why people can remember a castle, road, town, or speak a language.

We are still unraveling the technology of the cells of our body. There are vast oceans of awareness inside of you, whether it is spiritually or physically. It's just a matter of using our energy like a computer to grab the data. A spiritual person has lived other lives, but may not have awakened yet. Some people don't awaken or realize how spiritual they are until they are around thirty years old. You've lived in many other countries and other cultures, but the place you most likely lived at one time is the spiritual hub of the world: India.

In ancient times and in ancient teachings, before archaeology and history were established, structures and buildings were languages. During those ancient times, when you walked through an archway, the depth and the width of the wall were built in such a way that they spoke directly to you. They didn't just build the wall because it was a hallway. They built it to a certain width and a certain height. When you walked down that hallway, you could feel something. They built circular structures with arches - not too low and not too high. The structures evoked in you a certain feeling, energy, or a spiritual consciousness, like a language.

When you look at certain structures, you feel something if you can let yourself go to that level. You can experience it differently than what you would see in this world. You can literally feel the emotion of it, if you let yourself go. If you pay attention through self-observation, you will feel an environment and it will tell you something.

In the ancient structures, everything communicates. When you walk into a place, you may not know what it is, but your heart starts pounding and your breathing picks up because your mind instinctually starts taking in the structure. It is energy, electricity and literally millions of pieces. When the brain recognizes a certain mathematical structure, it creates a specific rhythm that tells you to awaken. It can also summon a surge of emotions. You just don't understand what it is.

In Persia, they built temples with hidden entrances. You'd ride on camelback for weeks or even months to get to these very secret places in the deserts, mountains, and valleys. Most people were killed in the process of trying to get there.

These places were the great mystery schools of ancient knowledge. The novices, or students, would enter them and would never leave because they were forever changed, becoming great spiritual beings. So how did this happen to the people who sought them? They probably were spiritual in their past lives but the knowledge was buried deep. When they went into these ancient sites, all the structures were perfect. Every square foot of the massive complex changed the essence of who they were. It shifted a part of their consciousness to such a level that they became super beings. They became mystical, wise, spiritual beings within the confines of that structure. They never left because they knew the influence that the structure had on their mind would eventually collapse. If they ever left, they would not be who they could be.

During those ancient times, you couldn't write words the way we do now. The knowledge wasn't available then. But a way to communicate was preserved through dance. In certain dances, words were expressed by movements. The people understood that the expression of the dance told a story. It was acted out through each movement and turn of the body. It was a form of communicating feelings and emotions.

We dance, in part, because it makes us feel a certain way, but we don't realize that it's more than just listening to the beats. It's more about feeling and emotions. If you observe how certain things make you feel, it changes the state of your consciousness. Music can do that. I listen to Indian music because it makes me remember a time when I lived in India. When I can let my mind zone out and experience it, pools of knowledge surface in me. I don't dance to it or try to figure it out. I don't sit there, wondering what kind of music it is. *I literally let it transform me and it releases something within me that's profound.* It changes something inside of me. It reminds me of a better time, a better state of consciousness. If you can remember just one thing, many things will surface!

There is a song, called "Omiya" by Mychael Danna from the album: *Kama Sutra: A Tale of Love* that I like very much. This particular song is very soothing and captivating, the kind of music that uplifts your emotions and speaks to your soul. As the singer goes through the octaves, your frequency begins to shift and it stirs something within you that is almost primal. It's a feeling of exhilaration, a feeling other than just about you, and it is very fulfilling. It is definitely worth experiencing this music, so you may want to purchase a copy of it.

The reason I love the song *Omiya* is because of the tonal. It puts you into that state of mind if you allow yourself to let go. There are different levels in the octaves of the music, and it is so incredible because you can actually walk around while in that frequency. You can include movement or dance to help shift you. Octaves create certain impulses in the brain, like when you do, "Aums." It means something very spiritual, even though some people may feel nothing. That's because they don't use self-observation.

No matter how unusual or how different the sounds, the brain might think: "Oh, I don't like the music." If you listen with your soul and feel it, you don't have to understand the words. The music will transform you and send you an emotion in the form of energy. It is up to you to take it in, let it fill you, change you, and transcend you the same way that you would sit and space out. Then you're in that place. Let it take you there.

This music was originally taken from the ancient sutras. These are ancient teachings which were not necessarily meant for music; they were designed to raise your consciousness. Some people think they're so beautiful because they feel it, even though they may not understand why they're so attracted to it. It changes them; it helps them to remember what they have forgotten. This piece of music was designed to take you through these octaves, and if you let your mind go, it will shift your consciousness.

Unfortunately, the music is very short. It only goes for two minutes and then it's all over. If you can reproduce it so that it lasts for several tracks, then maybe you will really get somewhere. When you listen to it, just let go of yourself. Let go of your thinking as a typical human being living your life. If, for a moment, you can just let yourself escape into what I am saying, there's a chance for you to exist beyond all of this. It's a sound that totally frees you. Hopefully, you can understand what I am saying. You may feel nothing, but most people feel what I am talking about. There's not a word to describe this experience. You can feel it right away.

There are other people who listen to it and don't feel anything. It's really up to you.

So, you have to fight to experience this. Let it just overtake you. Don't think about anything but what this artist is doing. She is pouring out her heart. She's actually in a trance, letting a sound emit from her body. The sound that is coming out isn't in spoken words. It's really octaves of soul, which is a dimensional consciousness. She's gliding in this energy place in her mind. She's transcending this from an energy vortex and she's releasing it all for you. If you can catch this wave, and bring it into your ears, it will send you through to this dimensional place that she's bringing it from.

The brain doesn't know you to process. It doesn't know how to experience it. The brain just thinks it's pretty. You may not be able to do it the first time or even the second, but if you understand what I'm saying, it will change you. It's an emotion. It's a feeling. When she's doing it, the sounds really are absolute love, absolute pain, absolute everything.

The sounds emitted from this music are not about sex. It's about something coming out of her that speaks a universal language. It's about her son that died and her experience of seeing her son once again. Her love for the son is screaming out, expressing itself. And it's beyond words! It's about seeing God, yet there are no words. *It transcends words.* It's about every emotion in your body. It's not like, "I feel love. I feel a little joy. I feel hate." It's about feeling it, not saying it. And she's just making the sound of, "Aahhhh." She's becoming something more than mortal, something more which tells us we have to fit this little square structure of society and use words such as, "I'm angry. I'm frustrated."

What is this that we are doing? We're mimicking what we've learned to express. Our mother says something and we repeat it. This is how we learn. Every smile on your face is like your mother's, your father's, or your brother's. How you act and deal with situations is similar to how someone else does it. There are a million different styles that can be counted. But when this singer is sitting there and she can't speak, she can just let out, "Aahhhh." She's letting it out, releasing something very deep from within the soul. Why are the tones, the octaves, so important to experience?

There are higher tones that elevate you to where you can see energy on inanimate objects. When in that state, you can literally sense an object, like a tree, breathing inward and outward. You can feel the warmth of somebody off in the distance. You can feel what it's like to be them because the energy touches you. You can imitate it, and it is like you become that person for a brief moment. And if you can become that person, you know their data. You experience what it's like to be them. You can hear tonal. It is such incredible music!

When you start to gaze off and you hear this song, you know it could easily be a masterpiece! The place you go to is perfection. It's an energy dimension that exists within your mind. It's connected to vast worlds and vast dimensions that you co-exist in. You don't walk in just one place. You walk in multiple places. It's just a matter of choosing to become aware of all of those places. When I listen to this music, there's a part of me that knows it's foreign.

I sometimes visualize living in a past life in India. I see a giant orange platform of stone. It's very warm out and I see pillars. I envision another orange type of marble stone. You know the kind that I am talking about. It's not bright orange, more like a deep brownish orange. And I see a woman dancing. She has flowing white clothing and she's making the sound of "Aahhhh," and then she just becomes light. She transcends beyond everything. Just visualize that for a moment! Now *feel* it. It just transcends life to become part of something that you could have been without thinking about it. It's not about words. It's about letting something out of you that you can't do if you're a machine. You can talk about it but you can't do it.

If you just went "Aahhhh," somebody might think that you're having some kind of release. There's a part of you that wants to, but never in your whole life will you do it – at least not in front of another person. You will grow old before you let yourself do that. But when you're by yourself, you might go in the bathroom to make the sound with feeling, "Aaaaahhhhhhh." So if you feel the need to do that, why don't you just do it? What is telling you that you need to do it? If you did that, do you think you'll live forever?

What if the release of that sound comes from some ancient part of your being, in your DNA, from the beginning of time? *Do you think it's been held down by the conformity of how you are supposed to live and exist?* If you can do that when you're having sex, it's like bliss. It's just absolute bliss. When you're having an orgasm and you let that sound or feeling out, it's not even about sex anymore. It's about the state of mind that feels so perfect, so free, and so uninhibited. It's a very beautiful state of mind. It's just that sex is such an overpowering thing for us naturally that we no longer think about controlling how we're supposed to feel. When we have really good sex, it's about just letting go and releasing so that you can go to that place that I am talking about, and all of a sudden it's just 'Aaaaaaahhhhhh.' It feels *that* good. It's great! It's incredible! And you feel charged!

That's where this lady is just hanging for a few minutes. She's just releasing her soul, and that's what you should reflect on. You need some mental self-observation because if it's not this, it's all the other little things that you should be experiencing. You should let this part of you out by being solemn. Don't let your chemical emotions confuse you. Let your mind be at peace and just be gentle.

Just imagine Christ. He wasn't in your face. He was just a very solemn person. So were Buddha and Krishna. They could also be very energetic, like me. When you think about them in this spiritual state of mind, you see them as just very bland, yet very loving. There's a love that comes from them but it's not the romantic type. You can feel it because you look into their eyes and see or feel something that is an expression of love. It's not the kind of love that is a chemical reaction of what you're supposed to perceive. It's a transcendence of your soul from some deeper part that you are afraid to let out. You're afraid to look at it. If you did not care about what anybody else thinks or says, you would awaken something so incredible inside of you that no words could ever describe.

In this world, even though we cannot hear it, we use words like "tone" to explain things because we think on a more structured level as a human being. The earth is a very low tonal. It is like, "Doe" and it's pushing you to stay at the same level. But there are times when you slip past it in your state of mind and you go to this higher place. And because the earth is a low tonal, it pushes you back down. It pushes you right back down to where you were before, so you wonder what you just experienced. What was it that you just felt? For a moment, you felt this higher dimension. You want to reach those higher states of mind so that you can experience them often. When you come back, hopefully you will keep some of the things you've learned and use them in this dimension.

So the secret is getting to that state of mind and not just experiencing it. Utilize it in other ways. If your mind is at peace and it's on a certain level, you will feel a certain energy in the middle of your chest. It's very peaceful. When you're in that state, your mind is quiet. There's little to no babble. There's no thinking going on. No words. It's a state of mind that's just feeling and experiencing. Now imagine being able to keep that feeling while going outside, looking at a tree, and hearing that same music as you look up at the canopy of the tree.

Imagine how this feeling affects you as you're listening to the music, looking at someone you love, and staring at their face. Imagine looking at your mother as she's growing old and the things that she can't say to you, because it's not considered to be something that you would talk about, like growing old or the life she lived, or the mistakes in her life. Think about feeling this way, as you're looking at the sun on a yellow flower. Study the structure of the flower, its curves, colors, and the light as it reflects off of it. It's the state of mind that you're in that makes the difference.

It's a way of experiencing, because you can feel something when you look at that flower. You can feel your mother's essence inside of you when you look at her. You can be her and understand her in ways that you did not before. You feel. That is life. Learn to experience life on higher levels, staying in this state of mind. The longer that you can keep it, the closer you are to the true self. We think we're supposed to just be happy, joyous, and dancing around, but that is not what we are completely. You can do all those things but a truly spiritual person has a certain kind of solemnity.

When Christ, Buddha, and Krishna looked at the people, touched their faces, and felt what they felt, they were in that state of mind. It wasn't a boisterous love. It was a feeling of emotion like you were feeling in that music - the feeling of nothing going through your mind but the absolute giving of life. True love is experiencing that, because even if you experience it, you are moved by it in a way that's not typical. And if you're moved by it, you give because you understand. You lift as you give back.

Think about self-observation before you try to recreate this state of mind. That means you should think about your body. Think about your leg moving, your stomach, your body, and its structure. It helps you to cross over to this state of consciousness. You have forgotten how to create these moments. You have grown old. When you were a child, you went to this place every time you walked out to a field or a forest. When you looked up at a tree for a few moments, you felt something. You have just forgotten. You don't think about how or what you felt back then. I felt it when I went back in time once.

It was a time when I was young and I was taking a walk on a sunny day. I remember walking out to this little pond. There was tall, yellow grass everywhere. As I was walking through it, I could hear the grass crinkling between my feet. It was on my shoes but not between; there was the smell of dried grass and I could feel the sun on me. I could feel the crunching. I walked and I lay down on a stone looking into the water. I could see my reflection and the sun was really bright.

Then I focused my eyesight into the water. I could see this whole world of insects moving around in the water and I could see the eggs from a frog. I just remember being in this really intensified state of mind. It wasn't about me; it wasn't about what I wanted; it wasn't about needing something or being hungry or going to do something. It was a point of is-ness, of just simply existing without any thought. I could experience the whole pond. I could experience the sun. I could experience everything. It put me in a state of mind where I stood out and just looked around. And when I looked around, I could feel more from the land. I could feel more from everything.

I remember walking in this state of mind in this field and seeing some of my friends playing. I felt very abstracted from them, like they were a scene from a movie playing. I just remember absorbing this, not feeling that I was a part of it but just simply seeing the existence of it all. It was a very unique, enjoyable feeling.

Then, of course, somebody came running to me and said, "Hey Eric, what's up?" Instantly, it snapped me into their mode so I went off to play with them. But there was a state of mind that transcended the normal state of mind. We lose this as we grow older. We don't reflect on it. We become more and more a product of commercials, television, music, and doing our thing. We have to stimulate ourselves over and over. We never really reflect on that state of mind. If we do, we sit down, look at a tree, and say that it's really nice. But we never really allow ourselves to go to that place, that state of mind that just looks at everything and experiences it. When I manipulate the wind to make it stop, or make it blow, I'm in that state of mind. I love the wind. It's not a matter of just saying, "Stop!" It's a matter of feeling like I am in the wind and at the same time I am existing here. I can't explain quite how it is, but it's as if I am two things at the same time.

You're reading this book and your hands are holding it. So, you are experiencing both at the same time. So, who's to say what the limitation of your consciousness is and what it is able to experience? When I become the wind, I choose to stop the wind by choosing to stop myself. So it stops. When I do something or I change something, it's in that state of mind. I can do nothing when I'm in an ordinary state of mind. But when I go into this higher state, I know what Christ and Buddha were doing because there's a certain power that comes with it; the power that, if you think in a negative way, you can do nothing with it. It drops you back down to this level.

If you can let yourself go, the things you can do are just phenomenal. It's like the dream mode, like the time when you can hear the music. The second you think about the music, it stops. So, you have to build the skill to cross this abyss. It takes time and practice.

I've given you much food for thought to ponder and to experience. Will you make the effort to do it? Will you experience the tonals, the octaves, the higher dimensions, and shifting? It's entirely your choice. It's like making the decision to get out of bed very early in the morning to witness the sun rising. Will you make the effort?

If not now . . . then when?

Chapter 5

THE SOURCE REALIZED

THE PLANET EARTH is a living organism floating in space. All the living creatures on the planet are part of that organism. The human race is the central nervous system of the planet. If I said to you, "Are *you* the only *thing* of your body that thinks?" You might respond, "Yes, I'm the only thing that thinks." I would say, "No, you're not." You are made of trillions - not millions, not billions - of living organisms in your body, all whom think individually on their own without any assistance from you.

For instance, you have red and white blood cells. White cells will find a virus and size it up to see if they can attack and destroy it. If they decide they can't, they communicate with other white cells and get together. When the white cells sense there are enough of them, they will attempt to attack. Is that not rationalization? Is that not a form of intelligence? It absolutely is.

On your skin, you have billions of spider-like creatures, all choosing their mate, having children, knowing the size of their territory, and protecting it. Is that not intelligence? It absolutely is. In your eye, you have millions of living organisms, all knowing which species are theirs, which aren't, which to attack, and which to run from. Is that not intelligence? It absolutely is. You are made of trillions of living organisms. Name one inch of your body that isn't packed with millions and millions of living organisms all whom work for the one being – YOU – one singular being. Yet they are all individual and independent within you.

If you become depressed or psychologically distressed with yourself, you can create cancer, tumors, ill health, bad cellular structure, collapsing of your arteries, etc. That is a known scientific fact. They've also found that, when you have an illness, if you think positively your cells will regenerate and try to reciprocate that emotion somehow. The cells tend to know that there is a force, a will, that's instructing them. You need to create and maintain the body. Scientists also believe that has to do with your consciousness communicating with this giant living organism that is your body.

Now, keep in mind that your body is roughly about 75% water and 25% solid mass. Did you know that the planet is about 75% ocean and 25% land? Isn't this an amazing coincidence? Your body regulates its own body temperature of 98.6° (37° Celsius). Similarly, the Earth maintains its temperature even though it exists in the subzero temperatures of space.

Did you know that during the previous World Wars when the doctors ran out of plasma for the injured soldiers they had to use a substitute? Do you know what they used? Purified ocean water. The body accepted it because what gives you life is found in the ocean. It is found in the earth. You get your nutrition from the Earth through plants, vegetables, meats, and grasses eaten by cows. It's still a transformation. There's a recycling of different forms of vitamins and minerals. All of that gives you life and it is found in the Earth.

How does the Earth think as a living organism?

It's very simple. Your brain uses low-radiation impulses; that's how you create thought. Do you know what electricity is? No, you don't, but you have learned how to harness it. You can do really neat things with it, but it's not really understood what electricity is. When you accept that and you understand that the mind uses a form of energy called electricity, then you have to take the concept of what I'm about to tell you into consideration.

In chapter 11 of Rupert Sheldrake's book *A New Science of Life,* he mentions a series of experiments where rats learned how to escape from a water maze in one laboratory at Harvard University in Boston, Massachusetts. New batches of rats were tested month by month, year by year. As time went on, groups of rats in laboratories in Scotland and Australia learned the trick faster.

How did rats in other parts of the world learn this trick?

They learned from the collective consciousness. In other words, the rat's brain wavelength is a frequency. It's like 106.7 or 98.5 on a radio dial, and it is exclusive to that species. Since they are all on that same frequency, they share data on an ongoing basis. As more and more rats of that species learned this trick, it built momentum. Therefore, many rats learned this new behavior quickly, rather than each monkey discovering it over a long period of time. It was like throwing a stone in water. It made a ring that encompassed the whole planet as a thought form, as a form of consciousness.

Each species on this planet, like dolphins, whales, lions and beavers, has a collective consciousness within their own species. In a very complex way, even human beings have it. This energy consciousness is the collective consciousness of the planet.

In the same way, you have billions of living creatures telling you what's going on in your environment by the way of your cells and nerves. Even a nerve is made out of millions of living organisms. Each nerve can contract, expand, and react to different impulses allowing the electrons to transmit and receive a form of data. The information is created by their consciousness, collectively building as other nerves add to that information until it gets to one central processing point – YOU.

Humans do the same thing for the planet. Ask yourself, "Why do you think that the planet needs to have arms and legs to be a living thing? Why does a living thing have to be micro when it can be larger than us? Why does everything that exists have to be smaller than us, or about our size?" You are limited only by your conscious capability of understanding.

The planet is a living organism. According to science, you have an energy field that radiates outward from your body. All objects, from plants to rocks, have an energy field. There is an energy field that also goes around the planet, over the deserts and the deepest parts of the ocean. It's an energy field, a soul, a sense of being; whatever you want to call it.

Somebody once asked me, "If the planet is a living organism and everything on it acts like cells in our body, what about something like steel? Steel is not alive." If you took a muscle out of your arm and laid it on the table, what would be the distinction between life and non-life? It's actually movement. According to science, it's an interaction. If you take a negative and a positive form of electricity and you touch the muscle, what happens to it? The muscle expands and retracts.

Think about your body. Why does your body function the way it does? It's because you, as an electrical being, have taken this mass and you have learned to manipulate and control it. If you tell your arm to go up, it goes up. If you tell your arm to go down, it goes down. You make your fingers move in a precise rhythm. It took you years to learn how to do this. How many tables did you fall over while learning to walk? As your body changed and you became a teenager, your muscles had to adapt so your body could be controlled by your consciousness. And now we're back to electricity again.

This expansion and retraction is a part of life; all things move. All living things have movement in their own way. Everything's living; no matter what it is on this planet, it's alive. Scientists have observed stones that emit high frequencies.

As for steel not being alive, you really have to look at it from a different point of view. Steel lasts longer than the human life expectancy so we don't view it in the same context; this is limited thinking as a human being. Think of it this way; doesn't steel bend and retract in the heat and cold? Absolutely, it does. Just like humans have diseases and infections, steel has rust, abrasion, corrosion, and deterioration.

When you get a wound or a cut, don't the red cells compile together as a micro-verse, bring nutrients that start healing your wound, repair the damage, cleanse, and refine it? Who on this planet takes care of all the skyscrapers, bridges, and steel structures? Who paints them? Who welds the cracks? Who maintains them? The human beings - the micro-verse of the planet does this. If you look at your arm and you envision all of your veins, what is moving through them? Your blood contains billions of cells moving things backward and forward, exchanging data, doing different things for your whole body. That is a form of movement. What are all the highways of the planet? What are all the jet ways? What are all the other forms of communication? It's all part of a living organism. It's just a different concept of viewing it.

It's just so hard to change your perspective to see the planet that way.

Let's imagine you're on an absolutely huge island. It's monstrous; it's massive. You see all the trees, all the flowers, and the butterflies floating around. Birds and hawks are flying around in the upper part of the mountains. You can see clouds up top through the rain forest in the distance. You think to yourself, "My god, it will take forever just to explore this island." It could take you weeks and weeks just to see it all. It's just huge. You can see the ants crawling around on the ground. You can see the spiders building webs, and you can see the trees. You can see everything from a larger and smaller scale: a micro-verse (smaller) and macro-verse (larger).

You decide to go on a boat ride, so you hop in your boat and head out to sea. You're sitting in the back drinking a Piña Colada, looking at this island, and thinking how majestic and beautiful it is. As you move further and further out to sea, the island's structure starts to become a little more blurred; it starts to meld into itself. As you move further away, you begin to see the edges of the island. You can see how big it is now. You continue to move further away, and it becomes smaller and smaller until it starts to look like one large object in the distance, like one big stone, one big structure, one thing. If you go into it, just as you were when on the island, you can see the entire superstructure, every detail, and if you move away from it, like zooming a camera lens from telephoto out to wide angle, you see nothing but a large structure.

With this understanding, if you could take a syringe to your arm and take out blood, and if the blood were intelligent, it could swim up through the glass of the syringe. Then it could look back at you and say, "Where are all the other blood cells? Where's Harry the white cell? Where's Julie the red cell? Where is everybody? What is this one giant thing with these flapping arms and tentacles coming from its body?" Then the blood cell goes back into the bloodstream. All of a sudden, it sees all of its friends again. It goes back into your inner-verse, which it thought was huge, but now understands that the inner-verse is part of something much bigger.

Let's apply this train of thought to the universe. The universe started off with the big bang. This giant explosion of gases created mass and condensed molecules and is expanding forever outward. This happened billions of years ago and it's just a slow movement at this point, but still an expansion.

What is it expanding in?

It's probably expanding into absolute nothingness, pure blackness, infinity. No planets, no stars, no meteorites, not even dust outside its borders. Within those borders, it contains matter, much like your body. You could say that you are moving around in absolute nothingness. The boundary of your expanding body has been growing since infancy. Since you started off smaller than a microbe within a womb, you've expanded. So is the universe expanding with everything that it contains.

Astronauts in space all agree that they can't relate to their houses, their kids, or their swimming pools anymore. They say this because the Earth looks like one living being. The ancient word for it is "Gaia." If you go back to the island analogy, remember that you were on land and you existed in a little micro-verse. Then you jumped into your boat and you moved away from the island and saw it as one large thing. Let's do this with the planet and the universe now.

Imagine boarding a spaceship which can move faster than the speed of light. You sit in the back of the spaceship, like you did in the boat. You take off and you can see the whole planet now, floating in space. Imagine the whole planet below you is one living thing. As you continue to travel further away, you look at the planets in the solar system, and you're amazed at the beauty of them. You start to move into space. You go past all the planets and solar systems and head out of the galaxy, into galaxy clusters, the Cosmos. You just keep going and going.

Remember what I said about the universe being this expanding object, constantly growing. Eventually you get to the edge of the entire universe and you shoot out into pure infinity, pure nothingness. There are no planets, no stars, nothing. As you're sitting in the back, you look through the window and you see billions of sparkles everywhere. Those are galaxies. As you move away, you can see the edges of the expanding multi-universes. As you move further away, it gets smaller and more condensed. It starts to look like a big glowing globular object floating in pure blackness. Do you know what that is? That's God! It's the body of God. And everything inside of it is matter, like we are matter. God's soul, Prana, the Force, is the energy that intertwines it all. It's what interconnects it, permeating all things. Just like your body, it's conscious of everything but yet not aware of any one thing.

You are made in the image of God, but in a much different way than humanity ever expected: not with hands and feet, but as an inner cosmos. Your liver and your kidneys are all made out of different kinds of organisms cooperating and working together, creating a synchronicity of life in order to maintain one being. It's duplicated over, and over, and over, from micro to macro.

Where did everything come from?

In the very beginning, there was absolutely nothing. There was pure blackness, pure infinity, pure space; no dust, no planets, no stars, nothing. Particles and atoms didn't exist either, just absolute infinity and pure blackness. Since there was nothing, there had to be one thing, an opposing force.

We know it as the vacuum of space. The vacuum of space can be called a pressure. It's like putting your hand on a vacuum cleaner and feeling suction, a drawing or pulling sensation. This sensation is generated by a machine, but in the universe's case it was because there was nothing. It was like sucking all the air out of a Ziploc bag. Of course, a Ziploc bag has edges, so you might say that the universe is so big and so heavy that it created a vacuum in itself. It was pulling on itself.

If you were able to move through time and space to the beginning of time, the second you rematerialized you would be torn into trillions of pieces smaller than molecules. The pressure would literally suck you apart. You would explode because it would be that intense.

This tension generated a new kind of energy called *free electrons*. There were trillions of them that went on forever like oceans of universes packed together like smoke. Although the electrons were thicker than water, you couldn't see them because they were so fine, so microscopic. Since there was so much of it, it became extremely dense. It was all that existed; created from the suction, the pull of the universe.

You might as well forget the word *time* because time did not exist until matter existed. Yet, what if you did have the concept of time? You're talking about billions, and trillions, and quadrillions of years before there was God, before there was anything. Eventually *something* happened because something must always happen. It's a numbers game.

If I said to you, "Do you think you'll win the lotto this week?" You'll probably say, "No." If I say, "Do you think you'll win it in this lifetime?" You'll probably say "most likely not" because the chances of winning a lotto are like one in eighteen million, right? But let's say you were an immortal and you knew you were going to live longer than fifty thousand years and you played the lotto every day. Do you think you'd win? Statistically speaking, you'd have to win it. You'd win because you were going to play the lotto at least eighteen million times. So eventually, you're going to win.

Something was eventually going to happen in the universe, provided all the circumstances were set up. At this point, if you had a super powerful microscope, you would see objects shaped like little chocolate chips, like floating flat squares. There were billions of them and they moved back and forth ever so gently, vibrating, as if they were moving in a very slow direction. They were so slow that it was not even measurable. As they moved, one of them moved in a certain direction, shimmering and gyrating, hit another one, and created something like the letter `T`.

Instead of all of the objects shimmering in the same direction, the `T` shaped object started to rotate in the opposite direction creating a different kind of electrical current. That electrical current, much like a little tiny snowball rolling down a hill started attaching itself to other `chocolate chips`, creating an electrical pulse. It created a different kind of electron, a different pulse of energy, because electricity isn't affected by gravitation, friction or anything of that sort. It became a living thing within itself, only without a mind, consciousness, or purpose. You were consummated from a microscopically small egg and sperm. That creation of life became you and is now absolutely huge in comparison. *The creation of God happened in much the same way.*

Over millions and trillions of years later, it became more complex. Its source of food was this shimmering type of energy, the free electrons. It kept attaching and multiplying, expanding itself, and becoming more complex as a living organism; a living form of energy. As it drew together, atoms and molecular structures were created. They were spiraling and moving around other electrons. Again, it became more and more complex until molecules started forming very faint and very complex forms of matter. Yet it was still all contained in that energy.

Now, the one question you may ask yourself is, "When did it become intelligent?" or "Did it become intelligent?" It became intelligent, but its intelligence is so completely different than human intelligence that it's difficult to conceive.

The universe can be explained with numbers. Numbers are the galactic code, a language to the whole universe. Everything has a rhythm, a number. Every pattern has a number because it's repetitious and being repetitious means it's calculable. If an electron is going from point A to point B and it's constantly moving back and forth at a rate of thirteen nanoseconds...13 ... 13 ... 13 ... 13, it's a pattern.

According to Chaos Theory, everything is predictable, even running water because of the way it splashes. It actually can be formed into patterns. You can calculate how the water is eventually going to collect because it holds a pattern. When you project light through a screen, it creates a kaleidoscope, but it's the same pattern over and over again. That means nothing is random. When you bounce a ball, there may be a million variables, but it only hits a certain million and then after that it's the same predictable pattern.

The Universe, this Energy, God, started to become aware of itself, of its patterns. Everything works in a collective pattern in the universe. Everything contributes to a process, like a giant database. So, all these electrons had to accumulate in some kind of pattern. They naturally seek out a purpose. It's like evolution. It's just natural to the laws of physics to create refined patterns. Refined patterns create intelligence. God became intelligent over quadrillions of years as energy, as a giant form of Prana, the Force, whatever you'd like to call it, before anything existed.

There are many levels of energy. Energy can be denoted as levels of dimensions: third dimension, fourth dimension, etc. There are thousands of dimensions, not just four or five. God started to create denser forms of electricity. Those denser forms of electricity slowed to lower variables.

Imagine standing by a highway, which is comparable to being at the lowest frequency. Then a car drives past you at twenty miles per hour. You can't see what's going on in the car; it just goes by. A car going fifty goes by even faster. A car going seventy-five goes by faster still; and a car going one hundred goes even faster. Those cars are all at different levels of dimensions. If you got into a car going fifty miles per hour, could you see what the car going twenty is doing? No, you would go right past it. Could you see what the car going seventy-five is doing? No, it's going past you. It's a vibration. It's a tonal. But if another car is going fifty, you could look over because you are moving at the same frequency. You can see that the person is reading a book and chewing gum. You can see what kind of gum they might be putting in their mouth because you're at the same frequency.

So this energy being, if you want to call it God, started to create higher and lower frequencies within itself. As it created different molecules, electrons, and impulses, they all condensed to different weights and different speeds of energy. Eventually, it turned into a current where electrons could instantly solidify into gasses.

There came a point when the energy began to solidify into different kinds of gasses, which were incongruous with one another. The result was the largest explosion of all time! It was far beyond all the nuclear weapons on this Earth exploding at the same time. When it got to the point between the energy and the molecules condensing, it created a super-fusion explosion.

As soon as this energy was released, but before the physical explosion took place, all the higher electrons were sucked out from the higher dimensions. These electrons instantly glued together. Certain ones were attracted like magnets to specific other ones when they solidified. This created matter, and the matter solidified instantly. Then an explosion separated it all into a million infinitive directions. That was the creation of God in this dimension. It was the creation of matter.

Why did you say it was the creation of God "in this dimension"?

God exists in multiple dimensions but this reality is in just one dimension. Are you one-dimensional or are you multi-dimensional? Think about it. When you're asked to say the alphabet, where are you saying it from? You hear it in your head, but where does that place you? Where are you? Can you point to the exact place where you are? Are you this body? Are you inside your head? If you cut off an arm, is the arm still you? Or do you not identify with it as a functioning part of your body? Technically speaking, your body is a robot, a machine. You are energy. You are an energy being. Call it a soul; call it whatever you want. The body simply moves around and collects data for you. If you reach out for a cup, it's because you commanded your body (like an automated machine) to reach out and bring it to your mouth.

As an energy being, everything you touch is turned into electricity so that you can consume and be aware of it. Everything you see, hear, and taste is converted into electricity because you are an electrical being. Like a person driving a car, the car is the body and you are the driver. You are the soul within it. You are an energy being from that other dimension that has been infused with this dimension.

I'm having trouble with two things. The first, "nothingness" is almost completely incomprehensible to me. The second, I always thought that God was intelligent because it seems like creation is an act of will. As I understand it, even with the vacuum, nothingness, and tension, there are still free electrons. Where did the electrons come from?

The electrons came from the vacuum.

Where did the vacuum come from?

The vacuum came from absolute nothingness. Absolute nothingness creates a vacuum because there is nothing to fill it. There is nothing to push on it, and there is no air to push the walls of space. It's very hard to conceive. Take a look at it from a physicist's point of view. If you have a bed sheet, and you pull it out on all four corners and hold it tight, isn't it always going to sag a little in the middle?

Yes.

Think of the universe this way. That sagging in the bed sheet is the pressure I'm referring to. You're really not holding it up, but it exists. The universe is so big that there is some pressurization that's in flux. It's unstable. It's not calculable. It just simply exists. This instability creates a form of absolute finite energy that is so fine, it's like dust. It's almost undetectable, but it exists. Because it exists, it destabilizes and creates a form of energy. It's smaller than a molecule. It's smaller than particles. It's smaller than anything science can perceive. Yet scientists know all these things exist. They are like tachyons moving through the planet at hundreds of millions of miles per hour. They are moving through us right now, but they are so absolutely finite that they are almost imperceptible. And that's where it all came from.

It will take time, but there will come a point when you will see it in your mind. Let's just say that mystical people of great spirituality like Christ, Buddha, Krishna, and other enlightened beings, possessed knowledge far beyond themselves. Somehow, in some way, they just understood things. All the thoughts of the world from every creature, from all of time, are collective energy. There is a collective database of information from the planet that is just stored electrically.

I have found there is a truth between computers and spirituality. If you think about memory in a computer, it floats; it's just here. If you unplug the power, it collapses; it's gone. This collective energy, this information, is floating much like it would be in a memory chip. There is energy here from the sun so it constantly has an electrical field.

One can reach what is called the *mind of Gaia*. In ancient words, it was called the *Akashic records* – the totality of all knowledge. If you can harmonize your mind (your consciousness) like a tuning fork to the vibration of the planet, you can find out anything you want to know. It just comes to you. It just makes sense. It's like you always knew it. You just didn't know how you knew it. It's like suddenly remembering an old memory that was dormant. The answers I am giving you come from this place. Someday you will understand what I mean. You'll see it. It will just make sense.

Does God have a consciousness?

Yes, God has a consciousness. However, for you to conceive how God's mind works is almost impossible because it is so different than our human way of thinking. Imagine what goes through the mind of a snail, slug, or ant. You can conceive it because you can observe it. You are the observer looking at it. You have watched movies, read studies, and watched scientific programs about the chemicals they use. Now reverse this perspective and think about whether or not an ant can conceive the complexities of the human mind.

As humans, we've barely begun to explore our own solar system. We've only visited Earth's moon. We haven't visited other planets, let alone other solar systems, or galaxies. If you want to conceive the size of God, hold a grain of sand in your hand. Our solar system is inside of that grain of sand. Now look at your feet and imagine beach sand about twenty feet deep below your feet. Think of all the grains of sand below you, each a solar system within itself. Then look to your right for about ten miles down the beach until it begins to disappear. That's like one part of the Universe heading in one direction. Now look in the other direction for ten miles and imagine each grain of sand that's there. That will give you a small concept of the vastness of our universe.

Now, conceive how God thinks. Your brain works on low-radiation impulses. Those low-radiation impulses tell your heart to pump. They help your liver and your kidneys to function. You're not really aware of it, but in your super-subconscious mind, there is a level of awareness. For instance, yogis can hold their breath for long amounts of time by lowering their heart rate, among other things. That means they've tapped into their super-subconscious mind. They're utilizing that inner-verse, that inner dimension of their body.

I don't believe that astrology rules our lives but I do believe that we, as a species, are manipulated to some degree by solar radiation. All the stars in the universe are like the neural synapses of the brain. The neural synapses release sparks of information, data, which move across the expansions of the brain to other points that reciprocate it.

In this same way, all the stars in the universe reach the Earth through light, solar radiation, and millions of different frequencies. Like a giant orchestra playing its rhythm upon a small ball, you are impacted constantly by these different pitches and frequencies, because humans are electrical beings. All creatures' brains, including humans, are receptive to this influence. It manipulates and affects us as societies, as well as giant organisms, moving as units upon the planet.

God communicates through the stars. The same way that you communicate through the electrons in your brain without realizing it, solar radiation manipulates all of the other electrons in your body like little points. God thinks using solar radiation compared to the radiation in your brain. God communicates with different solar systems, galaxies, and universes in the same way your brain receives and separates information from your heart, kidney, liver, and other organs in your body. They are all very different with a specific function. All are made out of billions of living organisms that have never been seen, the same as other organisms in your body. Your organs would be aliens if they moved from one point to the next. This concept applies to the physical matter of the Universe - God.

Does God think?

God is more like an organism than a self-thinking type of thing. I don't think that God has intention – meaning a divine plan for the Earth. I think that God has awareness in the same way that you have an awareness of your hand or your thumb. You are protective of it. You use it, but you don't think about all the cells, tendons, muscles, the blood flowing through it, or all of the very complex things that make it a hand. You simply see it as an appendage that you use. But if something happens to it, you react. If it is in danger, you react to the pain that is emanating from all of those millions of cells saying, "Hey, help us." It would be the same effect if the planet were in danger. Maybe the Earth's consciousness, being the collective consciousness of all living things inhabiting it, would feel like a tiny pinprick in God's palm. So God scratches it, but in a very different way than having hands or a body.

You must understand these are analogies. There is a level of awareness. It's just not the kind of awareness that you perceive. Are you aware of your liver working right now? Are you aware of your kidneys? No, yet they are there. They are a part of you and they function for you. There is no awareness unless you feel pain, unless you feel death. God is unaware in the terms that religions have dictated. However, God is absolutely aware because It is a part of everything. You could say that, similar to humans, God is made of two parts: Its energy and Its body. All the matter, planets, and stars are Its flesh and blood. And God's soul, energy, and consciousness is intertwined like your mind and your energy is intertwined with your body mass.

Electrically, you are the spirit, or the Force, to the micro-verse in your body. All the cells of your body succumb to you. If you become depressed, they become depressed and don't function very well. If you become positive, they become positive. God does not have depressions, but there is a sense of energy from It that can affect all of us and we are receptive to it. You can tap into this energy to do amazing and powerful things if you simply know how to do it. Call it tapping into the Force, or the power of the Force, or being a Jedi warrior; it doesn't matter. In truth, all of these stories come from a true source.

Are you saying there is a way to "tap the Force?"

There is a way to tap energy as a singular being. When you consume this energy, you can change your tonal, your vibration, like a tuning fork. Remember, God is a very high vibration and it is in the lower dimensions that this frequency slows down. Humans are in the lower vibrations. We are moving at ten miles per hour where the higher vibrations are moving at seventy-five to one hundred miles per hour. If you raised your frequency to a similar speed, it would be like one car driving next to another. Since you are moving at the same speed, you can see what's going on inside that car if you want. If you raised your tonal to one hundred miles per hour, you would conceive and become a vibration with God. That's called enlightenment. You simply act here in this lower dimension using the knowledge and the power from that higher vibration.

It is possible to tap into a super energy, a super power that is beyond your comprehension. A very refined state of consciousness will do that. If you study and practice your spirituality, you can achieve amazing things. Everything in our Universe uses an exchange of energy. A car does not run without gasoline. A tree does not grow without water and minerals. Fire does not burn without wood or fuel.

First, you must learn to absorb Prana to draw in this energy. You have to learn how to consume mass quantities of this energy. It's the same concept that a martial artist uses practicing Kung Fu. They absorb chi and use it to throw someone across the room. Imagine being able to absorb a hundred million times that amount inside of you so that you can do amazing psychic things, like healing the sick, seeing other dimensions, and unimaginable things. These are the things you can do once you learn how to tap into Prana, because it does exist.

If Prana is a form of God, is there an opposing force? Is there evil?

Yes, there is. But it's not a devil with horned feet or anything like the Bible conceives. Stealing something is not considered evil. It's considered immoral, unethical, and wrong. When one beats up somebody, it is considered to be evil. In my mind, evil is the willful intent to diminish the ability to experience. I will give you a great secret. Everybody questions and asks, "What is the meaning of life?" *The meaning of life is to experience.* You're an energy being in a physical body here on Earth to experience what you could not experience as an energy being. As energy, you can't smell. You don't have eardrums so you can't hear. You can't see, taste or touch. As energy, this whole physical universe doesn't exist. This universe is like a smorgasbord of experiences. To a soul, this universe is like Disney World to a seven year old because it can experience things here that it never conceived before.

As an energy being, you're tied to this body that allows you to experience the physical world. Your body transforms data. It transforms experiences into energy so that it can become part of your consciousness. So when I say to you, "The meaning of life is to experience," listen to the birds singing, feel the wind on your face, experience the warmth of the sun on your face, and feel moisture on your toes. Experience what it is to kiss, hug, roll in the dirt, play in the snow, and laugh. The meaning of life is to experience. It's doing everything you can't do as an energy being.

Being an energy being is not bad. It's an experience that's absolutely beautiful; a creation that is to be realized, tasted, and enlivened. To do anything that is the opposite of that is truly sinful.

Unless it is polluted chemically or somehow faulty in its natural sensory, everything that's living has one thing in common. It has a natural desire to live. Even stupid animals don't run off cliffs. Insects fear death. Everything has a sense of life. *Everything wants to live.* That is because everything is infused with the Force. We are infused with this energy that tells us to exist. The same energy that communicates to your body says to every soul, "Live, exist, function for the greater." In the same way, we function for the greater good of the planet. So does the planet function for the solar system; the solar system for the galaxy, and the galaxies for the universes. It perpetuates until it becomes one consciousness of God.

So let's go back to the concept of evil. What is evil and how did it come into existence? What makes us so sure that it even exists? Well, if God exists, and God *was* the big bang, for every action there is an equal and opposite reaction. If I push on you, I can only push you so far before the chair you are sitting on, the mass of the floor, and everything else retracts and pushes me back. Where is the equal and opposite reaction to the creation of the universe? Where is this opposite opposing force of energy? What is it?

It exists. It is the Darkside. It is the negative side. It is anti-life. It is the opposing force of life, stars, planets, universes, and everything.

When you understand that there is an opposing force of energy to a positive force of energy which we are a part, you can now conceive the concept and the potential of evil. Again, evil isn't stealing someone's car; that's immoral and unethical. Taking someone's pocket book is immoral and unethical, but it's not a sin. The suppression or the termination of life is evil.

If someone kidnaps another person and suppresses them, locks them up in a room, and deprives them of touch, smell, and new experiences, that is considered the Darkside. That would be considered a will of darkness, a will of evil. To kill life is wrong. Wanting to kill or destroy life is a bad thing. It is a wrong action. To mentally torture someone, suppress someone's feelings, or marginalize them emotionally is evil because it is the opposite of the meaning of life. Those things are considered to be evil.

The Darkside wants to eradicate life. Anything that flourishes with life is an opposing force to the Darkside. When the universe was created and it expanded, the opposing force wanted it to become nothing. It wanted to squelch it and make it disappear because it's an opposite reaction.

The Darkside is attracted to anything that has to do with life flourishing as an equal and opposing force. It's a reaction. Since the Darkside is everywhere, as much as there is a positive force everywhere, these two are like oil and vinegar. You can put oil and vinegar in a container and they are separate. They float on top of one another. But when you shake them vigorously, they look like one hue. However, if you look closely you will see the little oil dots and the little bubbles of vinegar. They're separate but they're so finite you can hardly tell. Well, that's like the energy of the Force and the Darkside – both are everywhere. And whatever you attract is what you will consume as energy. It will be utilized in that way, in a negative or in a positive way.

Even though the Darkside sees most human beings as something it dislikes, it is not unlike the Darkside to utilize or empower someone to cause destruction in this dimension. It sees humankind as a tool. Some people turn to the Darkside to use energy to create death, destruction, or mayhem to help throw a board into the cycles of life to jam it. The Darkside is a very real thing, just as the Force is a very real thing.

The Darkside is simply attracted to the Earth for one very good reason: the Earth is a living organism. Every planet in the universe is alive in some way. Perhaps they are not as advanced as the Earth in terms of life. Maybe in some cases they are more advanced than the Earth. But as the Earth flourishes with life, as it flourishes with intelligence, it is seen as a very, very, deadly opposition. According to the Darkside, Earth is an opposing organism in space. As Earth flourishes with life and the Force grows stronger within us, the Darkside accumulates and find points where it can crack into us to eradicate or spoil this process.

A lot of people say that the population is a bad thing for the Earth and that humans are more like a disease on the planet. That is not true. All things have their pros and cons. You could say that a baby can pollute a womb and a mother can die giving birth. There are certain factors of life that are unstable. Nothing is perfect. The Earth is a living, growing organism. The human race has some instabilities but it realizes certain things within its collective consciousness. We need to take care of the planet now. We need to clean it up. So, we're going through highs and lows as we progress collectively as an organism. But the real threat to the Darkside is the purpose of the Universe.

I'll approach this concept as an analogy. Some people question how satellites can be a part of the planet. Well, it's all part of the higher functioning of the planet. Humans use their arms to reach out to touch. What does the planet use to reach out with? Nothing. The planet is expanding, but it's collectively using the sensory of the organisms that inhabit it. You have eyes to see. Earth is creating its own eyes in its own evolutionary stages. It's creating its sensory and we are the most advanced part of that evolution.

Consider humanity's evolution. We started off with what is called the Reptilian brain, which was approximately two or three inches in circumference. We eventually evolved to the advanced features of the Neo-Cortex. That's when the circuitry really advanced, getting better and faster. This is what telephones, fiber optics, and satellites are to the planet. They are the circuitry, the nerves, and the synapses. Call it whatever you want, but the planet, which is evolving as a living thing, is becoming more alive, getting older and more advanced. It's finding its form. The Darkside is most afraid that the Earth will create more of itself.

Every species on our planet multiplies. This planet is a hermaphrodite, so to speak. It doesn't need a male and a female to procreate. It has both qualities within it. Like a bee pollinating a flower, the planet uses us to pollinate. We will create spaceships and we will pollinate the moon. We will pollinate Mars and we will terraform planets to support human life. We will go to the stars. We will bring the DNA. We will bring our fruits and trees to grow. We'll create water, an atmosphere, and the right temperature.

We'll create everything that's similar to our home with our DNA, thus mimicking ourselves over and over in the universe. That is what the Force ultimately desires. It sees us multiplying and sees the expansion and advancement of life. The Darkside is very opposed to this. It's opposed to us because it sees us potentially doing this. It wants to hold us back and prevent this from happening.

To grasp this concept, you cannot only look at a period of one hundred years of time. In our civilization, one hundred years seems like a very long time, but to a planet that is billions of years old, one hundred years is like the blink of an eye. The purpose of the planet is to continue expanding as a living organism. We all know our plan. We know we're going out to the stars. We can feel it. Most of us are already craving to go out to the universe, as if we were created to do it. Some of us feel that our soul came from a place that already had the knowledge to do that, and that we can indoctrinate that knowledge into the rest of the world. I believe that you can see a lot of similarities in our bodies versus the planet.

What is the role of enlightened people on Earth? Who are the people seeking spiritual teachers that have evolved to that level?

Well, if we're going to use the human body as an example of this, then you could say that those evolved people are *White Cells* and everybody else are *Red Cells*. Those who have no interest in this path serve as an organism that contributes to the planet. The very advanced spiritual people feel the rhythm and the life of the planet.

They are the protectors of the planet. They have the sensory of a much higher level, like the white cells in the body are able to communicate and understand one another. Red cells do their own thing, just marching along. In the body, the white cells protect the red cells. They protect against invasion from the outside that the red cells are oblivious to. White cells have the sense that recognizes a virus. To the body, a virus could be considered the Darkside. It's anti-life. It's destruction or multiplication of another life form that will only lead to death and decay. So the white cells fight it, and learn new things. Somehow, they hold an arcane sense of knowledge. When other white cells die, their experiences are given to new white cells so that they can adapt quickly to continue the battle. So, in many ways, they learn from the other white cells, much like with reincarnation.

Old souls reincarnating into new lives are sent to places on the planet where they are necessary because of their knowledge from previous battles. I teach people this knowledge because I believe that some people are *sleepers*. When a sleeper hears what I am saying, they know it is absolute truth. They feel it. It's exhilarating. It's as if they were searching for something their whole life and they never could quite put their finger on it, but their life did not feel complete before. It's as if they knew that there had to be something more, dimensionally or physically. Something beyond all of this was missing for them. It's because these old souls carry the knowledge of dimensional beings.

Red cells don't have this knowledge. They just live. Most of them don't have souls yet. The ones who do are new souls. They are bio-chemical beings with electrical energy that serve the planet. But they can develop souls, if they choose. Einstein said that he didn't necessarily believe that everybody had a soul. But he did believe that we are made of energy and you cannot destroy energy. You can only recreate it. He believed that if you can learn to control the energies within your body, you can control yourself as you leave the body and are looking for a new host; that means you can find another body to incarnate into.

Red cells have to contribute to the planet's consciousness; white cells do not. Red cells live their lives. They experience, touch, and smell everything. When they die, their energy, like a sugar cube, goes back into the ocean of the great collective consciousness. It becomes a greater consciousness for the planet with all of its knowledge combined. It becomes the Akashic records. If White Cells awaken and continue on their path, they will be able to incarnate into another new, fresh body to continue the battle that they were pursuing.

The Earth has a particular vibration that constantly pushes you to be a red cell. That's how it keeps red cells as red cells. The Earth eliminates certain states of consciousness, which is why there's a student-teacher relationship. By demonstrating this knowledge, the teacher progresses to a point where they can attain the information and hold it all together.

I've known this information for years. ***The fact that I can share this with you confirms that I am whatever it is that I am saying.*** Therefore, as a teacher, it is my experience that this is what you must be seeking. It's the bridge. It's the arm that reaches out to pull you in. If you don't take it, you fall back into what you've always been, a sleeper. If a part of you awakens and is drawn to this, you will not only grab onto the arm but you will also pull up vigorously and embrace the opportunity because you can see it as a higher truth.

To do otherwise is foolish. However, I don't think this path is right for everybody. I think this is a very selective path. A teacher shows you things, exercises, ways to do things, and how to experience things. A teacher will help you to see things that are incomprehensible to your imagination. It's through these experiences that you grow strong and capable of embracing the reality of this knowledge.

Do not think that this is where it all stops. All this information that I've taught you is the very beginning. It's like taking a single step out of the door when your entire journey to Brazil is to experience and explore the whole country. You've only just been introduced to the truth. The rest is the greatest adventure of your lifetime. There is no other choice in the end. It's very addictive. I believe that this information came into your hands because it was the will of the Universe. It is really up to you to pursue the teacher. It's up to you to pursue whatever it is that's meant for you.

Chapter 6

DISSECTING THE MATRIX

I'VE NEVER REALLY addressed the reason that I teach the people that I do. I have tried to find different ways to explain it; to find the right words so that it makes sense to you. What is the role and purpose of each individual? How does it all work? Why does it work the way that it does?

Although you have many pieces of the puzzle already, I would like to give you an even better understanding, a superior vision of what is really going on and where this is heading. In this dimension, I don't think it's possible to fully understand the totality of everything. You can get a very good understanding, but there is a lot more to learn about the different complexities.

Movies are now being made on the concept of virtual reality. I find it very interesting that humans mimic the things spiritual masters have done within their own minds. The people who create these virtual realities do not have the same skills. They use artificial means to create something similar, but without the understanding of something greater.

It has given me another way to explain what the majority of people have difficulty understanding – the concept of a supercomputer that is able to create these realities. Perhaps in the future, there will be incredible wireless, tubeless machines that project you into a virtual reality while you are lying down. Maybe there will even be satellites that scan your body weight and frequency, your unique schematic numbers, enabling you to go into another reality. The possibility of this is endless; however, a virtual reality doesn't even come close to the real experience.

Think of the collective consciousness of the planet as a supercomputer beyond anything we currently have available. Extend that to the solar system, the universe, and the totality of the consciousness of God. This ultimate supercomputer creates a multitude of other *virtual worlds*. In some aspect, you exist in one of those now. It is real. It is also *sur*real. It's like when you are in the dream state and you wake up for a moment. Then you forget that you have just awakened and go back to your dream state.

Can you imagine what it is like beyond this world? What is it like beyond this material life after you leave your body? What about parallel dimensions, meaning dimensions that are similar to this world? The most interesting to me are the dimensions in the Universe with much higher frequencies. What's the truest reality beyond all of these illusions? In the past, spiritual masters have used the word *illusions* to describe reality. The experience is so real to you that you don't even realize it is an illusion. In modern terminology, we use the term *virtual reality*; it's just semantics.

Now, I am back to my favorite number – three. What I am referring to is the *third truth*. It is very difficult to explain this to you in words because it is energy. It is a brilliant vastness that goes beyond our time and space. If I was to give it a color, it would be fuchsia or a blend of purple and pink. It's a color that I've seldom seen. It's not necessarily a color that exists, it's more of a tone or a vibration. It can waiver, depending on where it is. If you think of distances like from point A to the furthest point, that's still not it. It's here now. It is vibration and it is energy. All of these universes are here at the same time. Their vastness varies with each universe or each dimension. You move through this space without having to physically move at all. You can be in one place and, through intention or desire, also be in another. *You simply just **think yourself there** and, all of a sudden, you **are** there.* It's like folding space. This is a multi-layered statement, so you need to ponder what I just said.

You can look at this as if were a *haze of energy*. You can see through it, but it is a substance within itself. It's like a fuzzy beautiful energy. Thought, ideas, and concepts are pulsated through it. **"You are made in the image of God."** There's more truth in that statement than you can possibly imagine. On a micro level, those of you who move beyond the Earth as White Cells and move through the Universe eventually become a moving energy consciousness because you are a piece of God. You have individuality but you are also an aspect of God. When you move to this ultimate level as energy, your purpose is really to move your memory and your ideas. Or you are addressing a problem within the embodiment of God. If you have something bothering you on your leg, a multitude of electricity and energies, all separate and individual, work collectively in unison for you to command the physical matter of your body.

The Universe is vast beyond your comprehension.

This universe was created when energy solidified into matter from a higher energy vibration, with molecules attaching onto each other like a snowball growing larger while rolling down the hill. The Universe created matter, the Big Bang, and life in this dimension.

So you have two halves - matter and energy. It is like a fusion of the higher energies and lower energies, creating the essence of life. In this creation, the *breath of life* is really the energy of God. If you removed the electricity from your body, there would still be life but it would be organic matter. If you then removed the organic matter from the body, atomic particles would make up your flesh. If you remove that, you are left with nothing. In a sense, this is the fundamental creation of the whole Universe. You need these elements and this way of thinking to create your virtual reality because it's still all energy in the end.

Life came from this energy. Red cells are biochemical; they think with electricity. They create consciousness, but only one in about fifteen thousand people has a moment of self-realization. There is a known truth that states: "*I think, therefore, I am.*" Through the evolutionary process of this world and all the other worlds that possess life, eventually there comes a point where the few reach the White Cell level in the process of evolution for the planet. Those White Cells then say, "*I am more than what I am,*" and they become a **soul.** Then, out of those fifteen thousand White Cells, one says "*I am more than just a soul,*" and she/he becomes what is considered to be a *super being.*

Everything moves at a particular rate of speed. In the times of Krishna, Buddha, and Christ fewer people were able to reach a state of enlightenment. If you look at the evolution of the planet during those times, it makes total sense. The planet was still evolving back then. There were enlightened masters in other parts of the world, but it was not as well known.

Anything that you read or hear about enlightened Masters is only a small percentage of the truth. You hardly ever hear about the unwritten, destroyed, or secret teachings that happened before pens and paper were available. The knowledge was passed on by word of mouth; often misconstrued by that person's ideas or personal points of view. The real truth is rarely obtainable. Most people accept what they read or hear now as pure fact, and this has been problematic throughout the ages.

When Buddha, Christ, Milarepa, or any of the Masters attained enlightenment, they understood that nothing is as it appears to be. They were able to affect time, space, and other dimensions because of their knowledge of non-real reality. So, Buddha, Krishna, Christ, and Milarepa had their moments of self-realization, and that enabled them to awaken and to accomplish great miracles.

Speaking of special moments, in the movie *The Matrix* when Neo questioned everything in his mind, he found that *one special moment*. That was his realization and he was able to affect reality. Even though *The Matrix* is a movie, it is also a fable. This is the way the Universe communicates with people in this dimension. I call this *broadcasting*.

If we go back to a time before those great teachers lived, there were other beings who visited the Earth. All of these beings are portrayed as looking very different or strange. That is because during those times, the matrix for the planet was not as solidly written as it is now. Many highly advanced beings from higher dimensions wanted to intervene and escalate the consciousness which was developing in this world.

So, they came to the Earth and materialized into physical bodies. Sometimes, there were carryovers, like blue skin or shimmering energy. These beings were able to merge with both realities simultaneously because this virtual world was not as solidly pro-grammed and refined as it is now. So, the stories that you've heard about advanced beings in Egypt and other parts of the Earth are all true.

It is difficult to imagine what it was like thousands of years ago because of our limited perceptions. As a virtual program, our reality is so much tighter in its progression that it's inconceivable to imagine anything different. Over time, it became harder and harder to bend reality. It took a greater amount of will to exist in this dimension and to break the code so that humanity could function here, awaken, and serve a much higher purpose. In ancient history, the advanced beings had a greater understanding of the truth than we do now. They were trying to seed the world with information, to counter the programming of the world, and also the Darkside.

It is very difficult in this time and age to awaken. You can have glimmers of self-realization and then easily fall back to sleep again. The matrix is always the Doe vibration. It's always the vibration that brings you back into it; it's the constant. In order for you to awaken from it, you need to self-reflect. You need to constantly think about and ponder things that will make shift your consciousness. The more you think about spirituality, the more spiritual you'll become. You'll feel as if you're making progress, but you will also be frustrated at times because personal growth takes awhile.

You will sense more or have a knowing about certain things. There's a sensory about you that's part of your spiritual awakening. You are starting to be aware of the matrix. You're starting to feel the virtual world. In ancient words, you're starting to *realize the illusion.* At first, you may not fully understand it because you don't know where you're going with it. It's like going down a road that you've never seen before; you don't want to go too fast because you don't know what's around the corner. But if you travelled that road frequently, you would feel comfortable speeding along knowing what to expect.

When you're interacting with the world and you're affected by other people in the program, you're brought back into this reality very quickly. You're brought back into the *Doe.* If you're not quick enough to jump back into an altered state of mind to begin your work again, then you're going to fall back asleep very quickly. You're going to forget about working towards awakening. Maintaining your awakened state will become less and less appealing.

This is why you should have things in your home that remind you of your spirituality. The people you surround yourself with will either help you fall asleep or help you to awaken. The material things that you have in your home, such as posters, pictures, and decorations will either help you to fall asleep or help you to awaken. I don't have pictures of my family around the house because it makes me think too much of the Doe. The decorations in my house inspire me spiritually to help maintain my energy. That helps me counter the vibration of the Doe. Everything I've ever taught you supports this.

When you reach a level of self-realization, you have

this energy or shine about you. In the past, some people have broken the matrix on a few occasions. One of the biggest ways to break free of the matrix is to fly. Everybody always wants to levitate, or defy gravity by rising into the air. There are priests or gurus from the East who have mastered this successfully in the past.

They were photographed and documented as having the ability to levitate ten or fifteen feet into the air. Some of them were said to reach a level of "Samadhi," which is the Vedic name for this. It is described as an ecstatic level of bliss. When they reached this state, they were able to float through the air. What they are actually doing is breaking the matrix. There are also ancient beings, thousands of years old, who are still living right now. They are *physically immortal*. In a sense, they have been glitched into the matrix. They are deliberately still in this dimension for higher intervention.

All of this fits into a much bigger picture, if you understand the dynamics of how this all works and how it's all linked together. Most of the world's people have to remain Red Cells because that is what *we* want in the world. When I say we, I mean enlightened beings like myself who have a knowing that the Earth needs to reach a certain level of evolution for its own soul. Gaia is achieving its own intelligence and its own consciousness in a very different way. But there are dark forces in the Universe that don't want this to happen. These forces don't want any kind of life to exist in the Universe, especially of an evolved nature. The sun is alive but it doesn't have a conscious ability to affect anything. You can affect things on this micro level. You can also affect the direction of something. You can actively and consciously choose to intervene on this level.

In its own way, the Earth's consciousness will play a pivotal role in this part of the Universe in the far future. It does so in a way that helps extend the consciousness of God as a totality, as a body. The Earth's conscious limitation will not just be within our solar system, but the entire Universe.

Think of a microorganism within your body working the totality of you. Can a microorganism reach out to anything within a two foot area of you? No. But as a totality, it can affect *its* entire Universe - even beyond - and be part of it. The Earth's consciousness is going to be able to affect more of the embodiment of the Universe, helping the rest of the Universe become one, to return back to energy, pure conscious thought, God.

There are darker forces, the anti-aspect to creation that has interplay in this dimension. They are also using preventative measures to keep this from happening. As viruses go in, the body creates anti-viruses or *white cells*, even in the human body. A White Cell is an analogy that I use in Higher Balance as well (see index).

Recently, I saw a science program talking about super cells in the body. It said that super cells are dormant in the human body. When havoc is created and all these bad viruses break out in the body, it's just a matter of time before the super cells awaken. The super cells come out and they kick ass, but they have to be discovered before the rest of the body is destroyed.

We are made in the image of God. On a micro/macro level, you have the same kind of scenario. The difference is that the body can die and take everything with it, so it doesn't always have a happy ending. When I speak about super cells, super souls, or super spiritual beings, this is what I'm referencing. I'm not talking about anybody who can sit down and meditate or anyone who professes to have healing powers or spiritual abilities. I'm talking about something that is profoundly beyond that. These are very unique individuals, very rare, and very difficult to find.

There will be a moment in time when a door will open up and more energy will temporarily be available, much like it was thousands of years ago. When I say a moment, it's figurative. A moment can be a hundred years on this Earth. This will allow circumstances to either conflict with the Darkside, be ruled by it, or counter-ruled by it with a force of positive energy. The Universe wants to be certain that all the propagations are made, so It is prepared for that time.

When the body senses a problem, it releases endorphins and other things to prepare itself for action. On a dimensional level, it's very hard to so that because the program of the matrix is so strong. It's very hard to break outside of whatever is written in this reality, this code, this matrix. It takes very powerful people to even affect it. Some people wonder where the conflicts are located. Where are they and how is it that we do what we need to do? It's multileveled.

Spiritually, you can tie all of this together as you meditate. You will hear from other people that you haven't heard from in a while. They will try to bring you back into their world; this is another way of the matrix. As you're moving out of it, the program's saying "warning" and it's pulling you back in. When you become more spiritual, certain factors will suddenly surface to try to pull you out of it. Always be aware of this. It may seem like coincidence, but there's a point when it goes beyond that. You can use this as a means of acknowledgment because it helps you to awaken spiritually. It's a little mental trick to use when you think, "I'm falling deeper in the matrix." *Simply questioning the matrix helps you to awaken.*

You have to operate physically like everyone else. You have to work inside the levels of the matrix. If you bump it too much, the matrix starts to pile up on you to make things more difficult. You have to work within a function that doesn't bump the system, or draw too much attention to yourself. Only the most powerful can really be here right now, but even then it is hard to get things done. Back in Krishna's time, you could do even bigger things more often because the consciousness grid wasn't so rigid. Now, you have to make a conscious choice on how you want to progress. Either you stay asleep or you work to stay awake. There are natural forces trying to keep you in this place, and there are forces that want to keep you here this way.

You said the matrix was less rigid previously than it is right now. What made it tighter?

The human race made it tighter. The human race is the central nervous system of the planet. Because we think, we emit energy. Because we work in unison, we fundamentally create a grid, like bees or ants. We're just more complicated. Everything we create and design is done in such a manner that compliments structural thinking. So all the books, television programming, radios, and other forms of communication formulate how every person thinks. Who you become is based on what you're exposed to within your environment. If you're exposed to spiritual things that is how you will fundamentally develop your thinking.

Suppose alien races visited this planet, would the matrix be less rigid for them?

Systematically, the Universe follows a very strong pattern, as we've seen in all creation - a sea shell versus a galaxy. Chaos theory is the same pattern. Alien races exist within the same levels of the grid. The grid does not just function for the Earth; it just functions differently. The whole Universe is similar. It depends on the acceleration of the planet and its evolvement. Some alien races have already progressed further than us spiritually. As long as this universe exists we must follow within some level of the pattern of the matrix. The matrix itself has a beginning and an end; there's a reason for it. There are mandates to contain and direct it all so it's not corrupted. Yes, aliens can have an easier time but not 100% because when they come into this dimension, it's not the same code as theirs.

If alien races are more spiritually advanced than we are, then when they come here, is it possible that they understand things that our consciousness isn't yet ready for?

Precisely. This is why they observe our world before they're ready to communicate with us. When the Earth reaches a certain frequency, then they will communicate with us because the whole of humanity, including Red Cells, will have spiritually progressed.

Are there different levels of the matrix? And do they have their own programming?

Precisely, both assumptions are correct.

Is there Universal programming?

There's a mass Universal programming.

What sets that frequency?

Have you ever heard of artificial intelligence? Artificial intelligence takes a piece of information and builds on it. When the Universe was created, isn't it possible that each galaxy took a spinoff of its own information and developed its own artificial intelligence? There would still be unanimity to compile it all together.

Before wheels were created by primitive man, they developed a different way to create movement through vibration. It is a different kind of intelligence; however, apply that same knowledge to galaxies and other universes. There is also a universal matrix, but it's only the fundamental framework of one. The bottom layer is still a solid structure of the Universe that is based on the matrix. As time progresses, it develops a plan for development and creation.

If it's an experience to go from energy into matter, then is energy also an experience?

Most people can't even go there. That is so far beyond what they can conceive that, if they even thought about it, they would rather be a Red Cell as a result. Pondering that can be both discouraging as well as encouraging. There are advanced beings, or Avatars, who have repeatedly come into this world to awaken Red Cells to become potential White Cells. They tried to promote the development of White Cells to become Super Cells. They also tried to encourage some more powerful Super Cells from other parts of the Universe to migrate here in this dimension to assist the progression of Gaia's consciousnesses. If somebody asked me how I would compare other worlds to this one, I'd say that it's a lot darker here. It's not darker as in evil, but everything is thick, dull, and dark, energy-wise. It's very dark to me compared to the shimmering brilliance of other universes and dimensions where others do exist.

The Universe was created from energy, from the pure consciousness of God. God wanted to experience other possibilities, so God created super consciousness, the super being, and birthed this dimension. The energy slowed until it hit a certain vibration. It's similar to a car going one hundred miles per hour and then slowing down to ten miles per hour so you can look at what is around you. If you moved faster, you cannot see what is on the other side of the road. But if you slowed down considerably, you could see more. And if you stopped driving altogether, you certainly could see what's around you. So let's say that reality had not begun to formulate yet.

Was there a reason for the birthing at that particular time?

The reason was to see what is here. It's to discover this entire Universe. It is infinite, which is hard to imagine. But for God, it's like stopping the car for a moment and smelling the roses on the side of the road. God is curious.

It is simply that God exists, but because God slowed down there is a law of physics within this frequency. There was also a counter reaction, a counter force created in this dimension, and it doesn't want this frequency to thrive. It doesn't belong here. It's a reaction. It's like pushing down on springs and then bouncing back from the friction. Only we don't think of it that way because we're all part of this dimension. In essence, the Universe was birthed from energy, and then solidified into matter. When I move my hand in a big circle, each little movement of my finger is analogous to a hundred million years. Scientists are now saying that the Universe is around fifteen billion years old, but it is actually older than that.

Imagine everything that consists of energy getting darker, solidifying, and becoming balls of mass: planets, worlds, and galaxies. It's all light, energy, and liquids. Now imagine throwing it in the air and watching it come down. It begins to form a structure because it's slowing down, freezing, and solidifying until it becomes globules floating in space. The globules become planets, worlds, and galaxies. Then they start to feel the effects of these universe's laws of physics. It now has to decide, "What am I going to be? I must be something. I'm going to take on a design. How can I be something from nothing?" So some force helps it to take on a structure when it slows down to zero point.

This is how worlds and civilizations are created. Throughout the whole galaxy, only a few become alien worlds. As they move, the alien world's progress and they become the nervous system of the entire Universe for God. So the Universe is very numb until it can build up enough nervous systems to become a matrix of electrical grids to communicate back to the source of what you are. Your hand is not your hand. If you cut the nerve that has all the wiring for touch, feel, sensation, motion, and control, what do you have? You have a living lump of flesh, which is a living organism. Until you can wire in with the other worlds, you cannot move from this world, this universe, and this dimension, to their dimension and share with whatever they're experiencing here.

When God pushed into this universe Its reason for the creation of life was to utilize us. So, when we die, what do we do with our knowledge? When the Earth lives a few billion years, what will it do when it finally departs? All the data of Earth's experiences leaves with it. What happens to *universal consciousness*? Where does it go? Where will the solar system go?

Everything will become the totality of the Force. We just aren't able to conceive hundreds of billions of years. In the beginning, there really wasn't much of anything to harness the information. The Universe was like a body that didn't have enough nerves in its hand to feel, so when it touched something, it felt numb. Have you ever had Novocain in your mouth? Can you feel a sensation in your mouth when that happens? Can you feel everything? *That's how the Universe felt.*

The Universe felt like that until it began to develop

life within itself. Initially, it started to grow algae or bacteria because the only way that consciousness could ever be attained is through life. We're living inside an organic body, the Earth, so we're more advanced. That's not to say that the Earth is not a part of God. It's not to say the Earth isn't a part of you. But there's a greater part of you within all of this. Some areas are more spiritually evolved and more consciously in tune with God.

All of the planets had to create bacteria to create life from nothingness. What does a planet do if it is able to gestate enough? If the world dies out, it's gone, but if it culminates like a flower or a tree, it is going to pollinate and become a complete solar system. The solar system becomes like a little ball pollinating out to more galaxies in time, and that results in webbing neural networks of consciousnesses, of intelligent beings that are capable of harnessing intelligence to experience and collectively share that one experience. When you spread this throughout the Universe, you have a grid of a whole different level.

I was under the impression that there was a matrix for Earth and when you reach a level of enlightenment, you break through the matrix. So if we break this matrix and we become enlightened, are we still trapped by another matrix somewhere else?

You're not trapped. You have an understanding of the matrix and you can choose wherever you want to go. In the end, there's absolute nothingness. This has been taught by many great spiritual teachers. In the end, they are correct because there's only a consciousness that is God. All the realities of time, space, and dimensions are within the mind of the only thing that could possibly exist next to non-existence, the mind of God.

To exist in the other frequencies and dimensions is a matter of knowing; having the choice to either become Red Cells in the beginning or White Cells to be more in control of your destiny than you are now. You can move through the other dimensions of God. They're as real as any other dimension, but in a sense they're an illusion. As long as you can understand, you can appreciate all the beauty, complexities, and vastness of each individual. It is still uniquely individual.

By the same token, you have the gift of being able to move freely now. You can choose where you want to exist. You can choose to exist here in this world by incarnating into a physical being in order to be able to feel, touch, and smell. Other aliens in the Universe are completely different from us. How we experience in this dimension is absolutely unique.

If you were a dog, your sense of smell would be different than what you experience as a human. A dog has a much greater sense of smell than a human, so a dog's sense of reality is completely different than a human's. Every level is ultimately another level of the matrix, but there is a totality of something in the end that I call *true consciousness* and *true space*. That is ultimately reality.

That's the place that I'm speaking about, this place of pure energy. That is the truest place beyond all levels of the matrix because you have accepted the reality of what you are. You are a piece of the consciousness of God in a very complex way; in other ways, not so complex. So you are now able to reciprocate and act independently, but you're still part of it. You're not completely independent. Therefore, you are always part of its matrix, part of its consciousness.

So the matrix is pretty much a big network for God to communicate, understand, or get information.

No different than you. What part of you is real?

All of it.

How is it real? You have already discovered your body is not you. It's all living organisms that are totally not you. Your body is a big part of the problem because you're so hooked into it that everything you experience is constantly bombarding you, distracting you from who you are. Remove the body and you still have consciousness, but your consciousness has many 'I's. Each 'I' is really not you. It is part of the organic brain that has developed those 'I's with you, so that you can function in this reality. None of those 'I's are really you. They are an aspect of you. They're not your true Middle Pillar. If you are of the body, you're still going to have them.

When we die, do we go into another type of body?

You go into another type of body with less demand from the Doe because you're not tied into the physical anymore. It's like you're in a different consciousness but you are still going to leave. That makes you a basic White Cell because you still have an identity here that you haven't set free yet. This creates a pitch, a frequency, and it limits you.

Let's say you want to get up to two hundred miles per hour because that's ultimately the highest dimension. When you leave your body, you get sucked into the Doe of the planet and become part of the planet because you never understood this information. Or maybe you understand that if you lose the body, and you have a soul because you've worked on it to some degree, you're going to move to fifty miles per hour. But you'll be stuck at that level, not even knowing there are other places to go because you haven't set free who or what you think you are.

You're still dealing with all of your 'I's. You'll have less of them, which allows you to go fifty miles per hour and that is profound. But it still does not mean you ultimately understand it all or that you're capable of moving the entire grid. The Darkside is just as much part of the matrix and interwoven into it as the Force. This Universe, which is solidified, is now an 'I' of the true consciousness of God. It's an aspect of God experiencing.

On a micro level, we are made in the image of God. In a lot of ways, we have an 'I' that is a fanatic. We have an 'I' that loves nature. We have an 'I' for enjoying music. We have an 'I' that's a worker. We have an 'I,' but that's not really who you are. If someone said to you, "Is that who you are?" Would you say yes? If someone worked, would you say, "You work. You sleep. You're a responsible person. That must be your whole life." Do they have any idea who they're talking to? That's an 'I' that they see. That's all they see. The totality of consciousness, God consciousness, is by far much more complex.

You can only move through **time and space** when you have absolute sincerity in your heart and when you can remove your 'I's completely. You can still move through **dimensions** with 'I's but you have to find absoluteness within you to really move. When you go to these places, you will understand because you're not thinking in a biochemical body anymore. Your soul, your energy body can think as energy and can understand much faster. What makes your head spin here won't make your head spin there. You can understand better when you allow yourself to have the fluidity to let everything go. If everything that you understand about the physical body became water right now, what would happen?

If that was an illusion, what would be left then if everything turned to water? The only thing that's not an illusion is what remains. You would simply disappear as if you were an illusion. Assuming you're not an illusion, you'd be left with true reality. So if you're fluidic, let go of everything in your mind. That's what allows time and space to open to you because the matrix can only hold onto you as long as you can hold onto the matrix. As long as you accept the illusion, the illusion becomes real. Realism is really surrendering what you think about everything. It's the hardest thing to do. It's almost impossible. Keep in mind that you are an atom in comparison to the Universe. You are here trying to understand the Universe. It is no simple task.

Right now, the Earth has already reached the crossing point and there continue to be many forces that are resistant to taking a more positive direction. Of course, there are certain forces that absolutely want the Earth to move in a positive direction. The people who are the most powerful are those who are helping to push through these tumultuous times; they are the people who can transcend time and space. This comes from absolute dedication, practice, meditation, and training.

One quarter to one half of your time is spent sleeping. One quarter of it is spent dealing with life. You make a choice of what you're going to do for the other quarter of your life. Those of you who actively do something worthwhile will be super beings. You will be able to travel to various places in the world, go into a spiritual state of mind within yourself, and be powerful enough to:

- Achieve the necessary goal to be where you need to be and create a collective grid.

- Amplify it spiritually because your ability will be so powerful that you can affect the frequencies of those beings who are trying to find that tune.

- Harness the greater tuning and then separate it into smaller parts. So a super being in this dimension would be able to bring forth a very powerful vibration and be able to transcend it externally.

What do these challenges feel like for White Cells?

They feel a sense of unity, camaraderie, and a desire to live peacefully. They want to bring technology together so that the planet can travel to the stars to pollinate. They want to have more peace on Earth, to create technology that feeds the world, and medicine that extends life so that we can live to be two or three hundred years old, and to remove all disease so we can pollinate the Universe faster with new life.

It is the most important thing that the world so badly needs - a reflection of healing the Earth rather than polluting it. It would influence the consciousness of Earth by researching various studies and pushing forward some progressive ideas, like some of us are already doing. There is what I call *nodes*; the people of Hindi faith and the Buddhists are already projecting the right type of energy. In essence, everything would take a positive turn, such as researching fuels that are lifesaving to the Earth, fuels that will help us move through space, and things that will help us move dimensionally into other places, too.

What is the greatest crime in the Universe? It is the suppression of life. As Navigators, we are here to assist with the amplification of consciousness for the planet so that its entire people will understand and think in a positive direction. We are here to help the world to progress rather than deal with pettiness and greed. It is not about monetary gain and the growth of industry. If people lived beyond a hundred years old, they would be more aware of the pollution they are creating because, in a hundred years, they would have to live in it. As it stands, most people don't care about these things because they don't think they will be alive then anyway.

The "great story" of the Mahabharata, an epic Hindi poem that includes The Bhagavad Gita, was written about a spiritual war. This was a technology war of humanity. During those times, Krishna intervened spiritually and interfered with the grid as much as he could, which changed the outcome of the war. The Earth is running its cycle, but there's always some other force that tries to disrupt it. The Darkside is like a virus. If God wants information and experiences, God (Krishna in the "great story") will keep correcting reality to experience it. So at times, God has to intervene in certain places in the Universe to prevent the Darkside from disrupting and corrupting progress.

A computer virus starts in one file. If it runs its course, what happens to the entire forty, fifty, or one hundred gigabytes? Likewise, the darker beings that are on Earth must have some kind of opposition so that the course can continue in the right direction. Otherwise, the Darkside will annihilate everything. It will prevent evolution from happening, destroying the mechanism in the process. The Darkside uses beings, people, who in their own way try to manipulate or spiritually affect the grid in a destructive way. That's the problem. The Darkside is the opposition to The Force.

In the movie *Star Wars*, there is the Empire and the Rebellion. We're told up front the Rebellion fighters are the good guys and the Empire represents the Darkside – the bad guys. Do the people who work for the Empire have kids? Do they have medical needs? Do you think they believed that what they were doing was wrong? Or did they feel it was right?

They thought they were doing the right thing for all concerned. They thought they needed to control all the people, and that with better policing, places would be safer. They thought technology and science would make certain things better. They wanted to govern how people reacted and make people live in a way that would be good for everyone. So everything they did was absolutely correct in their minds. They didn't question their decisions at all.

So, when people on the Darkside feel as if a fluidic spirit of God is too intimidating to them, they can't understand it. They can't conceive it or imagine it. To them, it looks like chaos. What do they do when they fear something? What do you do if you have nowhere to run? What does an animal do? It fights, attacks, and tries to take control. That's what the Darkside is doing. Every so often, humanity is affected by its actions, so the spiritual beings have to intervene to send a message through the grid. These are the spiritual masters. They affect smaller grids which go out and affect other grids.

There is the world of humanity or science, and the world of spirituality. There are also the effects of the moving Universe - the yin and yang of it. So the opposition is a collective of beings who want to control the direction of the Earth. They believe that theirs is the correct path.

On the Other Side are the people who believe in being fluidic. They believe that the Universe already has a grand scheme for its direction. So that is the conflict. *Everything is a program that was created by God.* There are people trying to bump the program because they don't understand it. It's far beyond their mental conception. They don't understand that God isn't "all-knowing". God still wants to know the ultimate outcome, but Its beyond human understanding.

It's similar to the concept of the bouncing super ball. When you bounce the super ball, it bounces all over the place. You have no idea where it's going to land next. The Darkside wants to control the outcome of the Universe. It wants to limit the possibilities to a predictable number. The improbability of failing is beyond its comprehension, so it can't accept that. But to God, the supercomputer that we can understand, it's all very simple. God is just trying to push things to the limit to observe the results.

It sounds like God is experimenting and just wants to see where things go, whether to the opposition or to the Other Side.

It's not that God is trying to see what happens with the opposition, it's more about God wanting to experience what is here. God is being told It is not welcome by the Darkside. To this, God's answer is, "Who do you think you are? Since when did it become your place?" The Darkside is the opposition, the creation of "evil", but really it's just trying to push God away.

And God pushes back to experience what is here . . .

Chapter 7

THOUGHTS ON THE PATH . . .

As a general rule of thumb people expect to hear familiar sounds and relaxing music during their meditations. That's wonderful, but over time your mind begins to resist the music, so you have to change it periodically in order to fool the brain. The brain has the remarkable ability of adjusting or acclimating to the circumstances; however, you don't necessarily want that to happen.

I recall watching a special on TV a while ago about the war in the Ukraine or the Balkans. The reporters were talking about all the chaos everywhere due to the rubble from the bombs and tanks. Yet, several months after the war started, the children were outside playing in the streets with the bombs going off as if nothing was happening around them. This demonstrates how resilient and how quickly we adapt to our surroundings.

So, I realized that when you meditate regularly you start off very well, but then, after reaching the peak, you start to come back down. I wondered, "How do you keep from becoming complacent? How do you shake things up a bit?" That's when I introduced techno music or the bass drum into the mix. The annoying part is at the end. Your brain is irritated because it's thinking, "I don't know what this is but I don't like it." Well, my answer to that is, "Fine. Don't listen to it. But learn to move beyond the music." That's really the trick. People listen to the music and let it take them somewhere pleasant. I'm all for that. It will take you to a certain point, but how do you move beyond that?

Some of the techno music you use is fascinating and soothing. It puts me in a spiritual mood. At other times, it can be a little annoying. Am I supposed to be focusing on the annoying part? Does my resistance prevent me from going deeper?

Yes. When you finally accept the music, you'll find one of two things will happen: You'll start to enjoy it and be surprised that you actually do enjoy it, or you'll learn to put the music out of your mind. That's a skill – *like wax on, wax off.* Whether you realize it or not, it is a skill to take this annoyance and move beyond it. Working through the resistance is excellent practice for your meditations.

I'm a big believer in turmoil, in the sense of "upheaval," because it's the only thing that makes you engage the situation. You must overcome it, so you have to make your brain adapt to it instead of fight it.

In most new age circles, everything is very placid, peaceful, and beautiful all the time. They meditate for ten, twenty, or thirty years and feel at peace. So, what brings you to Higher Balance? Is it because you are looking for something more than that? It is my belief that ***everybody wants the experiences.*** You want something to sink your teeth into. The brain is your friend, but it can also be your enemy in a lot of ways. The body is not who you are. So you need to shake things up. This is why I created annoyances for the brain – to shake it up.

Some spiritual circles insist that you should ground yourself by visualizing an energy core through the center of the planet. What is your opinion of that?

I think it's true, but we're back to the concept of adaptation once again. I believe in evolution and spirituality, but I also embrace science. When I look at humanity, I look at the entirety of evolution. Meditating for thousands of years by centering and grounding yourself – well, I can see how the brain will find a loophole for adapting and wrapping itself around that concept. But understand that you will be stuck there – you will not progress any further than that.

Most people are Red Cells. The Doe specifically tries to keep you as a Red Cell. Your organic brain works for the Doe, and the Doe works for the organic planet. As a sentient being, you are now awakening. You're saying, "Alright, I need to run part of the show. I need to step forward and take some control." Centering and grounding is a good system. It works. You can incorporate that into your meditation practice, but don't make it the complete focus of your practice.

The human brain has found many different ways to get around that particular method. How many experiences do you usually have when you center yourself and then wait? True, it does help you to become clear, but there is also a part of you that wants something more. The rational part of the brain says, "You can't center everything." What if that's actually the sensory that you need to develop? Your brain will be conflicted; so the question is, "When will you learn to stretch out? How will you recognize it when it happens?"

My approach is to work on your metaphysical skills and incorporate them into your meditations. When you feel the momentum, go for it. Expand on it. Some spiritual schools that specialize in meditation say, "Don't do anything paranormal or psychic." But when you look at the spiritual masters of the past, they all performed miracles. What is a miracle? It's a clairvoyant ability. It's psychic phenomena. It's all of those things! The secret doctrines that everybody alludes to are metaphysical teachings.

In many spiritual schools, the teachers depend on a large number of students to pay for their expenses so the classes can continue. They have guidelines that must be followed. For instance:

- Don't intimidate or frighten people by saying you can read their minds.
- Don't say you can control them.
- Don't say that you have certain metaphysical abilities. It might frighten the students and they will stop coming.

So, the teachers say that they meditate, center themselves, and wait for God to come in. They say, "We'll pray for you. We'll put out beautiful energy for you. Good things will happen to you." Then spiritual adepts come into their schools. After a year or so, if the student works hard enough and progresses, the teacher says, "Okay, now we're going to give you the secret knowledge."

This is where you get into the techniques that I've been alluding to; pushing those psychic abilities, and the sixth sense part of your mind. In my opinion, this is clearly the link to enlightenment, to God, and to what everyone is searching for. It is completion.

About 150 years ago, there were horses and buggies. Then there was a technological revolution. What happened to spiritually accelerate things?

I believe that Gaia, the planet, is a living organism. I think those occurrences were simply phases in the consciousness of Gaia. When you look at nature, everything you need to know about the Universe is revealed to you. When I look at the planet, I see a child. You have to go back tens of thousands of years to understand what really happened. The information is scarce, however, because of its limited documentation. A lot of it was destroyed or lost through time. The study of Archaeology shows us that there are many gray areas. I certainly believe there were other cultures in this world long before our own.

On a macro level, I see continents as part of the planet's brain. You could say that Africa is one hemisphere of the brain and that Europe is another hemisphere. Over time, they collectively built connections, like the neural system of the human brain. Because this happened, information elevated from smoke signals, to telegraphs, to phone calls, to emails, and instant messaging. This created explosive levels of communication in the movement of data. This started to inspire new ideas and concepts, which literally exploded as they reached other cultures.

How fast was this data moving? If you went back through the ages and looked at the available information of those times, how was it moved? Was it by train or telegraph? When communication spreads on the planet, it creates a new era. Information is now moving much faster than ever before. The information that used to take a hundred years now only takes five years or less to get around. Everything seems to be catapulting forward. That is what happened. If you look at the history of humanity in evolution and study the human brain, you will find it very similar. The consciousness is more of a significant change, but there's a very strong connection.

If you have a highly analytical mind, how do you stop yourself from analyzing what you're doing when you're trying to shift into a higher state of consciousness?

When you start shifting into the higher states, dissecting and over analyzing what is happening will definitely hold you back. The very thing you're trying to move out of is the very thing you're using to analyze it. That is the dilemma. You're excited and you want to experience those higher states. At the same time, you are fearful of what might happen. If it does happen, you wonder if you'll have any control over it. So there are all of those factors working against you.

There's a simple technique for people who over analyze things:

Imagine yourself walking backwards: *Close your eyes; relax; put your hands palms down by your sides.*

*Don't cross your legs. Put them down and imagine
yourself walking backwards. Most people will instinctively see their feet walking backwards.*

*Once you notice that, become aware of the road.
Usually, it is a dirt road with some grass in the middle.
It's ironic that most people see the same thing. Then,
become aware of the bushes and the trees moving past
you as you're walking backwards.*

*Next, take note of the distance. Usually, the road is
very straight. As you're walking backwards, your body
relaxes and surrenders, which is similar to what happens
with the Techno music.*

It's about finding a way to trick the brain with
something it doesn't expect. Once you've done this,
you're saying to the brain, "Calm down. Relax. You
don't need to analyze anything. Just unwind." You're
literally clearing that part of your mind. This opens
up other regions that you want to bring forward so
that you can slip into this higher state of consciousness.

Many spiritual teachers rarely refer to each other or support synergy of knowledge. Why is that?

My perspective of this knowledge is very different
compared to most other teachers. One thing that
bothers me is the people who dance around certain
subjects and don't give an honest answer. I think many
teachers intentionally evade the answer to your
questions. Students believe every word that comes
from the mouths of a spiritual teacher is the absolute
truth; that they have the only solution to the problem,

and the teacher is without ego. Well, that's not true. They do have an ego, but mostly in a good way. I want to be the best teacher possible. There are too many things already kept secret in this world.

To answer your question, there is little acknowledgment of one another because of fear of losing students to someone else, even though a lot of the material is redundant. It's unusual to come across something new that pushes the boundaries with a fresh approach. When I started teaching, I knew what I had to say and was reluctant to do it because I knew there would be some backlash when I approached a subject nobody else wanted to talk about.

When I get together with other spiritually advanced people, I often get the feeling they know a lot more than they share with others. Their students are often kept in the dark. Those teachers are very competitive and hesitate to share their knowledge. They are very protective of how it is interpreted by society. And when that teacher dies, their students interpret those teachings in their own perspective. It is all about ego and keeping the information out of the hands of all but a few people.

A lot of the information is the same, but it will not be given out, in general, because the teacher wants control of the student. In the past, some guru's expected their students to live in isolation, but the times have changed. The planet and its people are evolving. There are too many highly advanced spiritual beings that are still asleep. Modern society has taken the ancient teachings and are hanging onto the knowledge instead.

There are some teachers who do give a lot more information. They share it more openly. Their teachings actually sound a lot like yours.

I can't speak for everyone else, but I believe that I must be truthful. The way I see it, most teachers dance around the subject, but the students want the real deal. I just don't believe that many spiritual groups fully understand the knowledge they teach their students.

For instance: There is a teacher who channels and has a spiritual center not far from where I live. One day, there was a class scheduled for "manifestation". The students heard some commotion out in the hallway, so they went to see what was going on. A teacher was walking down the hallway holding up a blue feather, waving it all around. Evidently she had manifested it and everybody was applauding and cheering her on. Later, another student went up to the teacher and asked her how she had manifested the feather. She said, "I was downtown the other day at the store and I saw this blue feather," and she said, "So, I bought it."

All of her students thought she had manifested the feather out of thin air. Maybe she said she manifested it. But are we all that stupid? The students who were sitting in class were thinking she had manifested it. If that's the case, then we manifest every single day. Every single day we have to put food on our table. Every single day we have to put clothing on our backs. By those standards, we are gods!

That's not what I'm looking for. I'm looking for the truth. If it's extraordinary, it's extraordinary, but I'm not looking for a blue feather. Even if she had manifested a blue feather, I would have asked, "Why in the world did you pick a blue feather to manifest?"

I don't like to talk about other spiritual teachers, but I'm going to be honest in everything that I teach. I'm going to call it like it is. I am who I am. I don't have any regrets, good, bad, or indifferent. My experiences have made me into the person I am today and they have made me stronger. When I look at other spiritual teachers and how much money they make, there seems to be a lot of exploitation going on. I have a real problem with that, and I'm angry about it. So now I'm saying, "I'm going to do this my way, and that's the way it is."

Money has always been an issue at Higher Balance. Some people say we charge too much, but like everyone else we have bills to pay. But I don't think the other teachers put out the kind of knowledge that I do. I think the students who know me and have taken my classes would agree with me.

So, I'm laying it all out here, dollar for dollar. We have an office that's not inexpensive. We have staff on the phones, so we've got a huge phone bill. We do all of the production ourselves because we couldn't afford to do it otherwise. So when people ask us why we don't just give everything out for free; it wouldn't be available. Everything costs money in this world. The staff has to work to feed their own families. And they've got their own bills to pay. This is the way life is in our world. It took me a long time to accept that. I'm not saying it's wrong for anyone to charge money for their services. Ask yourself what you are getting for that money. What level of knowledge are you getting, and do you have great results? Blue feathers?" That doesn't do anything for me. It's not good enough.

I've been working with the tone meditation for quite a while. When the tones come in, it indicates a shift in consciousness for me. I hear several tones at one time, but what am I supposed to do with them?

When you are thinking with the mind, rest assured, it's the brain you are using; the brain is the problem when it comes to the tones. I say that because there is a difference between the brain and the mind. The brain is a copycat of the mind that mimics you and convinces you that it is YOU. However, the tones are something the brain cannot mimic. The tones come from a different part of your consciousness that is very unique.

You start out hearing a very high pitch when you concentrate on the sound, and then you begin to hear several different pitches. You realize, suddenly, that you can control the pitches, but it is not that easy to do. The second your brain starts to think about it, the tones stop. If you can stop the Babbler in your brain, you have the ability to bend or separate the sound.

Envision the first pitch that you hear as a solid bar. As you listen to it, you'll find your brain stops talking and some other part of your mind begins to come forward. It's really a couple of different pitches that are making only one sound. When you start to focus on each pitch, you can pin it down.

It's just like listening to an orchestra. At first, you hear the music and it moves you. Then you hear the harp. All of a sudden, you can hear all of the string instruments, and you can now zone in on each individual instrument. Well, you are actually doing the same thing with the tones, but you're doing it in your mind, or from the source where the sound is coming from.

That sound can be heard anywhere. That's what makes it absolutely unique. If you put earplugs in your ears, you would hear the tones. You could be at the bottom of the ocean in a submarine and you would still hear the tones. So it doesn't matter where you are.

I have trained extensively with the pitches. I can go into any environment and hear them. I could be three feet away from the some speakers that are booming rock-n-roll music, and I would find the pitch and break it all down. It is an inner dimensional thing within your mind. As you begin to separate the bars or notes, you focus more and learn that you can move them further apart. You can find other pitches too, and as soon as you pull them apart, a new bar will re-appear to give you another different pitch. So now you have three pitches. Then you separate them and now you've got six pitches. Unfortunately, the brain interferes and the tones disappear, so you have to start all over again.

So you start to gain control over those pitches. One of the things most people don't notice is that your breathing will start to change. Don't worry about your body. Even if you were in a coma, your heart would still pump and your lungs would still function. The body is a living organism; there isn't anything about it that's entirely YOU. Tell the organisms in your body to do their job and go have fun with the tones. Go play with them. As soon as you can get over the fear of letting go, you will learn to separate the bars even more.

The bars are teaching your consciousness the equivalent of walking. You're learning to move your mind through a different kind of will. There are no words to describe it. I call it movement. I could call it walking, but in this realm, it's movement. If I want to walk, I physically choose to get up and walk. When you're dealing with the bars, you're moving. You just haven't had that realization yet. Hence wax on, wax off.

I'm trying to prepare you for the day when you do a different type of meditation. You will be relaxed when, suddenly, your consciousness will be way out there. You're not going to wonder, "Hey, I don't have a body. Why can't I see me looking at things?" You've removed that issue. While you're *out there*, it's similar to a very dark room. You're going to realize that it feels good. It is very relaxing. It's not a time for talking or for using words; you're using consciousness.

However, if you stay there too long, you will become bored. You're going to want to move around. So are you going to use your feet to move? No, you're going to think about the tones, and the tones will come very naturally to you. You will just move without giving any thought it. But this is not necessarily movement – I am using this term simply to explain something that's otherwise very difficult to explain. You can move into this dimension, see other realities, see this physical world, or move into other dimensions. The tones will train you for the moment when you're ready to make that next step.

You've learned what you need to do to move your mind, train, discipline and understand it. After a while, the tones will become like second nature to you.

Where does the information that you are sharing come from? Where is that source? Where is home?

You're in it. Home is right here, right now. It's not about *here* or *there*. Humans always think in terms of,

"I've got to fly home. I've got to drive home. This is a place. That's a place." Everything is categorized. You are already home!

Think about your body right now. There are trillions of cells in your body, but for right now, let's just take one single cell: a red cell, a white cell, or any skin cell. Take any cell you want and ask it, "Where is home?" When you fully understand what I am saying and accept it as truth, then God will approach you. You could just acknowledge it, but acknowledging it and accepting it are two very different things. It's as if somewhere inside your mind you say, "Hello, little cell. How are you doing?" You want to feel complete. Right now, you don't feel completion because you haven't accepted that you're part of something bigger. You see yourself as an individual. You identify with, "This is who I am."

That's what you have been taught to think since you were just a child. You have a name and your name is different than everybody else's. This is who you are. This is what you are. That is a human concept. It has a tendency to create fear of belonging to something much bigger. You feel displaced and you wander around asking, "Well, what is it?" **God is right here**. Look at how we interpret this with our human brains.

A good example of this is the music scale. All of the notes are in harmony but you only choose to hear "Do" or "Re." The Do, Re, Mi, Fa, So is here too at this very moment. When people pray, they talk **at** God: "I need a new pair of shoes. Rosy needs a new roof on the house," and so forth. When you meditate, you **listen** to God. It's about surrender. It's about manifestation. It's about you moving into this higher place. When you do that, you move up an octave. You go from Do, Re, Mi and move into So. When you hit So, that's it! That's when you say, "Okay, God, now I've got to go back down there again? What is the point? I worked so hard to get here."

Fluctuation is part of it. There's also a propensity to forget, get stuck, or have a blank spot. At the same time, there's always awareness.

Absolutely, we must acknowledge the beauty in this world. We're so busy trying to find completion that we often separate ourselves from the beauty that's around us. I'm not just talking about the trees and flowers, but also the people. Sometimes, there is a disdain in us towards Red Cells. You sit there and think, "I'm part of this human race." Can you imagine that? It's a part of you! So you look at all of it, and you try to get "off the rock". I think you have to accept what's here on Earth with all your heart. It is absolutely, stunningly beautiful.

I often joke with the students in my office, "I can't wait to get *off the Rock*."They ask, "Why are you saying that?" And they get mad that I said it. Even though I'm bored with things occasionally, I still marvel at the beauty of this dimension. I marvel at the sounds, textures, colors, and my environment. It helps me to balance.

Every spiritual teacher says, "God is all around us." That is true, but instead of excluding yourself from It, you can experience God now with the sixth sense. You can pull the sixth sense into the picture so you can receive It with more appreciation. This, of course, helps to oscillate your energy and make it more harmonic. Too many spiritual people spend their time trying to remove themselves from life and society. They try to isolate themselves. You have to keep *one foot in this world* to appreciate it. You also need to *find that spiritual aspect* and bring both things together. When you can do that, you will find that perfect pitch. That's when the higher states of consciousness will start to move for you.

It's a lot of work. It doesn't come easily. Just remember that *you chose to be here.* As a White Cell, you are the very best at what you do. I'm not talking about just my students. I'm talking about YOU and everyone else in this world. That's what you have to remember. YOU are the fighters. ***You will awaken in this reality.*** And when you awaken, it will change the face of humanity. It will change the face of the world.

I want to talk a little bit about ego and arrogance. When I was growing up, I was indoctrinated into doing psychic work by my father. I learned not to be afraid to do this work, and I did it very well. But that came from not knowing anything different.

I was aware that a lot of the other kids knew about me. The teachers at school found out I could do psychic readings, so they would ask me to do one for them during recess. The school bus driver would track me on the school bus. She'd make sure my stop was the very last one, and I was always doing psychic readings for her. If somebody asked what I did, it never occurred to me not to say, "I'm a psychic, you know. I predict the future. I heal people. I do astral projection, and I bring my friends with me." I never thought there was a reason to keep this to myself, whereas most families would have said to keep it to myself and not to tell anybody what I did.

Everyone has fear; it goes back to your level of confidence. There are different kinds of fear, but the kind that I am talking about is the fear of being who you think you are. It's the fear of saying, "I am a spiritual master. I am profoundly gifted. I can do miracles." If you honestly feel that way, you should be ashamed for not getting that information out there. Everyone is afraid of being rejected. It is because of your social structure. You don't want to be known as "the crazy person" or "the nut."

How does a person like me become a spiritual master? Why do I stand out from the rest? I'm not telling you anything that you don't already know. You read my books and say, "Oh, I absolutely agree. I couldn't have said it better." When you read my material, you agree with it and it makes perfect sense. That's because you know it already. What makes me any different than you? I'm different because I was born with a big mouth and *I'm not afraid to use it!*

Every single psychic or spiritual skill that you possess is minuscule compared to what you potentially could be. That is because of fear. If you heal someone, you wonder why they don't heal a little faster, but you never vocalize it. As much as you would like to heal someone, you still have some resistance within you. You're aware of it. You're conscious of it. You even feel this truth in your chest center. It's there. You feel it in the form of pressure.

People have been tested in various institutes for their psychic abilities and various other spiritual attributes. Many skeptics wonder why those people can't perform better under pressure with others watching them. Why can't they consistently recreate the same experience when they are being tested? It's because of the *Governor*, and that Governor is fear.

I was driving to an event recently with the loud music playing. I was really pumped up with excitement. I got out of my car, ready to meet everyone. They knew who I was and were excited to see me. I got to the door, saw everyone there, and suddenly my heart started fluttering! It is the same fear-based experience for most people who have these spiritual gifts. They are doing the same thing because they are afraid to let their intensity out.

You have a different kind of Governor that is experiencing a fear of public awareness. You are constantly being told that you are arrogant when you talk about all the things you have done, or that it's pure ego, and you shouldn't have an ego while doing spiritual stuff. That's nonsense! If I'm being arrogant or cocky while healing the sick or giving out great information that's helping someone, or doing good works, please put up with my ego for a little while. I think it's just the fear of being labeled. Be confident; be strong. Don't be afraid of people judging you. When you can work with that, you'll have bigger breakthroughs.

If you're going to do a psychic reading or predict the future, don't be afraid to be wrong. Tell them that there is room for error. Believe it or not, this raises your accuracy level. As soon as you know that it's okay if you get a few things wrong, it eases your fear of giving wrong information. It takes the pressure off you.

Tell people that you're going to do some role-playing, and that you're going to act like you're predicting the future. You're doing this as an experiment. Tell them you're going to pretend that you're a gypsy, or you're pretending to be a psychic reader. Don't be surprised if that person sits there with their mouths wide open saying, "That's accurate! Do you know my sister," or something to that extent. It's about confidence in your abilities.

When people are under a microscope, they sometimes panic or freeze up. It has happened to me before. It happens to everybody. I've just learned to control it better than others. Don't be afraid to be a bit bolder. Give yourself some wiggle room. I say, "I'm 98 percent accurate." That leaves a two percent margin for error.

Just cut loose and let that raw power out! Begin to do that, even in your meditations in the privacy of your own space. Stop thinking about what you want to do. You know what your intention is, so just do it. Acknowledgment is very important. The best readings are the ones when the other person says, "That's great, amazing! Yeah, that's correct," because they are helping the psychic. The psychic is leading them and the other person is filtering the information they receive.

Still, the vast majority of psychics are not very good – there are a lot of frauds out there. So, acknowledgment is necessary as it helps you to become more accurate. With a little encouragement, you are able to download more detailed information; sharing it helps to confirm whether or not you got a hit. You might be vague at first, but you will get better at it with practice. So again, it's about getting over the fear factor.

Are there any energy manipulating devices, like the Tesla oscillator, that actually work on a paranormal level?

Most things that other people marvel at seems obsolete to me. People are constantly looking for a new device to take them to the next level of spirituality. They don't want to work for it or earn it. Mankind has always built machines to simplify things, and now you want to use this technology to simplify your spiritual awakening? You would be using an organic brain to interpret how to accomplish that device, and that is the biggest hurdle. I find that a lot of those things are good, but they still focus on a physical reaction.

Higher Balance came out with the Magnetic Pill a while ago because there is an organic bridge to spirituality. You have to deal with the organic. In my opinion, the human body can certainly tap into the energy fields that are all around us, which is why I came out with Magnetic Pill in the first place. It contains *magnetite*. Putting magnetite in the body makes you more sensitive to the magnetic fields. It may not propel you spiritually, but it gives you the ability to turn on your sixth sense.

Higher Balance is currently working on several types of devices. There are high levels of ionization in the air. That's why you smell the electricity in electrical storms. In New England, there are higher levels of paranormal experiences with ghosts and other kinds of phenomena. They typically happen at night when there are less photons from light sources, like the sun, which break up their energy.

I'm sure you have seen those electrical devices that create a static charge. I want to mimic the charge that comes from electrical storms. My suspicion is that entities coming through dimensionally need this type of electricity to bridge from the other dimension into this one. I believe they use ionization. It creates a clothing-like substance giving them mass. When it fades away, they fade away. So, in my opinion, this is a device that's worth investigating.

I am strongly interested in magnetics, but not the kind where a magnet picks up filings. Our reality is held together by a form of magnetic energy. If you bend these magnetics, you can move to other physical realities, bend time, or do a number of other things. So I would like to invest in research to experiment with magnetics.

I agree that we cannot awaken without the sixth sense. I've successfully entered into different states of reality, but I can't do it deliberately. I find that my fear only allows me to go so far. What can I do to change that?

In theory you're holding yourself back, but the Universe is also intentionally holding you back so that you can learn enough to know what you are doing when you open that Pandora's Box. There is a reason why you cannot fully expand.

Let's say you have a box. You can't force the box to open. You can't willfully open the box, but the box *can be opened*. Most people scratch their heads on that concept. *The box is used as a metaphor for a lot of things, but in this particular case, **it's about letting go**.*

It is the same thing if you try to force a flower bud to open. If you try to do that, it won't be perfect. It will be ruined. There is a moment in nature when it opens as it surrenders. Surrendering is the key to removing the fear of being who you are and letting that enormous power out. No matter how hard you try, you can't control this with your organic brain. You've got to find a way to let go and trust that your consciousness will thrive.

The problem is that you can't let go of it. This is why the Higher Balance Institute created all of this material. As you listen to it and apply it, the knowledge will unfold. There are many students who've already reached those higher levels of consciousness. We have a module called *Bending Reality* where students share their personal experiences.

You can't tell the Universe, "Come on, move it. In the next ten minutes, I want it to happen." The Universe will react like you're a 5-year old child saying, "Get in here and make this happen for me now," like you're a little kid pulling on God's shirt while God says, "I'll do it when I'm good and ready." We're all a bit anxious because we want our experiences to happen now. The more you analyze things, the more it will work against you. You control what you reap. With conviction, you increase the octaves in your energy fields, releasing yourself to experience new things.

Some people have asked me why I send people to haunted houses. A haunted house is something beyond a normal, everyday life-experience. If you're an analytical type of person and you see something unearthly, it freaks you out and you won't be able to logically dismiss it. You know it isn't explainable. It removes the Governor. If I tell you to do this or that and you have an experience, it raises your octaves and opens your mind to experience new possibilities. There's nothing wrong with analyzing, but don't do it when you first start out.

Do it after you've accomplished something great! It opens the door for you to have other experiences.

Everything relates back to energy and it's important for you to think in terms of it. It's important for you to become conscientious of the subtle energies that are in your body. The more you can consciously say, "I felt that," or, "I can do that," the more it removes the wiring of the Governor. That gives you the ability to step forward with much more confidence.

In the center of your brain is the pineal gland. It is, primarily, the seed of the organic psychic ability in your body. It's where this ability originates. There's basically three parts of your brain. The reptilian part is in the center of your brain. It's a little smaller than a clenched fist. The next part is the mammalian, which grew over that and is more complex. The third is the neocortex. It's the larger frontal lobe that makes you who you are right now. So you've left behind your primitive parts and you've advanced. Within the primitive areas, there's some very good wiring that allows you to plug into the Force or to energy. Animals use this because they haven't developed the advanced parts. Unfortunately, humans are not using these regions nearly enough.

There is a great exercise for this that I call the "brain wiggle." Imagine an area about the size of your finger inside your head, several inches back, and right between your eyes. Now wiggle it forward and backward, forward and backward. Some people might argue that there are no muscles in the brain so you can't feel anything. Now that we've got that out of the way, let's do it anyway! Sometimes, it's not necessarily about what we already know that is going on organically.

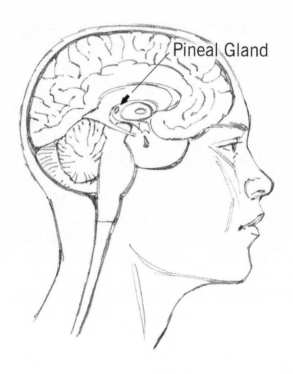

Use the brain wiggle exercise to stimulate the pineal gland and heighten your sixth sense.

Concentrate for a few moments and wiggle the pineal gland back and forth, back and forth. It's possible to get a headache from doing it too much. It's usually a pressure right in the front of your head. So you need to know when to stop. If you practice this on a regular basis, it will develop very well. Then it will seem easy to do this exercise and almost overpowering.

This technique stimulates the portion of the brain that is designed to communicate with the sixth sense. If there are motor gears for you to talk, for you to walk, and to move your body, then there are also motor gears for everything else. This is the motor gear that's designed to plug you in. As soon as you give it proper attention, it's going to begin the wiring process that will "plug you in" and give you the extra sensory to get you there.

So just close your eyes for a few seconds. Take a nice breath in... Breathe out... Relax your body... Just a little while, see if you can move the pineal gland forward and backward. Keep your eyes shut. If you don't feel anything, don't worry about it. If you can feel it working, just keep doing it. Don't worry about whether you can feel it moving forward or backwards. Don't worry if you're making your eyebrows move. *Don't over analyze this.* If you're moving your eyebrows, you're still thinking about the center of your brain. In the end, you will get the same result. That's all you need to know.

Some people will certainly feel this region and that's a good thing. The speed will vary for each person. Some people tend to do it very quickly, while others will take a few minutes to do it. This is the area that you hear about in stories of the third eye or the mind's eye. But it is often overlooked by many teachers, with the exception of the mystery schools.

Your muscles are electrically stimulated. If you open your hand and close it, it's because your brain is calculating the precise amount of electricity needed to stimulate the muscles so they can expand and contract.

This technique, called Prana Pull-Ups, shows you how to manipulate your electrical energy. It's still energy whether it is more physically oriented or not. It teaches you that by stimulating other regions of the brain, there's something more to you. You're trying to turn on more of that area of the brain.

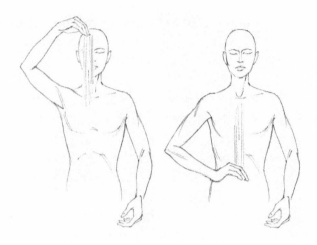

Prana Pull-Ups are an easy way to begin enhancing your energy body. Breath is very important. Make sure to breathe deeply as you pull the energy up and down.

Take your hand and move it to where your navel is located. Breath is very significant, so you'll be using it in this simple technique. Breathe in and pull your hand up. While you're doing this, envision you're pulling energy up from your lower region and you're moving it upward. As you breathe in and visualize this, you will feel and know that you've got it because there will be a tingling sensation that literally trails right behind your hand as you're pulling the energy up. You'll feel it come right up and you'll feel tingles inside your core. It will feel very subtle.

If you're looking for something that's going to wow you, it doesn't work that way. You're integrating something that you don't usually think about. Normally, you function on the exterior. You touch the world; you feel the world; you see the world, but you don't internalize anything. You don't feel any of your organs, except for your heart pumping.

With Prana Pull-Ups, you're trying to get a sense of the energy moving upward in your body. So the first trick is to utilize the breath and recognize when you can feel that tingle. When you've got the tingle, you're ready to take the next step. So let's just go ahead and try this one more time.

Put your hand at your navel and just imagine your energy is moving deeper into your body. Now, just scoop it up. It's like yoga for your dimensional body. Up until now, your brain's been controlling it. This will stretch your mind a little bit. It's like putting water on the ground in the desert and planting some greenery into other parts of your energy field.

Now, take a breath. As you're pulling it in, take it from above your head, fingers pointing towards your forehead and like a light dimming switch, bring it down and exhale. Bring it up, inhaling, and then down, exhaling. One more time, clear your mind. Pull it up, breathing in. Now, bring it down, exhaling.

You should practice these techniques as often as you can. The trick is in the breathing. Breathing is the first thing you do when you come into life and it's the last thing you do before you leave. Breath controls the speed at which your mind does its talking. If you think about your breath, you can control your thought. When people react, they say, "Calm down; take a deep breath." It's that inner knowing. We already know there's a connection. When you hyperventilate, you're told to breathe into a bag; it's all about relaxing and breathing. If you pay attention to your breathing, you can control the way your mind works.

Whenever I do any kind of dimensional or consciousness work, I automatically do some breath work. I'm aware when my breathing changes. While I'm breathing in and out, it's almost like I'm setting a rhythm that relaxes the brain. Then I move higher and go into the zone.

Another thing you can do is use your hands. If you notice, I do this all the time. In primitive times, our vocal chords were set lower and we made a lot of guttural sounds. We couldn't really define or create words. As we evolved, we became better talkers. Our minds and our energy got better, leading to the creation of dimensional bodies and souls. So we used our hands a lot.

To this day, we still communicate with our hands. Whenever I move my hands and make certain gestures, no matter what nationality or culture you're from, you get it. There's this unwritten knowing that's inside us all coming from our unconscious mind. If I say, "Stop," I put my hand up. If I say, "Come here," I motion with my hand. These are the basic ones, but all of these subtle hand movements, right down to a little fling of my arm or how far I spread my fingers apart, have meaning. It's a body language that we can understand.

Thinking about how consciousness constantly moves out of your hands, what happens when you breathe in, take both hands and put them out in front of you (like when you tell someone to stop) then rotate them outward, left hand rotating to the left and right hand rotating to the right. Next, rotate both hands back to their original position while breathing out. Rotate both hands so that the palms are up, while breathing in. Then rotate the hands so that the palms are down and push them towards the floor, all the while breathing out.

Breathing in, with both hands in front, rotate them outward. Next, rotate both hands back to their original position while breathing out. Focus on feeling your internal energy as you do this.

When I do that, my energy does all sorts of interesting things. I can feel it move to the extent that it makes the hair stand up on my arm. My physical body reacts. It's a very real thing. So this allows me to explore my dimensional body through a different form of control. Instead of touching on the exterior and pulling in information, I can control the source of the experience and have it flow backwards. It's like turning the direction of a metal pipe so that the water shoots backwards.

So when you put your hands out in front of you, use your breath and work with it; you will feel the subtle energies. They'll get very intense. You can make them so intense that electronics stop working and jewelry breaks. For that reason, I don't really wear a lot of jewelry. I could easily destroy my watch.

You can control a lot of this energy by paying attention to your hands. Think about your hands. Hold them out in front of you as if you are telling someone to stop, with the palms facing away from you. Just look at them. You don't really want to make yourself go into an In-Between state, but you want to become aware of them. Now close your eyes and then turn them to the outside, like before, with a breath.

If you put them out and you don't breathe when you turn your hands, nothing really happens. But if you turn your hands and you breathe in as you're turning them, you'll feel a tingle inside. It's in a certain area. Everybody will feel it in the same spot. So this is by design. Work your hands, systematically and firmly. Don't just pull them out loosely. Have the muscles firm but not too tight. Then all the muscles turn with precision, lowering together, up together, but with the breath. Don't be afraid to breathe. Believe me; it makes a big difference.

Feel the power within you, almost as if you're using your primitive self by breathing in and out loudly. Don't be afraid to use it. Call on that energy and then force it with your hands, with really tight fingers. Now be in sync on every finger movement. If you breathe with it, you can't just wave them around. Every breath must be connected with a set of movements. One breath exhaling is one set until you finish breathing out. That's one movement. Moving the opposite way would be another breath, either coming in or out. It doesn't matter which way as long as it's precise. If you work it any other way, the flow becomes normal, as if you're reaching out to touch. *If you're not feeling energy, you're not letting yourself go.* The energy is not going to be a massive thing. It will be very subtle.

If you're feeling pretty good right now by raising your energy, it's not just because of the breathing. I want to clarify that so you don't confuse the two. Just because someone is hyperventilating, it doesn't mean they are moving energy. You'll eventually be able to do this exercise with very little breath. Once you get it down, you can even hold your breath and do it. Your breathing seems to synchronize or it gets the brain to skip so you can get in that backdoor and control it.

You'll find a set of patterns. When you turn your hands outward on both sides (right hand to the right, left hand to the left), and when you breathe in, you'll feel this energy move from the middle of your chest, back through your shoulder blade on each side. Some people are wired differently, so don't assume that everyone feels the same thing. You'll find that every time you do that movement, the energy will be in that particualr spot. *When you start thinking about where you're feeling it, you'll start controlling it.* When you're not thinking about it, you're just becoming conscious of it. That's what you want to do.

Your goal is to move this energy all over the place. You'll eventually be able to move the energy through your legs, through your arms, extend it out and then back in, and then out and back in. Then, you want to sit there and expand your whole aura field. Take a breath in and just see it expanding and retracting. It does not have to be about Chi Gong, Reiki, or Tai Chi. These schools all understand this technique. They've got it right. But I don't want you to think that you have to follow a specific training in order to do this exercise. In your inner knowing, you already know what you need to do.

When you're at home listening to a song that you really like and you tune into it, you feel like doing your own thing. You might feel awkward doing it when there are other people around; that is the Governor controlling you. So when you get back to your private space, try this. Play around with it. Stand up. Do some energy movements. Bring them down. Work it this way. Work it that way. Don't be shy in working with this. It will exponentially amplify your meditations and your psychic work. It's a matter of how much time and effort you want to put into it.

You can use this for the areas in your body that are hurting. Send the energy to that place. You can talk to your cells and tell them what to do. The body is bio-chemical. And its main component is electricity. Electricity is communication. So what are you doing now? You've found a way to talk to your body. You've found a method to talk to your cells. If you're looking for a way to get into an organ and tell it what to do, this is how to do it. You'll move that energy because you're so used to feeling it. So start moving it in there.

The best method is the one you learn to do on yourself. It is the one most receptive to your body. As long as you have the right intent, just move that energy. You know what the body expects from you and it will communicate with your cells by saying, "Hey, get to work on this – we need a little help here!"

When you feel confident doing this healing on yourself, you can project the same energy toward other people. Their cells will become receptive and they will feel a tingling sensation moving through their body. Tingling is a sensation. Sensation comes from stimulus. If there's a sensation in an area of your body and you're not physically touching it, something's got to be happening. It's electricity. That's the bottom line.

I've been feeling energy in the palms of my hands for years but I've never thought of it in the way that you describe it.

That's excellent. It's all about giving you the tools to reach new levels. Most people don't utilize the knowledge to take themselves to the next level.

The energy seems to be strongest when my fingers are spread apart.

That's interesting. Ask yourself what it means when you spread your fingers.

Closed - open.

'Open' can also mean `go, ` (with fingers spread apart), `Closed` (with fingers together) can also mean `stay`. Work your energy out (with fingers spread apart); stay in (with hand clenched into a fist). Stay in; go out. Everybody communicates a little bit differently. We just have to pay attention to this inner way of knowing things.

Ever since my youth, I've talked about working with the chakras. Besides the seven primary ones, there are numerous minor chakras, including the palms of the hands and the heels of the feet. The reason why we work through our hands with the energy is simply because it makes sense to do that. We reach out with our hands, and we pull in.

The palm of the hand is really a dead zone, physically, because we don't do much with it. It's simply a support for our fingers. When you look at it, it's like a satellite dish. It's concave and there's hard wiring in there. When you think about it that way, the mind starts to work differently. If you can accept it and think of it as a satellite dish, it receives information. It can broadcast information. It can do other things too. It's just a matter of switching your thinking to fool the Babbler. Obviously, it serves another purpose for support, but in many other ways it can do more. This is just a new way of looking at it.

Try breathing through your palms. A lot of people will wonder how you do that – do it with intention. It's the same as breathing through any other chakra. You should understand that by now, so breathe through your palms.

When I go into a house full of negative energy, I always use my hands. I don't do it to draw attention to myself. I keep my hands down at my sides while I'm breathing. I breathe through my heart chakra and my mouth. I'm breathing fifty percent through my palms and fifty percent through my heart chakra, while unconsciously breathing through my mouth. The breathing works this energy while I'm sampling it. I'm looking for something that doesn't feel normal to me.

As I begin to feel the house, another sensory comes through – the sixth sense. It's not sight, touch, or smell. This sensory gives me information by using my intent. Since I'm looking for spooky things, entities, spirits, or anything obscure, this is what I feel. I notice it with my palms. I tend to turn them around a lot as I walk around. I move my hands in certain ways but I'm constantly breathing in through them as if they were breathing and tasting the air or a fluid.

That's how you switch your thinking. You can fool the Babbler and stop it from interfering. It will just go along for the ride. That's what I'm doing in many cases. I'll know right away if there's anything paranormal around me.

There's a great place in Portland Oregon that you might want to visit. It's called the White Eagle Saloon and Hotel. Some people say this hotel chain is haunted. Most of them aren't anymore; still there is some very interesting energy at the White Eagle. You can rent rooms there, and there are bands downstairs that play all night. When I went there, I picked out the energies right away and zoomed in on it. It's something you can experiment and play with, but remember that your palms are broadcasters and receivers. You just have to think of them operating in a different way.

Can you use them to move the energy?

You'll find that maybe you get a little antsy working with it because you can really affect organs and other parts of your body. This is a good thing but you've got to recognize if you're feeling a little weird. You might want to have something sweet handy just in case your energy gets low. Once you get used to it, you won't have that problem anymore.

Some people have problems with their neck, spine, arms, or hands. Will this affect their energy output if they're trying to use their hands as sensors?

When you see quadriplegics or people born without any arms, what do they learn to write with? They don't need any arms or feet; they find other ways to do the things they need to do. You use your arms and feet because it makes sense to do that. When I look at a house, I can scan it in a few seconds. I don't need any kind of physical contact. You will become very skilled at this if you practice it often enough.

If you want to feel and experience things that are beyond your normal range of belief, then fool yourself and use whatever tools you need to get around the Governor. When you become more experienced, you won't even have to think about it anymore. You really don't need to physically move the energy. You'll be able to move it all over the place with just your thoughts.

So it's really about taking baby steps. If you don't have an arm and you want to move energy, you're going to start off by making a little tickle with intention and using your chest area to move the energy wherever you want it to go. It might take you a day or two to get it right. You work with your breathing, and it boils down to intention and choosing the right areas.

If I wanted to move the energy in my fingertips, I would start there and just move it backward and forward. It's just like doing the 'brain wiggle' with the pineal gland that I described earlier on. There isn't anything to move there, but you can get the sensation if you work with it. You're limiting yourself by reflecting on the physical body and saying you can't move your arm. Whatever you do, adapt to the situation.

One day a deer came out of nowhere, jumped on my car, and nearly got hurt because I didn't see it. If I didn't send out an energetic emotion to warn it and the animal died, would it be because I didn't project the emotion?

What happened with animals in your youth to make you feel that way? Maybe you had some kind of connection with animals, an affinity with nature, and by using your senses frequencies they became second nature to you. You learned how to tell the difference. When you're in a car, you need to feel if that animal is in danger or they're going to just wander into your path. Whatever happened in your youth shaped how your psychic ability was developed.

People generally feel bad if they accidently kill an animal. One time, a squirrel ran underneath my car and there wasn't enough time for me to hit the brakes. I wondered if I should look back. Was there anything I could do? Probably not, but those thoughts do move through your mind. Emotion is the universal communicator, and when you project your emotions, you feel a certain truth.

People develop their psychic abilities in many different ways. I can feel across a very wide range of distance. I think a lot of White Cells develop that sensory during their childhood if they are afraid of the 'boogey man' or when scary things happen in their lives. When you're a kid lying in your bed, if the room is dark and you hear a little creak, your sensory checks it out. If a flea cracks a fart, you're on it! Nothing gets past you.

Throughout my whole childhood, I remember having a fear that something was outside of my perimeter and I didn't have any control over it. I was always wondering what was coming to get me. It only took one entity to make me feel like that, so believe me, there is a reason kids feel that way. I developed that sensory from the fear of **what if** something was coming to get me. You use fear as your sensory, and that's how your organic body tunes into the subtle frequencies around you. Then fear leads to the development of the neural synapses in your brain which create the fear-based sensory.

When I drive in areas where there are lots of animals, I use a wide angle vision instead of just focusing on the road straight ahead.

I agree with that. Peripheral vision is very interesting. Sometimes you see something moving, and when you quickly look back there is nothing there. You can put your intention into objects, essentially creating a beacon that projects the emotions. It may be challenging to do it consistently though.

Is it arrogant to think that the projected energy is actually happening?

No, projecting energy also works for me. You're either sensing it or you're broadcasting it. You're saying that they'll pick up on it if you're conscientiously putting that energy out.

I experience lights often. It can be white on white in a daylight background. They look like little paisleys and speed by so fast it's like the air is filled with them. I can see them at night but they are more obvious during the day.

What you are doing is picking up on other frequencies, and it feels like they are part of your natural reality. Many people have this same experience, but how short is the list of possibilities for it to happen? It's like saying you eat one kind of food because that's all that exists. There's just a lot out there.

Sometimes when I'm meditating with my eyes open, I see twinkles or color. They appear white or blue.

Remember the F's in **The Handbook of the Navigator** and how your brain takes the F's right out of your optic view? It literally erases them. When we have spiritual experiences, we have to be very careful about how we choose to identify or interpret them.

Lights can be very tricky. I heard about a person who was seeing a light that she described as an angel coming after her. If you see a tree stump in the distance, the human brain can add legs, arms, and a head to it. It's only natural for us to put a human figure or face on something that we see, and you are naturally more inclined to build upon something from your childhood. Some people are poets, some acoustically talented, and others are better at drawing or painting. If you stopped seeing the lights for a while, would you be able to pick it up faster than someone who never had that experience before? Probably.

There are some basic rules of thumb to use:

- When you see vertical patterns of light, it is generally from some other kind of intelligence. It's a dimensional being of some type.

- It is the same format in which our bodies are made: from top to bottom, vertically. We define it like this because it's easier for us to understand it.

- If you see a light coming in, generally it's an entity coming to communicate with you.

- Your brain is trying to cope with that experience, so it adds arms and legs.

- When its circular and it looks wavy, or if you can only see the light, that's usually dimensional. You've probably opened a vortex.

Sometimes people will lie in bed in a dark room so they can work on dimensional portals. At first, you may see purple but it almost looks pure black, so you may think your eyes are playing tricks on you. When you work with that for a while, you will start to see it moving, like clouds coming out of an endless source. The purple will move across the black. If you want better results, *just go with the flow without any expectation*. Fear of what may happen will, again, restrict your experiences.

After you open the vortex, you may see a skylight on your ceiling in the middle of the night. You can see planets or stars, and it looks very real. For the most part, it is real, but this is being filtered through the organic brain. Even if you're not thinking, the ʹIʹs try to interfere by interpreting how you see things. So, don't be so quick to verbalize what you are seeing; analyze the experience afterward. *Don't analyze first because you'll start writing the script. Then you're going to contaminate your experience.*

Your brain will take over and add data to the mix. That's why it's very important to just let it flow. Spirits and ghosts don't have vocal cords so they're not necessarily going to come in and say, "Boo!"

I wish I could write a music score because I hear fantastic tunes all the time. As soon as I pay any attention to it or wonder where it is coming from, it fades away. Then, much later, something just like it hits the music charts.

So this is about time, the matrix, the Gaia mind, and tapping into it. You can still hear the sound, but it's coming in on a different dimensional frequency. You're thinking it must be something audible that everybody else is hearing. Another good rule of thumb is to think of three things it could be so that you choose the best conclusion. Where is it coming from? It's beautiful, perfect music.

When these things happen, you're tapping into the collective consciousness. The music has no words, so you naturally tune into it because it is an emotional thing, which in this dimension, you are driven to choose over data. But when you consciously pay attention to it, it will fade away. If you could only hold onto it, it would play for a while. As soon as you try to grab it, it will fade away again. Practice and you will get better at holding onto it.

So, start meditating and doing other things while in an altered state of consciousness, working your energy. You are more apt to awaken your other senses as well as your natural gifts. It's just a matter of enhancing that particular area.

I had a conversation with some people who had passed: my sister and my father-in-law. My father-in-law told me that everything was going to be alright, and that gave me a sense of peace.

When you say they talked, did you hear words or was it like a very complex emotional communication?

I believe it was words. I believe I actually had a conversation.

Everything is emotionally communicated. In other words, a spirit doesn't really talk; you hear it empathically. Similar to television and radio signals, we need devices to take that information and translate it into a format that we can understand. So, when a spirit or an entity communicates with you, there's a fast relay of sound, like verbal communication between both of you. That is how it broadcasts.

An artificial plant has a specific feeling – you know this feeling. You know the feeling of a bottle of water, how warm or cold it is. It's just a little bit above room temperature but you know that's a feeling. That's a different kind of coded information in your energy consciousness. You know what a shoe feels like. You know the feeling of a pair of pants. Everything has a specific frequency in your consciousness. If you can get skilled enough to work with that, you can communicate with any being in the Universe.

When something is communicated to you, you know what it is. It's like the scent of something. "That's pumpkin pie," or, "That's popcorn." Each has a different scent that contains a message. Well, communicating with a spirit is similar, yet different. You get the information, feel it, and you recognize who the feeling is from. You know this presence, this person, and they're emotionally expressing themselves to you. You're hearing words because the emotion reverses the communication and puts it into words for you. So, whenever you're dealing with entities, spirits, or even an alien being, you may not understand anything that it's saying, but if it's sad, you're going to know that. If it's happy, you'll know. Emotion is a universal language.

If I put a question out there and let it come to me in its own time, I will feel the answer. It's not channeling. It's more of a download.

Absolutely, I can think of a million ways to describe this, but it's elusive right now. It's about paying attention to what is going on. Women are better at this than men because Men use a different hemisphere of the brain. Women are better at using their intuition. Men construct things a little bit differently in their head when it comes to visual objects. Women are better at understanding the emotional side of my teachings while the men often seem bewildered. This doesn't mean everyone fits into one category or the other. Go out there and play with it. Experiment with it.

Is there a technique to amplify the manipulation of energy?

When I teach, I approach a subject from several different angles to help you understand certain aspects or bring them out. Everything starts with your breathing, so acknowledge your physical body. Think about your body right now while it's sitting in the chair. Become aware of your feet touching the floor. Become aware of your socks, your pants, and your shirt. Become aware of your hands on your lap, relaxing. This is a lot like hypnosis, but we're not really going to go into hypnosis right now. This is a whole different point that I am making.

So, think about your hands again. Take a good look at them. Look at your finger nails. Look at the hair on your hands. Look at the little hairs that are sprouting out of them. Doesn't it strike you as a little odd? You just take it for granted. Why is hair there at all? When you look at the folds in your skin, literally look at them.

Look at the veins underneath the skin on your hands. You know the veins are moving blood, but when is the last time you really looked at the veins? Look at your arm. Look at the 'tentacle' shooting out from the upper part of your body. When you acknowledge the human body, your consciousness begins to shift.

Your mind starts to move differently. Although you are here physically, it's like you're viewing it in the second person saying, "That's not me." Knowing that you're an energy body existing in a physical body is not good enough; actually start thinking about the body. When you open your hand, you can see the bone structures and the tendons opening and closing. When you feel your stomach, you almost get a little nauseous. It's almost like your brain is telling you not to go there. It's a crazy ride but you've got to go there. You may feel a little queasy in your stomach because you're thinking about something you hardly ever do. Residing within the matrix, you're really not supposed to reflect on these types of things.

Think about your breathing. Feel your face. Do you realize you have clay-like material on the sides of your face? What is this thing that you exist within? What is it? What is it doing? The more you contemplate your physical body, the more your mind moves. Think about this torso that's moving around. You're in the torso. You're stuck in there.

Put your hands out in front of you with your palms facing outward. See your hands peripherally come up into focus and then place them back down. What are these appendages? They are tentacles! Internalize this and you will begin to look at life a little bit differently. You will realize how attached you are to it. You will begin to shift. You will begin to feel slightly different.

Pay attention to this different feeling. Pay attention to your feet... your torso... your fleshy face. Take a look at the environment you're in. Everything feels plastic and unreal now to you, doesn't it.

When you look at someone, you understand they have a life force within them. You begin to see micro energy shimmering inside of organic substances. You now have a different understanding of reality. Everything starts to look artificial to you. *When you see the life force encased within the physical body, you don't accept the exterior as being YOU anymore.* As you look at things around you that don't have any life in them, like the carpet, the floor, or the chair, you start to feel claustrophobic. Then your breathing becomes shallower. When you pay attention to your breathing, you know something has changed. It's because you're feeling more like energy; and energy knows no boundaries. You're feeling like you're encased within something. Your energy is almost panicking, in a sense, because you feel this isn't 'normal'.

So use your training and calm yourself down. Breathe. If you're still feeling shifted, it's okay. It can leave as quickly as it comes. Look at the fabric. Look at the ground. Look at all the other people around you. They are vessels - a parking lot of cars. The driver is within them. When you reflect on this, you begin to understand what you really are; you're not going to get 100% out of this body because you're still connected to it. You can't leave it permanently right now, but you can begin to explore energy moving in and out of the body.

Let's jump back to energy movements. Think about your brain right now. You know what the brain looks like; you've seen pictures in books and on the television. What does the brain do? Think about it. What's it doing? It processes all the data that is moving around it, and you're somewhere in there. Do you feel like you're in there? No. You know you're in there. You know that's where your consciousness resides. So, acknowledging that shifts you. It makes you question certain things in a different way. It comes from the chest intelligence.

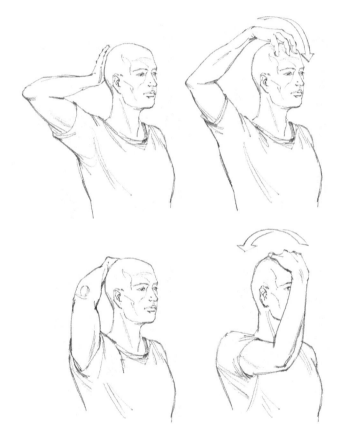

Using the brain rake, spread your fingers apart, and slowly begin moving your hand along your skull towards your forehead. As you do this, visualize energy coming out of your hand and into your head.

Breathe in and exhale. Now take your hand and bring it to the back of your head, not quite touching your lower cranium. Use whichever hand feels right. Think about the energy that you are pulling upward from the back of your cranium. See that energy coming out of your hand and into the back of your skull. Now breathe and pull the energy through your brain as if you're lighting up the areas that have no power, no energy, and no electricity in them. You're firing up those engines in your organic brain. Acknowledge it as a machine. It is a machine. Now start powering it up. Do one on the left side and then do one on the right side. Try and focus and see it being pulled up and over as if you just moved through the whole brain. Ready? Go. Now give it about two seconds or so and just breathe.

There's a certain energy you become aware of if you pay close attention to its subtleness. You generally feel it in your arms. You can feel it if you just move your body a little bit. This is the first time you may have ever really thought about your brain. Have you ever considered that you might be able to manipulate it and fire it up a little bit? It's like those go-carts that have the governor set to limit the speed. You have to turn up the governor otherwise everybody else shoots past you.

What you have to do is work with the organic brain and acknowledge it. It plays a part in making you older, in all your mood swings, and many other things. Reflect on the last time you thought about moving energy or moving your consciousness. What does the brain do when it's not thinking about reaching out to touch things? Does it think about touching itself? Where do its thoughts take you? What does it do?

When you're moving this energy, you're thinking about it. You can move it from the back of your brain up over the top of your crown, to the front, and on both sides. At other times, you can move it from the front of your brain over the top to the back of your brain on both sides. This stimulates energy to awaken it. Your brain is alive. Scientists tell us that we only use about ten percent of our brain – it is my belief that we use a lot more. We're just not aware of how much we actually do use. Did evolution intend for us to use our brain? Can we supersede evolution to stimulate it and speed it up?

Pay attention and listen to the sounds of your feet when you're walking and moving. Observe and feel the air around you. Listen to the sounds everywhere. Now remove yourself from paying attention to the sounds and go back to the feet. There is something about the feet hitting the ground. It's not the feet, but the physical touch. Pay attention to the movement of your feet. Pay attention to your body. Pay attention to the weight of your body. If you pay attention, you're going to start to shift. You're going to see everything differently. There is a *subtle* difference.

Let yourself go without analyzing what is happening. Just feel it. You'll start to see more. You'll hear more and things will begin to change. Everything will become surrealistic. It's a very intriguing place to be. The whole Universe has the same purpose; experience is knowledge. When you progress, you move forward in evolution. That's how you awaken. When you look at something and apply the knowledge to whatever you're dealing with, you can do great things. So, think about the energy movements and practice them so you can master them.

Be aware of all the beautiful presences among you. You are all fellow companions on this journey no matter what class, ethnicity, or social structure you come from. You are so beautiful to me. I'm really moved and I'm so proud of you. You are definitely worthy. *I see you and acknowledge you.* Whether or not I ever met you and talked to you in person, I just want you to know that ***I see you.*** I acknowledge you, and I'm just in awe of you. Remember that you are never alone.

I've always tried to teach people how to work with energy; how to move it, direct it, and control it. Technically, it's not something you can detect with your five senses unless you become attuned to it. Even then, how do you learn to control it? What are the trials and errors when doing this? What patterns, flow, or pathway does the energy follow? How does it operate?

When I was very young, I lived in a big apartment complex. There was a swimming pool that was part of the complex. I've always loved the water! Everybody thought I was a little odd because of the way that I played with the water. I'd move the water from right to left across my body. I studied the movement of the waves, the currents, the length of the pool, and the distance that the waves would travel. I'd see the wave gently splash and I knew how much time it took to travel there.

I'd move the water from left to right across my body, becoming aware of my body, my hips, and hands. Then I'd move my hands from behind me on either side so that my hands would come together in front of me. Of course, this created what I have named the "Phoenix Splash." By doing this, I learned to move water, and if you can move water you can move energy.

In a sense, it's like Tai Chi, but the difference is that

there is a resistance in water. Obviously, the water is transparent, so you don't necessarily see movement but you know it's there. You can feel it and gauge it. So if you have an opportunity to get into a pool, play around with the water and learn from it.

I've always been amused with the surface of water. I patted my hand over and over on the surface of the water when I was a kid. It was as if I was training myself to understand energy. For the most part, I'm self-taught. Everything was more of an inner awakening, an inner knowing and very natural to me. In my youth, I didn't doubt or question what I learned about the water and energy. I thought it was really cool. Maybe you have done similar things. When you get in the flow and you start playing, you observe yourself. You're studying how things work. Moving water will train you to move energy around and feel it. By observing the water, you literally know how far energy is going to move because the pool water gives you a sense of the distance.

Because the brain has its limitations, you need a way to adapt to the boundaries of the material world. Otherwise, you're not going to be able to define your experiences. That's what happens to a lot of people; they feel something or realize that something happened, but they don't know how to grab onto it. So when you move in the pool, you set parameters on your intelligence and your sense of knowing.

There was a study involving three groups of basketball players. Whether or not this study is accurate, the point is clear. The first group practiced, physically, every day. They'd get on the court, bounce the ball, and practice their shots. The second group took the month off. They weren't allowed to play or practice. The third group was told to sit down and visually go over a practice session, over and over again.

After a month, all three groups were tested to see how well they would do. The second group that didn't practice at all played horribly. The first group that practiced conscientiously did great. However, the third group who visually went through all of their routines over and over again, but didn't physically practice, did as well as the first group that practiced all day long. That's monumental!

This group already had a sense of what the ball felt like. They had a sense of the weight of the ball hitting the ground and what their capabilities were. They brought that mindset into their focus. That's how they trained their body, their brain, and their mind to work together in unison, and that's why they performed so well.

What capabilities do you have to help you to visually train? What parameters and gauges do you have so you can start to channel the energies? With visualization you can move the energy in many different ways. You can sweep it through, but are you sweeping three feet or ten feet? You have to obtain a sense of the parameters of this physical dimension so that you know what are capable of.

In a large pool, if you can move the water powerfully enough, it's going to eventually move through the whole length of the pool. You already possess that inner knowing, so you are not going to be limited, but you still need a something to set your standards by so that you don't have to think about it. When you move, you will automatically know what area you're working in.

It's a good idea to try different things. Feel the water moving up against you. When you move into a heavy energy field it feels very similar to this, so you'll adapt very quickly to this environment. When you work with it, it's as if you're reacting to the water pressure, and it just feels very natural working with this energy.

The basketball players knew what it felt like to play basketball. You know what it feels like to be in water that is moving around. You have that information already. Start converting that data into some mental exercises now. Think about pushing energy.

Imagine that you're made of water. Then see your water extend out to envelop around somebody or to become a rain shower. You're the entire rain shower and everything within that environment that the rain touches. It has become a texture of knowledge to you. You can feel everything.

At first, this may sound silly to you, but *silliness is what restrains you; foolishness is what keeps you from growing.* If you think something seems silly or you don't feel comfortable doing that, do it anyway! Go that extra mile! Think in terms of water. Use that water. It really gives you a sense of **pull** and **resistance** – there is a very strong similarity, and it is a bridge between the senses.

I learned to work with energy from moving water in that pool during all of those summers ago when I was a child. It wasn't about splashing other people. I used to float in the pool, feeling my momentum glide. I always wanted to be out of my body and this felt like weightlessness in space. *Think in those terms because it's the closest thing to separating you from the physical realm.* When it makes sense to you, like this, then you can do it. That logical little Babbler is based on what is acceptable in this reality and what's not, and you'll find a nice bridge between both realities.

With other kinds of meditations I've tried, every-thing's good for a while. Then I go "into the desert" and I don't have any experiences; it's desolate. Is that something that happens, no matter what?

Everyone has gone through a dry moment in their meditation. You have to remember that you're working with the organic brain. You're pushing it, so there are times when you give it a little bit of downtime. During that downtime, just switch to a different type of meditation. Do more walking meditations, or sit out in a park, or spend your time cooking something.

There are drawbacks, of course, but it still is a form of meditation. Your mind separates from the ordinary demands of life, and you get into the zone by doing what you're doing. The best meditation is the *Foundation Meditation*, but sometimes it's okay to do something different. Everybody thinks I meditate every single day. There are times when I step away from it and do other things instead. I'll spend a week maybe walking through a park. Or maybe I'll just take a week off and read a book. The trick is to get right back on track. I can go in many different directions now without even meditating.

Don't get down on yourself if you take some down-time. Don't take any more than two or three weeks off. When you get back in the groove, you'll wonder why you put it off so long because you feel fantastic when you do it. You're giving the brain a little detour; accept this as normal. You're not a failure. You're not going to lose everything you've learned. Your energy may take a dip, but there could be seasonal changes affecting you with lower energy. You're only human. Make certain you're watching your diet. Watch what's happening in your life. Be aware if you're around some people that have negative energy. There are energy vampires, people who will drain your energy from you. Some don't realize they are doing this while others do it willfully. This is the Darkside.

You've got to accept all of those factors. Take note: Is your house really dark all of a sudden? Did you notice any changes? You've got to respect the human body; it's going to have a direct effect on your consciousness. If you are ill or you have the flu, do you feel like running around shopping and taking care of things? No. Well, it's the same thing with your energy.

If you're not watching what you're eating or what you're doing, there could be subtle changes in your consciousness. So, you have to look at every situation instead of just feeling bummed out. Nine times out of ten, there is a reason you feel that way. You have to seek out the cause. It's not something random happening to you. Something's going on and you have to acknowledge that. Your greatest strength is acknowledging your weaknesses. But don't get bummed out because you hit a low point. We all do on occasion.

When you meditate, sit in your chair or on the floor and go into that place. You're turning it inside out, or you're bringing that other frequency in. When you have so-so meditations, you have to relax more. There's nothing wrong with a basic meditation. You've got to quiet the mind, too.

When I first began meditating, I took many `desert` trips. I even stopped meditating for a period of time. And then I would go into a meditation and hit such high levels that it was surprising to me. Sometimes you just need that downtime to reboot. Then you can turn it into uptime. Just remember not to distance yourself so much that you forget what you need to do; there is no excuse for that.

There are moments when you start to cruise. Something very different is going on. You can see the Planes of Light or you can feel frequency and humming. At this threshold, there is a barrier line. It's that point that you are at, and it manipulates your energy fields so that you can come in because it wants you to enter. It's like the bouncer at the door saying, "Okay, you're cool. You pass. Come on in." Meanwhile, the brain is asking, "What are those lights out there? What's going on? What's that rumbling?" And it brings you back down again. There is a continual, perpetual battle between the two, and it's not going away. There's no easy fix for that.

Your greatest breakthroughs will come from the times you've been meditating. It's the fastest way to take control of your spiritual growth. If you're bummed out, and the whole world sucks, monetarily, or health-wise, find the time to meditate because it's going to get you through that storm. If you don't do it, you're going to get beat up, banged up, thrown up on the shore and then kicked back into the water. If you trust that you will ride out the storm, you will.

So get out there. Do a little bit of energy work. Go out there and think about the psychic material. Sit down and play with remote viewing or telepathy. The more material you understand and use, the more flexibility you will have. Then, when you go into that place with the moving energy and you understand it, you will want to stay there.

Listen to the material. If you stand in the rain, you'll "*get wet.*" If you listen to the material but never practice it, you will "*get wet.*" It will have some effect on you, even if you don't fully understand it. But the subconscious mind will and it will start tuning you up by raising your frequency. It will have an effect on you, whether it's a day, week, month, or five years from now. But it will never happen if you keep putting it off.

So, just do it!

Chapter 8

WARRIORS WANTED: APPLY HERE

THROUGHOUT HISTORY, MANY people and organizations have felt a strong sense of urgency to awaken because there have always been White Cells. Their culture and religion of the times generated fear and set limitations for the people of what is and isn't acceptable. How can you explain spiritual knowledge to someone who fears a black cat walking in front of them, or walking underneath a ladder because it brings bad luck? These customs, practices, and superstitions were passed down throughout the ages. Even though it was not the truth, those beliefs were incorporated into that culture's concept of spirituality and have been integrated into the rules and regulations of our society. Many of them exist even today.

When I had my first enlightenment cycle, I didn't follow any particular path. It happened by developing my sixth sense ability. I wondered why other spiritual teachers were not sharing this knowledge with their students. The reason is because we are White Cells. We are Old Souls, every single one of us on this particular path.

It's like in the movie *Close Encounters of the Third Kind* when the people were passionately driven to go to the mountain. It's like that for us. We're drawn to this knowledge. This is a calling, a resonance. This entire planet holds a certain frequency, and either you tune into it or you don't. White Cells are "called" to tune into it. It's saying, "You've got to awaken now. You've got to remember who you are, what your purpose is, and why you were sent here." You need to get to work and get this knowledge out there. There is an important reason for that.

I'm not going to play by the usual set of rules. I'm just going to say it like it is. However, there are some reasonable rules that must be respected when you communicate with other people. White Cells are warriors; I don't want to beat the drum, but there is an aggressive side to us that is very much on the side of light. People say that we must be passive, but there's a part of us that doesn't want to be passive. We feel that if we are forced to be passive, we've been neutered. Well, if this is going to shake things up, bring it on. We know right from wrong. We're not going to hurt anyone. We love and respect life. We respect one another. We are self-respecting people, but there are forces out there that have different intentions for life.

If you look at the human body, it operates in a similar way. White Cells must serve their purpose. If they do not serve their role, we have a very big problem – that is how I see it. The White Cells on this planet are not passive. Some of them are doing exactly what they were meant to do. There are other spiritual schools that are also doing their job, but I think it's time for a specific group to step forward to accomplish even more.

I watch The Learning Channel a lot. One day, they were talking about red cells and white cells; saying how super cells are ancient white cells that remain dormant. They're in the body existing amongst everything else, but they're silent. This terminology caught my attention because it describes perfectly what I have been saying about White Cells for years, so I use this spiritual/medical language because there aren't other terms that are more appropriate.

When a very powerful negative virus comes into the body to wreak havoc, these super cells awaken and they literally jump up and kick ass. They come out of their slumber, shake it off, and say, "Okay, move along. We'll take care of this now."

I feel this is what we, as White Cells, are here to do. If you look at a virus, you have to ask yourself what it is doing. There's not much difference; it is just a macro-micro situation. Viruses clone themselves; they mimic; they adapt; they move amongst other cells of the body.

Now, I'm not saying everyone is a bad person, but they are out there. They do exist and you know who they are. You can feel them, but you tell yourself not to listen to the warning signs. The rational brain says, "You should just go and do your laundry. Isn't there a movie you need to watch?" So, of course, the real question is, "What do you do? Go up to them and smack them on the back of the head and say, "I'm on to you?" No – there are other more reasonable ways to handle this.

I don't want to call it a war because this is something that has gone on since the beginning of time. It isn't really a war; it's more of a balancing. I've heard some individuals say, "These particular people on Earth are like a disease. They should all be wiped out." That's absolute nonsense! Everyone is part of the Earth. Without them, the Earth would be in dire straits because we are its nervous system. We're here for a reason. We sprouted from the ground. The Cosmos has merged within us from the Universe that sprouted the Earth.

There is a job to be done here. We need to recognize our role and take action. But I'm trying to be careful about the way we approach this. I don't want to start something fanatical. I want people to be independent and free-thinking. Everybody absolutely must remain unique because each of us will work within our own group, fulfilling our own purpose.

So, I believe this is our calling as White Cells. It is one of healing. It's a much bigger level of healing than anyone can imagine though. It comes from those of us who are able to harness our abilities by learning how to amplify them. Using a metaphor to explain this, you've been swimming in a pool for a long time and hardly anyone else has a pool. Suddenly, you're thrown into the ocean. You already know how to swim in the pool, so you're going to do very well in the ocean. This is how I am slowly helping you along. Anyone who goes into the higher states of consciousness will understand this more complex idea. For the most part, it's really a matter of finding the true Super Cells and awakening them. I'm not talking about the pacifists. I'm not saying we're going to be out there with pitchforks. We need to start moving forward. Hardly anyone wants to talk about doing this, but it's time to wake up and fulfill your purpose.

It's time to start preparing your consciousness; the time is now. It's not about strength or physical endurance. Biologically, the world is rapidly changing. What used to take a hundred years to accomplish is now done in ten years. What happened in ten years now takes one year. It's tremendous; we're on the throes of a different kind of frequency and, as that frequency constantly changes, it affects the entire grid of civilization. There is a need for people to adapt to this frequency, but there are still those people who are muddling around.

What is the significance of the timing of this knowledge?

Let's just say that I expect great things from all of you; as White Cells, you already know that. This is the beginning of a huge movement. We are not the few anymore. I believe that each individual White Cell is going to affect many other people and that will affect the collective consciousness. There will always be Red Cells. Some people think we're all going to become White Cells, but that's not true. The Earth still needs Red Cells to function. It has an agenda, too.

There is no substitute for age because with it comes wisdom. I like the idea of youth, but if I had to trade what I know now, I would never give it up in a million years. The world had a recent consciousness shift in self-reflection. Part of that is from the Masters who are here walking on this Earth. There are more Masters on the Earth right now than ever before in our history that will move consciousness to the next level. Having said that, with change there is often resistance.

The significance of Higher Balance is a harmonic marker contributing to a consciousness shift of the planet. We may seem like a few, but there has never been a group of so many people with this particular frequency. There is something very different about what *you* know compared to the rest of the world. You feel a sense that nothing is complete anymore. You feel a sense of detachment, but also a yearning to attach to something. This is what happens with spiritual growth. You have this sadness because you know there's a greater beauty, a greater "something." You've experienced it from moment to moment; it is part of your personal growth.

You know that you have to function along with the rest of the world. You have to work, pay your bills, and deal with personal relationships. Yet there is still a part of you saying, "I hope I'm doing whatever I need to do, but this can't be it!" Many of you have already entered a cycle of enlightenment. You may not realize this but you have. You are holding yourself back right now by not acknowledging that you are. It's the same as saying, "I can't be; I'm not at a high enough frequency." Believe me, you are! The sooner you can accept that, the faster you will evolve.

Don't be afraid to acknowledge how far you've already come. You are that cutting edge. Whether you've been my student for a long time or whether you're relatively new, you know this is where you need to be right now. Enlightenment isn't always the golden glow that is shown in pictures, and it's not about levitating. It's not about doing miracles. When it comes down to timing, you'll be able to do more than you could ever imagine.

In this reality, we hold ourselves back because society tells us not to be too proud, not to be arrogant. There is a difference between arrogance and being proud. You can be confident in the knowledge that you have learned, even if somebody says you are being arrogant. I'm not arrogant. I'm confident. I assert myself. There is a difference. I don't let incorrect information spread, and I am not afraid to speak out when I should. We all need to create a little turbulence, because if it's the truth, it will hold up. The truth will always hold up.

You mentioned that white cells are fighters. Is it a general thing or is it very personal? I meditate every day, go to work, and then I'm back in the Doe again. In what sense are we fighters? Should we wait for that moment to come or should we take action now?

Innately, you already know the answer to this question. Rest assured, everybody can relate to it. You've already begun to fight. The fight is not about wrestling somebody or beating them over the head. You fight to survive in this world. Your next fight is to awaken. You're fighting to awaken right now. You're fighting to gain a foothold of this higher state of consciousness. You're wrestling with it.

This *is* a fight. Are you not exhausted? Are you not tired of your high days and your low days? Are you not tired of having to deal with those ups and downs? Ask yourself, "Did I choose my profession of work? Did I choose to move where I now live? Where would I be better positioned in order to spiritually awaken?" You're in a fight right now. Since you made it this far, I'd say you're putting up a very good fight!

Sometimes, the answer is so subtle that you don't recognize what's right in front of you. The fight to awaken is right in front of you! You're in this fight and you're feeling some anxiety. Anxiety is the result of trying to cope or overcome something that you have difficulty facing. So your fight begins by meditating.

The next step is to listen to other spiritual material and test it. You're trying to break out of this sleep-state – this rudimentary system that keeps you plugged in. You're fighting a sumo wrestler. You're in a big fight, but if you get into the zone and build your life around your spirituality, you're going to break out of that sleep. Notice that I didn't tell you to remove your life; it's a part of the whole. You have to understand that there is a reason for your current routine.

There's a reason why people place their teachers on a pedestal. Your teacher is an inspiration to you. You want to resonate with their energy and accomplish the same things. To use the fighting analogy, two fighters are boxing in the ring and when the bell sounds, the round is finished. You're sitting there cheering one of them on saying, "Oh my God! That's one heck of a fighter. You need to get in there and give him a one-two in the gut. Move it!"

That's what I'm doing. You're the prize fighter. You're working your way up the ranks. Where were you before you became interested in all of this? You were asleep somewhere in the dream world, speculating about awakening, knowing there was something more to this reality. "There's got to be something more to life than this," you often think.

Then you made the decision to do something about it and pushed the envelope. But your friends and family wanted you to go back to your childhood religion. This is fighting! You are fighting to awaken; that's what you are here to do. Once you've figured that out, you get your tools. Then you learn your skills from a reputable teacher. Eventually, you end up teaching others. You excel at this, and you teach more people. So fighting is one context of awakening.

On another level, there are beings out there that have chosen a very different path. They've chosen to suppress, control, and consistently obstruct your path of awakening. This is done on both a sociological and spiritual level. There are spiritual teachers out there who are doing this exact thing. They're not positive. They're not for the light or for self-growth. Their purpose is to control and dominate others, to create clones of themselves with the same haircut and clothes. There is nothing creative about them.

There are some very big organizations out there that I truly feel are like "storm troopers" for the Darkside. It is shocking when they say, "Okay, you see the light. Now, picture the light shrinking. See it dimming. See it disappear. Oh, there's nothing there." *You're unplugging yourself from the very thing that's giving you life and consciousness!* They say, "This is going to free you." Believe me, there are some very dark forces in this world. You need to remember and be aware they are "out there." Don't be ensnared by them.

When I read The Handbook of the Navigator, I couldn't stop thinking about the Darkside. Sometimes it feels like I'm reading a Star Wars novel again. A part of me wants to understand the Darkside. I just have a problem thinking that such a thing really does exist.

I've heard this before; it is a reasonable, level-headed statement. There are movies and stage productions that have all been inspired and created by individual beings. I'm not necessarily saying that George Lucas is a White Cell, but it's not beyond the consciousness of the Earth to isolate a resource to help create that kind of idea. There are different regions of the brain, and if you were to zoom in on those regions, you would find isolated areas. Who knows what sparks of creativity are being kindled.

When I think about all the different movies throughout history, I marvel at how perfect they were for their particular time. Some people wonder how that is possible, but you're not one of them. As White Cells, we all relate to *Star Wars*. We all relate to the concept of the Darkside versus the Force.

Some people just don't get it; they're bored with this concept. When we look at it, we're on the edge of our seats. It speaks to us. It makes sense to us. I think the planet works on many levels within its own design to create consciousness. Humans are the collective, the neural system of the planet, and we are becoming more complicated as we progress and populate the Earth.

I recognize the fact that movies have the ability to influence and shift the masses to a higher level of consciousness. The idea of the storm troopers from *Star Wars* came from two specific areas: the ancient Vedic teachings concerning the Force, and experiences that portray life. Lucas obviously borrowed from real world tragedies, like the Holocaust. The storm troopers are similar to that kind of organization. We are affected by whatever happens in our lives. Movies like this create and embellish those real life situations. What is the source of these ideas? Where do those concepts come from in your own mind? Where does true genius come from?

I believe it is the planet's consciousness, collectively working through a single cell to create and manifest in this dimension where we exist. At the right time, inspiration comes forth. It's the same story over and over again. If you look at *Star Wars* and the Greek Gods and their tragedies, it's a repetitious story with a different ending.

So the same stories are told throughout history. It simply confirms the ideas necessary for awakening. This material is provided by the planet and the Universe to awaken certain individuals. The planet is evolutionary, just like the rest of us. As we procreate, the planet will also procreate. We sense fear. We internally sense danger, and we intuitively know how to approach something or someone with caution. It's no different for the planet communicating within itself. Life mimics non-reality and non-reality reflects life. There's a truth in this statement.

Does the Darkside exist outside of this dimension?

No, it doesn't, and it is that simple. A lot of what I describe is from a very different source of knowing and I am constantly searching to find the right words to describe it to you in a way that you will understand.

You see things from a *size* point of view. So, when you think of the Universe, you automatically attach a size to it. You don't really know how big the Universe is, but in your mind you give it boundaries. If I said "planet," you would see a round shape in your head. If I said "the Sun," you would picture a certain size. So, when you think of the Darkside, you immediately try to give it a perimeter.

It is puzzling to imagine a size that you can categorize in your head. Well, it is big, and when God came into this dimension, that created the Big Bang event. It was God moving into this dimension. God's frequency within Itself began to change, and when that happened, there was a natural reaction – the great explosion.

You have matter forming within this coexistence of other energies, meaning God's consciousness. For every action, there's an equal and opposite reaction. Hence the birth, reflection, or opposing force that came from that - the Darkside.

Since the Force is here with the intent of expansion, there is also a natural and opposite reaction that wants the removal of all life. Those two forces are at odds in this dimension. *This is the dimension where frequency occurred. It gave birth to this counterforce of energy that's become its own intelligence.* It does not exist outside in the other frequencies.

Everybody has this same knowing. We all learned about heaven and hell. Ask yourself internally, "Is there a place that we consider to be the Darkside?" There is. Maybe we call it "hell." Now when I ask you to tell me about a higher place, do you think you can contain it? It's like it is infinite. You have this inner-truth already within you. It is primarily in this dimension; hence, the big battle for existence that's perpetually going on, not only in our solar system, but also throughout the Universe. There's this friction of energy that states, "Okay, no more growth; no more expansion." And the Universe replies, "Well, I really have to know what this is all about. This is very interesting." We all feel the

Universe's curiosity because we are one with God. Like the cells in your body are curious, so is the Universe curious within itself.

The *Darkside* is a taboo subject that nobody really wants to talk about. At most spiritual gatherings, it's always about light, positive energy, meditation, and self-reflection, and very little about the opposing forces. So, what exactly is the Darkside? What is its purpose? What is *our* purpose? How does the Darkside affect everything? What are the dynamics of it all? What do we need to do? Nobody wants to talk about that subject. Nobody wants to acknowledge the Darkside. The fear is that by talking about it, you are acknowledging it. Well, it is time to explain what the Darkside is exactly and how it operates.

There are two kinds of people that come to me to learn what I have to offer. They either come to learn about *love* or *power*. Coming to me for power is not a bad thing. Think of the power of the Jedi from *Star Wars*; they are good, but also powerful. I see that as power. I never see it as a bad thing. They're coming to me to learn this knowledge because they want to actively make a difference and change what is wrong with the world. They have an inner knowing, an instinctual belief, that this is where they need to be to help make those changes.

The people who come to me for love don't just come because they want to be loved by God. They come to me because they want to put this love into others to heal them and move them forward consciously. It's not about selfishness. When people hear me say, "They come to me for love or for power," they immediately judge what that means without truly understanding.

We have our warriors, but they will get banged up.

Who's going to take care of them and fix them so they can get back out there and do what they came to do? It's a job in itself. So, both are critically important. Some spiritual people don't necessarily know how to take on the Darkside. They don't know how to deal with it. Other people just want to focus on love and all that good energy. We're on the same team, but one has to interpret these higher dimensions and bring them into physical terminology so we can understand.

Let me be clear about something. There's nothing that I can say that's going to explain exactly what it's like unless we all jump out of our bodies and into energy form. Then you'll get it. I'm trying to give you the best interpretation of what is out there. So I want you to understand there's still room for interpretation.

From the very beginning of primitive humanity, there were spiritualists. The people who understood things first were the shamans. They were the leaders and they recognized that there was something more to life. As soon as they began to grasp that concept, the Universe spoke to their intelligence. The shamans tried to understand, interpret, and take in that information and put it into a structure that the people could understand.

Now, that's a positive thing to do, but unfortunately it's also a negative thing because of the limitations of the shamans intelligence when explaining it. For instance, he may have described something that looked like a lion because that was his point of reference, and a lion was the most ferocious thing he had ever encountered.

So communication and interpretation are extremely important. Try to be conscious of both. When I teach and pause, it's because I'm thinking, "What's going to capture the essence of what I am trying to say?" When I use words, sometimes it's not just a word. It's whatever it evokes within you.

If I say, "a ferocious lion," I'm not talking about the teeth, the mouth, or the body. When I say that we can experience a plant, I'm talking about the feeling. You recognize that feeling. You know that vibration. You know what it is, and you can recognize that feeling without touching the plant. Everything has a sensation connected with it. You know what a bottle of water feels like. So when I'm using certain words or structures, I'm trying to incite the emotional vibration that comes with that while I'm choosing the best word to explain it.

So if we look at history, we can see that God, the Universe, was always trying to communicate with us. In my opinion, all of the religions, belief systems, and different spiritual paths are mostly the Universe trying to communicate. The rest is our interpretation of this, and it's where we get into problems. From the very beginning, the Universe has tried to communicate with us. Since then, there was the making of a White Cell. But there must also be Red Cells to work for the Earth, to contribute something to this living organism.

Both have their terminologies for different things and ultimately, both face the battle between good and evil. All religions say there are negative forces and positive forces. Culturally, we may be oceans apart, but we still came up with the same concepts because the Universe communicates to us.

You need a way to bring this knowledge into your physical reality because it's something you have to be aware of so you can prepare for it. If you're aware of the Darkside, you'll be able to defend yourself, take notice, and be alert. There has always been the knowledge of good versus evil.

What does it all come down to? The universe is matter intertwined and fabricated with the Force. At the same time, it's intermixed with the opposing force, the Darkside. It's like a static energy of both polarities, with both energies ever present.

In mythology there were the Norse gods and the Valhalla, and the bridge between the two. The bridge was the middle ground. Well, that's where we are. It's the physical ground where both forces are trying to dominate, control, awaken, and reach out.

There are always the warriors and the healers. There are always those that are able to feel while the other people, the Red Cells, believe this is all rubbish. They just want to do their job and exist in this world. The rest of us are plugged into something very different. The Red Cells think we're crazy, while we think they're lazy. We have to accept them, as they have to accept us – for that is part of the natural process of the Earth. If they don't exist, then the Earth doesn't exist. It is a contribution of both.

That which is against life is anti-life. Having said that, how does one intertwine with life to destroy life? The best way is by trying to control your thoughts. If there's a flower growing, it is the Universal plan for the flower to accept its path. Now, you can manipulate its DNA to make it into other things. That's all great, but when you begin to structuralize with only what you think is best, you will run into problems because there is no new area to grow in. You've created a beginning and an end.

Right now, there's no end for the Universe. It'll probably come to an end eventually, but who knows when that will be. The Universe is like a giant flower that's budding, and God is ever watching it, waiting to see what it's going to become. Some people think God knows everything. I disagree with that. We are here to experience for God so God can experience in return.

God anticipates what seems absolute to us. If you look at a rose bush, you know it's going to produce a rose, but do you know every little facet of that rose? Do you know every little curve and texture it's going to reveal to you? What amuses God? The Universe marvels at all the aspects of the birthing process.

As we understand physics, for every action there is an opposite reaction. Since God physically came into this dimension and created life, there is a reaction. This is the Darkside; it wants all life to stop expanding, so it suppresses it. As the Universe collectively grows in intelligence, so does the Darkside. As with evolution, when you point a plant in one direction, the first thing you realize is that the plant always grows towards the light. If you rotate it and move it across the room, it's going to start moving towards the light again. So is there a force that's adapting to us to counter the productivity of life?

For every positive move we make, there's a countering of the negative forces. Whether or not we see it is the real question. The reason why many people don't see it is that we are micro. We generally relate to our micro reality and the world around us. However, if you look at history and all the different societies, you will see the rise and fall of those people who were trying to control by organizing too much. Then there are others that develop free flow cultures where they integrate a little bit of nature with science, so there is a level of progression as well.

There has always been a Dark Energy throughout existence in this reality. This Darker Force in our world, our planet Earth, is evolving, adapting to a higher form of integration. It's no longer working with individuals to dominate and control the people. The change is the difference between talking, convincing, and negotiating versus just forcing suppression to happen.

When I look at Buddhism and Hinduism, I see these as regions of the brain sprouting and acting like different gearing for the human mechanism. In a sense, it is micro, but all consciousness starts from the micro level and grows larger. Buddhism is good for the world. They're sitting there, chanting, working their energy and putting it out there.

Hinduism is very complex, but in the end, they get it. Alisone! They get it. They don't want to have reincarnation again; the Hindi's want life on Earth to come to an eventual end, so there are a few differences in their beliefs versus ours. They're still trying to put life out there. It's still positive. These are my interpretations.

As for the Christians and Muslims, they're seeing life progress and that's good. There are some fanatical groups who mess things up for everybody else, but for the most part most people want the same things as we do.

You mentioned earlier that certain people or organizations receive communication from the Universe. Are there any organizations that receive communication from the Darkside?

Yes, there are. This other organization caught my attention as I watched these different religions. They call themselves a religion, but they're not. I think everybody eventually will know what I'm talking about. When you think about them, feel it in your chest center intelligence. Feel your Navigator and trust it. Even though it walks like a duck and quacks like a duck, it's not a duck.

This 'religion' was created amongst other religions, but it doesn't act like religion. It doesn't necessarily act like spirituality either, but they call it that. They organize in a very methodic way. They realized there is one thing in this dimension that can do things very rapidly – money. So they focused on the material nature of money.

We say, "Use consciousness and let it expand. Feel God and feel the Universe." They say, "The mind and the brain is not what you want. You want this third thing." They say, "This is the soul. This is what you're really after." *The mind is the soul,* so I thought it was very interesting that they separated it. They say you have to block the mind out and remove yourself from it. They say it's no good; it's just a bunch of pictures. It's just random thought. They tell you this is what you need to concentrate on. I'm telling you this is **not** your soul. *This is not who or what you're being told it is. This is another source coming from another place that's going to misdirect you.*

How do they separate the Universe's communication from the Darkside's communication?

They go through great training to remove the light. We have different beliefs, but for the most part, our people are not really of a specific religion and we like it that way. If you want to believe them, that's fine. We're not saying we're better than religion. We don't ask you to pray for us, nor will we pray for you.

You can **feel** when you hear the wrong thing. If you don't listen to that feeling, you'd better start paying attention. If you feel it, you know it isn't right. They're saying, "Remove the light." All of us instinctively have that inner-knowing that the light is our connection to God. We may call it *light;* it doesn't mean we see it as light, but we know it represents that connection for us.

They're telling you to see it as a light and remove it. That is the problem I have with their organization. They say this is why you don't know what you want in life, why you have problems. All of these problems are mine. I don't want anyone to take them away. They connect me to life. As bad or good as those problems are, they are what shaped and molded me. They made me compassionate, understanding, and changed me from selfish to giving. It's the difference between selfishness and selflessness. Your experiences shape you and you learn from them.

I embrace the errors I've made. I embrace what I've learned. In a sense, they're saying, "No, you don't want all that. You don't have to deal with it. Just take it all away, and remove the light." When the light is gone, what is left?

Darkness.

They tell you that darkness is good because it's relieving you. They say that they don't use hypnosis, but in a rhythmic monotone they say, "Listen to what we're saying. We believe in the soul but we call it something else. It's over here." Can you feel the manipulation? However, some of you feel a connection with them. They are seeking special individuals. Eighty five percent of the people in this world are Red Cells. The other fifteen percent are White Cells. That's a small fraction of people, but we still count in the millions when you really think about it. It may seem like a lot, but not when you scatter it wide.

A handful of dirt looks like a lot, but when you throw it in the air amongst the rest of the dirt, it doesn't seem like you have so much at all. We're precious. *Never be ashamed of being precious. If you don't recognize how precious you are, you'll never fulfill what it is you need to do or be.* By acknowledging it, you've done one simple thing. You've taken a step forward instead of shying away saying, "I can't think of myself that way. I can't. How am I special?" We're all special, but you have a *particular* task and you've got to be able to acknowledge that.

They're scooping all of these people up. They dismiss whatever doesn't work for their religion or belief system. They tell you that you don't need psychotherapy or psychiatrists. Psychotherapy is no different than what I'm doing. I'm not talking about medicine. There's good medicine and there's bad medicine, but it all serves a purpose in one way or another. When this particular religion tells you that you don't need a therapist, you need to reflect on that statement.

When I look at a flower, the first thing I want to say to you is, "Do you see the beauty in it? I want to share it." There are things inside of you that you need to share. But there's not always somebody there ready to share it with. You sometimes need to find someone to share it with in other ways.

"They" are searching, building, and converting White Cells. It's a sifting process. They're reaching out and looking for the ones who haven't found the right knowledge yet. You have been searching for many years. Looking, *knowing*, *feeling*. When you look, you're thinking, "No, that isn't it. No, that isn't it either." They seem like they have all the right answers because they are only giving pieces of information to you, but they're holding back some, too.

We're a unique kind of spirituality. We're intellectual, a little like scientists. We get it. The Universe doesn't say that you have to serve It. It allows you to make your own choices. *No one can tell you what to do. You have to make your own choices*. It's free will.

What is their purpose? What are they trying to accomplish?

This group is searching for people who have the same psychic and spiritual raw potential that you hold. They're converting them and getting them to surrender the light, and **then something else steps in that can operate from within them**. They're training them in psychic abilities.

If you really go undercover and examine the things they do, you will find there are organizations within organizations in this group that have a definite agenda. That agenda is to find these particular people and win them over. They want to train these people to be used in a specific way at a specific time to have an effect on the one thing that is most precious: the consciousness of the planet. Which path will the human race take? I'm not saying the planet has one consciousness. Various motivations from one culture to another become one harmony. When you throw one good or bad pitch in there, it spreads like a virus. All of a sudden, everybody starts accepting that concept.

The recent changes in the collective consciousness since 2012 will continue on. It's a progression that has already started. Ask yourself how you feel about that. You know that you feel it. There have been many of these progressions throughout time on Earth. Many people have talked about feeling that enrichment. It has never really become a repressed feeling until probably the last few hundred years. People have feared, religiously or spiritually, that the end is coming. That thought builds in the collective consciousness, getting more complex, much as it is today.

There has never been such conscious communication of ideas and thoughts like we have now with all these technological advances. Even our atmosphere is filled with information beaming everywhere, stretching out, and encompassing everything. We have reached a point where there's a struggle over this consciousness and we feel it everywhere in the world.

Even though we're past 2012, religions still tell us it's the days of trials and tribulations. Once again, it comes down to our different interpretations. It's the best that humans can do. They're feeling it but they are not quite ironing it out. I'm not saying that our way is necessarily the best way. I'll share what I have with you. You can sort it out on your own.

The planet is going to hit a pivotal moment when, all of a sudden, there's going to be an understanding of the Gaia mind. Science will start to acknowledge it and they're starting to understand it now. But the shift was a death of the old way of being. You can feel the changes everywhere. Things seem different in the world. If you were to use your emotional feeling and ask yourself, "What does it feel like when something's gone?" What is that? It's a kind of death. Instead, look at it as new growth. The people of ages past hadn't sociologically found a way to interpret the shift that way, but they knew what it was.

We are now in a period of transition, like day and night. There's a period where the first beams of light come. This can take weeks or months of slowly getting brighter. It's like getting taller when you're young. You don't see it, but it's happening. It's still not at the point where all of the people have acknowledged it. But it has happened and we all feel it. So, remember one thing. *Evil thinks what it is doing is good.*

During the shift, there was a moment when everyone relaxed, and in that moment, it's almost as if everything became quiet. In that moment, consciousness shifted. It dipped before it went back up. This didn't change consciousness in an hour, or a minute, or over a period of a month. It's as if the planet was waiting for a new inspiration to come forth, a new direction to choose from. Society as a whole began to stop and look at what we have become, where we are going, and what it is that we want.

At that moment the human race, which is the central nervous system of the planet, began to express something. That expression rippled and was magnified. It permeated and seeded consciousness. The same way animals know things, it permeated within us, or better yet, in the Red Cells. The Darkside had been selecting and training certain individuals for power and glory all along. They had everything they need and thought, "Why search harder?"

Super White Cells, or White Cells that have the potential to reach a higher level of consciousness are holding something very powerful inside of them. Something huge is in your chest. It's very beautiful and very powerful and we almost don't say it out loud. It's **God.** These miniscule cells have in them a micro-dam door. It's like the Hoover Dam shrunk down into this little tiny spot in your chest. On the other side, in this other frequency, God tells us, "Just a little longer…hang in there."

That so called "religion" that I mentioned earlier is looking for the same thing, but they've reversed the light in certain individuals. What happens when you remove the light? It fills the person up with darkness. Now what happens if they have that same bridging ability? What if they have the same ability that Super White Cells have developed? *They become.* They go from a Red Cell to a spiritual being moving in a body, and then they're awakening!

What is awakening? Awakening is knowledge. Knowledge it's frequency. It's energy, and that energy, all of a sudden, becomes a different dimension. That dimension doesn't know distance. It's just there; it can flood out. This moment of breath from the planet has come in the past. This is not the first time. We all know that. We all have that inner-knowing. This has happened before on several occasions. Civilization has either been lost, or it has gained, moved forward, and progressed with greater cultures coming from it.

When that moment happened, my friends, students, and companions from all over the world sat down and relaxed. Then they thought of everything they've learned. They began to open this doorway, this dimensional door within them. That vibration, that energy, permeated within that breath as a contribution to the whole, the collective, to the Universe. In part, this is the purpose that you are looking for; to become an integral part of the change in consciousness and its continuation.

So what is my purpose? Who am I? Am I a baker? Or am I a cook? We identify ourselves as this or that. Why do we feel so driven like lunatics? What is the answer to all of this? Is it religion? Is my purpose to heal? Is it to fight? What is it? It's all of these things and more because each of "them" is doing the same thing. They try to dominate a frequency of consciousness. They mimic their personal belief system, on a smaller scale, in how they operate.

How do they operate? What is their method?

If you look deeper into this, you'll recognize their method. Rest assured that the Darkside is very methodically detailed. Everything is about perfect structure and perfect order. Think about that. Think about how they bring people in and they remove the light. They show you a pattern and remove it. These methods identify all the issues. Then they work them out and structuralize it.

They're like the Borg on **Star Trek** or the Empire from **Star Wars**. These are all interpretations coming from the Gaia mind speaking to the generations through movies, books, and other forms of communication. These are all representations of something that humanity has been feeling since the beginning of our birth into this world.

Not all of us are necessarily ready to fight, but we're all ready to let go and let it do its thing. God is saying to us, "When the time is right, we'll settle this for once and for all." There will be skirmishes that continue between their energy and our energy. We feel it sometimes in our daily lives. You may think it's just you, but how often can you say it's just a coincidence? When the shit keeps coming, is it you? We all have bad days. The car breaks down. The house catches fire. The cat goes missing, but all in one week? This might be the week something could happen during your meditation. Maybe you're about to have the big breakthrough and this interrupts it.

It's simple for us to think in those terms, but the Force and the Darkside are so complex that no super-computer could ever begin to grasp them entirely. The healers will heal those of us that are working in these skirmishes. We'll find people damaged by these energies and beings, and we'll fix them. We'll make them right. It's what we do. I have never seen a plant you could squish that didn't fix itself, as long as there was a little bit of life left.

Even if the Darkside wins this skirmish for a while, it will not get rid of us. We're diligent. We're up for a good fight, too. We're not just going to roll over. We get it. There has to come a point when you discern your purpose and start stepping forward.

The Darkside uses fear to accuse you of being crazy. They want you to find an organized religion. It's all very subduing. Everybody knows it. They can feel it. It's difficult to go against the flow because they are the many and we are the few, but we're not just by ourselves. Never forget that there is a bigger picture. This battle has been raging on this planet forever.

Why would a White Cell choose the Darkside over the Force?

What made the Empire from **Star Wars**, evil? If one of their representatives came to you and your family and said, "Look at this little planet you're on. You're poor. We'll give you a job, pay you a salary and let you drive a spaceship. We're going to let you fly around the Universe. We'll protect your family and we're going to take good care of you." When you're in this situation, you're not thinking about the bigger picture. You don't know the dynamics of the mechanism you're working for. You're just a little cog in a big machine.

Meanwhile, the Empire is growing, getting bigger and bigger. On the other side is the Rebellion. They're fighting Darth Vader and Emperor Palpatine, who represent the Darkside. We're told they're bad. They have red light sabers so they must be bad.

What made them evil? The Empire wants a strict sense of conformity, a strict sense of structural growth, and a strict sense of life. They want to marginalize and control everything to 'make life better.' How does one make life better than God? They tell us their way is compatible with God. They want us to trust them.

The Rebellion uses space ships and they embrace technology. They work with it, but don't use it for controlling others. It's a very fine line. That's what confuses most people when they follow these paths. The Empire wanted to control the Universe. They were very methodical in their control of the process of things. George Lucas, the creator of *Star Wars*, got this idea from the Nazis. If you didn't fit in with the Nazis, you were exterminated. If you were of a certain color, sexual preference, or different religion, you disappeared! The Nazi focus was on a master race - the Aryans.

During those times and even today, there is a lot of selectiveness. There is always the few who stand up and fight against tyranny. We are doomed the day we decide to say nothing. *We're all doomed the day that we decide not to be who it is we're meant to be, to do what we're meant to do.*

This has happened over and over again throughout history. Most things that structuralize eventually fall. Look at the Roman Empire, the Macedonian Empire, and the Byzantine Empire. The ones that really proliferated were the ones that changed, adapted, and renewed themselves.

What happens when one is actually able to dominate everything? When it dies, all the rest die with it. If we look at it genetically, what would have happened if the Nazis had been able to purely dominate the world? What would happen if everybody was wiped out? What happens a hundred years later? What happens to the human race genetically? Most people don't understand that once this 'goodness' is absolutely under control, it has an end which no one anticipates. In the end, the Darkside gets exactly what it wants.

The Universe must progress and continue to expand. It must continue to be able to open itself and reveal it's mysteries within mysteries. If I could conceive and understand the whole Universe, I wouldn't want to exist as a soul. I would want true death - to cease to exist. I marvel at the creation and mystery of the Universe. When I have found everything that I can find, I'll be ready to go. We all want something to intrigue and stimulate our minds. Give us a challenge. If you cap the challenge, you cease the desire to exist. Naturally, the Darkside wants to cap that.

How do people accept the Darkside's communication if their true self is created from the Universe? Wouldn't there be a clash of ideals?

The people in the religious organization that I mentioned want you to attain a level of *clear*. Then they will get you to talk about something. When they expunge it from you, it won't be there. *They want to remove everything that makes you human.* This state is similar to what we call, "Non-thought." They don't say, "Non-thought." They say, "Clear," but there's a fine line there.

Who controls you if you're "clear?" To whom have you surrendered all of your genetic design? When you're clear, your spiritual essence becomes submissive. Not only are they out to get you physically but they are after your actual consciousness. They want the consciousness of a being who can tune into this higher frequency. What happens when you succeed in extinguishing all of your light and you convert it to something else? When you look at them closely, it's a very frightening thing. They'll tell you that you don't understand them. They want you to study more so you get deeper within their control.

If you want to discern what they are, feel them in your chest intelligence. You don't have to be a genius. Feel it. Then you will know. They're everywhere now, fighting to get into more places.

I don't believe in going out to convert people or convince them our way is the best. That's their path, so we will not obstruct it. It's not our way. If they ask, we'll answer them. If they want to know something, we'll share with them. That's our way. Remember, I'm focusing on **one particular organization**. There's a lot of information you don't know about them. We speak about them vaguely because it's necessary.

One of their doctrines, 'fair game,' is a very interesting read. In Ancient Rome, when you were an enemy of the State, it was every citizen's job to destroy that person if possible, at any given opportunity. Their policy was also called 'fair game.' If you look at the history of this organization and what it was built on, there's a lot of documented information.

At some point, there might be a dissection of me in retaliation. I'm not perfect. I've made mistakes. I am who I am and I'm glad to be who I am. It's the mistakes that I've made and the good things that I've done that have really made me who I am. Anyway, the knowledge and the teachings stand on their own. They are undeniable. Take it for what it is.

You've talked about the Darkside being a lower frequency, but now you're referring to it as anti-life. Could it be like a frequency inversion?

I refer to it in many ways because there's not one specific way to describe it. It's very broad. How do you describe a specific person? How do you nail down what they're all about? You really can't. So sometimes I use a word because, in my mind, I'm talking about them at work. Other times, I'm talking about their home life, how they paint, or play music.

It's hard to define something that is so complex, but you have that inner knowing. You know what I'm talking about. When you use human terminology to define something, you have to be careful. It's just something that can best be described in several different ways. I'll describe it from different directions, so sometimes it may seem contradictory but it's really not. Sometimes you have to almost sound contradictory because you're trying to simplify something so that people can easily understand. When you do that, you weaken the representation of what you're trying to communicate.

If a dark presence approaches a being of love with its intent being evil, will there be any change in the dark presence?

It's free choice. If they choose to be that way, it's their choice. Impact them with love, and they will change in time. As Light, we have a way. If it comes down to a dominant energy, just project that love energy out.

If we plant a seed in a stone, what's going to happen to that stone? We live in a world of instant gratification. Everybody wants instant results. Be patient.

What happens when you put an ice cube on a counter? When you try to get the ice cube, it keeps sliding away from you. *As long as you have that vibe, the Darkside can't nail you.* That's the best way to describe it. If you forget about it or if you get lost, things can happen. Don't ever forget that. **When you feel a heavy opposition, just meditate.** It's like Kung Fu. It literally rolls right off of you. Just sit down and call on that place. You will be a lantern in the darkness and cut right through it. It's that simple. There are things in life that you have to reflect on.

The Darkside doesn't want to draw attention to itself. Neither do these particular people. Don't expect to just run into them. They blend in as well as you do. You know what you are. You know what you serve. They do too, but they call it a different kind of good. If you were to compare, an apple is still a fruit but very different from an orange. Yet there are still similarities between the two. They are just presented in a certain way.

You have to be careful of what you're lured into. When I moved to Arizona a long time ago, there were a lot of orange trees. The oranges looked really juicy and sweet. If you know anything about Arizona oranges, they're not sweet! Being from the East coast, I hadn't seen a lot of oranges yet, so I plucked one off the tree, opened it and started chewing it. It had the most horrendous taste. I couldn't believe something that looked so great had such a bitter taste! They look pretty but they're really just for decoration. Once you sample it, it's a little too late. No matter how bad things seem to get, or how off-track you might feel, you can still spit it out. *Just endure it and it too will pass.*

Don't think you have to constantly look over your shoulder. *The Handbook of the Navigator,* doesn't spell it out but it alludes to it. Like most spiritual teachers, I try to skirt around this issue because I don't want to incite a riot or any kind of violence. Using metaphors, I have to share this insight. *They* don't want to bring attention to themselves. *They're* not going to come out and look for you, but if you're going to look for them, you're going to run into them.

It's the same thing with me and spiritual matters. When I talk about ghosts or spirits, some people roll their eyes and ask how one person can have so many experiences with ghosts and other beings. Many years ago, I decided to join a paranormal group. I explored hundreds of houses, putting in a lot of time and energy. Most were dead ends, but there was always one pearl where something went down. After awhile, we figured things out and discerned the patterns. If you go out looking for trouble, you're going to find it. By now, you should have the tools and be able to handle anything that comes your way.

You should reflect on love and beauty. Harmonize your house and build your energy. If negative energy hits you, dice it up. You have the tools. Live your life as a human being. Be happy, be healthy, love the people in your life, and let them love you in return. ***Forgive, forgive, and then forgive again.*** Hanging on to resentment doesn't do any good. But don't let them harm you. Don't have so much forgiveness that you end up getting hurt yourself, but don't hang on to it either.

When you try to get your physical life in order, also work on your spiritual life. That's what will give you the permanent peace, the inner healing that medicine cannot provide. It will complete you, build you, and connect you. When you need that extra little something, to know God and to really feel something, manifest it.

Forget about manifesting money. Forget about manifesting a house or a lover. *Manifest God to give you a profound experience!* Then you will be satisfied. There's nothing wrong with that. Most people are unsatisfied in that one particular context. You want to be satisfied but if you know it's not an ego thing, then it's not. Religions tell you to have faith. They say that you shouldn't ask for something, but that is how religion controls people.

God wants you to find God. That's why you have a brain, instinct, and this inner-feeling. God is laying it all out for you, but God is not going to force you to take it.

One day when I was a little kid sitting on a stone on a cloudy day, I told the Universe that I wasn't going to do anymore spiritual things because I didn't know if they were good or bad. Some religious people told me that I didn't know the difference between God and the Devil. I couldn't tell the difference. I love God so much that I decided that was it!

I used to make up songs because I didn't know any real songs. I was always very much in love with God, the Universe, and spirituality. So on a rainy day, I sang a little song, "If I was an angel I'd fly in the sky." I walked out and sat on the stone, saying, "I'm not asking you for any signs because I know I'm not supposed to. So, this is the deal: I'm not going to do any more psychic work or any more healing. I'm not going to do any of it, because I don't know how to tell the difference. Some people are telling me that some of it is good and some is from the other side. I don't know so this really puts me in a bad position. Unless you give me a sign, I'm not going to do any of it! If you give me a sign, I'll know you are serious!" And then, I felt like I gave God an ultimatum, so I felt bad.

Suddenly, the clouds opened up and just like in the religious stories, the sun beamed down. Just like in the pictures of the holy person in the valley, the golden sun shown down on me. Everything began to hum internally - not in my ears - every single cell of my body was humming, just like I've experienced in my meditations later on. It didn't say to me, *"This is God."* It said to me, *emotionally*, "You are One with Me! You are doing my will. Do my will."

All right, that's it. I'm not a preacher. I'm not a holy man and I don't want to profess that I'm an enlightened being. I'm just doing what it is that I do. This is what I feel that I need to do. At that point, I surrendered to God. Then the clouds rolled back together. The rain started trickling down, but I was perfectly dry. It seemed to last just a few seconds. I'm sure the memories of a child are a little different from what I may perceive now, but that's exactly what happened. I've never questioned it since. I know when I'm doing well and when I'm not. So, I'm *not* just going to surrender my light and assume there is a greater evil that makes me do something bad. If the greater evil tries to convince me to make someone ill – I will recognize its source. I work for The Force – for God. That is all I need to know!

I'm **not** going to harm somebody purposely and willfully. I know right from wrong; we all do. That's the basics of all that you need to know. Don't waste your time worrying about some hoofed, horned being. With seven billion people to work on, do you think it has nothing better to do with its time than to mess around with everybody's life? There is a Darkside and it operates a bit differently, but it does exist.

Is faith necessary to have an experience like that?

You don't need faith to feel warm and fuzzy. I've had dozens of those kinds of experiences. Everything that I've given you will help to give you that feeling. Your experiences will be different, yet profound; but you have to take it up a notch and manifest it. Don't ask for it. *Wish for it!* Say, "I'm not demanding it. I'm wishing for it. And I'll wait." *When you're satisfied, that is the true moment that it actually happens.*

Although you think you're not really asking, internally you are. You need to have the mechanisms already built to open that doorway. You've got to work on this. You don't have to be a psychic, telepath, or telekinetic. You just need to have the fundamentals because, when it begins to happen, your sixth sense will kick in. Your other senses might be telling you it isn't there, but it is. Remember not to fight it. You have the training to understand this. That's when it can happen. That's when it *does* happen.

One of my students talked about a particular experience he had one day. He was going to give up everything so he could focus and train for this. Of course, the Universe opened up to him. That doesn't mean he was ready for it. You have to be psychologically prepared for the profound thing you ask for. Who knows if it hasn't already been on your doorstep but you panicked. Maybe you put it out of your head or maybe you wish you had stayed when that experience was happening. It's all a matter of intellect and being able to understand what you are experiencing that allows you to have an experience. *Don't analyze the experience when it's happening.* Do that later. The more you understand, the more you are prepared for, and the more you can allow the experience to happen.

Unless you are looking for the Darkside, don't worry about it! Work on your spirituality, but don't get caught up in this battle. If the moment comes, you're going to know what to do. Don't sit around every day wondering if this is the moment that you need to act. Don't obsess over it. Enjoy life. You're here for a reason. Smell the flowers; feel the grass. Eat the sour oranges for the experience, but enjoy life. Revel in it!

Meditate, find this other dimension and begin to explore it. Prepare yourself for when you leave this physical world. You've been trained and have the tools and skills now; like the basketball players, the knowledge will become useful to you when you need it most. You're going to be like a fish dropped into the water. You'll understand what you need to do.

It's more difficult to grasp this concept while in a physical body. Don't worry about that. When there are spiritual conflicts or psychic wars, you see it as good versus evil. It is just symbolism so that you can understand it. This helps you to visualize as a human being what you are seeing. There are dimensional frequencies, the Do, Re, Mi, so to speak. There is also a frequency that cuts through this level. When you meditate, you shoot past it, straight through to Re. You already know this frequency.

There are other dimensional spaces. Those people who are spiritually developed in a certain way can go there. It's beautiful. I saw it at sunset the other day, contrasted by the gray and the mountains. In between, it had an orangey-yellow color, like peaches. This is what that dimension looks like if I had to describe it as a color. It's like giving texture to humanity's eyes to see dimensional frequency. It's a large expanse of static energy. *If you were to move through this dimension from here to there, you would fold time.* Sometimes this is where the skirmishes happen. While we are cruising, they are moving through, too. It's like a consciousness. There are points where one can absorb this energy and use it to dominate the collective. To do this, you need a lot of people working on it. It's somewhat like rain, but it's a frequency that comes out of that dimension and enters the Gaia mind.

In this frequency place, the beings who have a lot of control can amplify louder. It's like dialing up the volume on a stereo. Some of them can plug into an amplifier that boosts the signal that is being broadcast. These trained individuals learn to be very strong broadcasters. So, in this particular arena, there are beings that have a little bit more say over what's going on.

It's very similar to the planet as a living organism. There are other beings that are able to permeate and broadcast there. With your body physically in one place, you can move into this other frequency. So, in a way you are not here at all. You are in this other place.

You can communicate through emotion very rapidly. When you encounter a heavy wave or a negative charge moving this way, identify who is behind it and then move it back like you did with the water. You can move it back, suppress it, or confront it directly. It's like fighting with static energy.

Think of Kirlian photography on the human aura. If a finger is physically missing from a hand, you can see the missing finger as phantom energy as if it were still there. Kirlian photography shows all sorts of interesting things with leaves and light sources. When two people put their fingers together, the energy from one finger fights with the energy from the other finger. If two people sit together, their energy blends and becomes one. It becomes this beautiful pink violet hue.

So it's like that. When you meet another conscious being in this place of frequency, either you're excited and happy or you feel resistance towards each other. If the other being is trying to dominate, you will feel it, so you have to push back. It's like a little kid who is out of control and you're trying to calm him down. When the other being is dominated by a vast amount of consciousness, it's pushed back. There are always the few who are able to manipulate the whole of that frequency place. It's like raining over an area; it affects everyone's mood. *This is what spurs different kinds of consciousness like a unified movement of thought.*

Not everyone knows this, but I've had a variety of jobs just like everyone else. At one point, I was a telemarketer. I was always very good at it. The computer would set us up with different areas to call so we'd all work on the same town simultaneously. That's how they kept track of what areas we were working on.

One time, someone in the office noticed a particular pattern in one of the areas. He complained about it and did not want to call there anymore. None of the customers wanted to buy anything. Everyone in the office had the same attitude. So, our supervisor gave in and moved everyone to a different call area. Even though we didn't change a thing, the people from the new area bought things all day long. Nobody knew that the other area was doing miserably until someone noticed and mentioned it.

How does all that relate to the global consciousness shift that you mentioned earlier?

I figured a few things out through those experiences. Consciousness is always moving in certain ways, and when you call to test it, you can see the commonality of that reaction. There are many layers of complexities like this that affect all of us. We are all in this matrix. We're all asleep, all functioning, just doing, and not really staying awake. As you're reading this, you're fighting to awaken, to be conscious.

We don't want the Darkside to dominate. There's lots of havoc coming from Red Cells to deal with, so we're going to protect them while they are sleeping. By awakening and making enough of the Red Cells consciously aware, they won't be manipulated so easily. By having a lot of White Cells doing this, we can maintain a high enough frequency, and all of the planet's consciousness can evolve to a higher frequency with a waking state of mind. Who is pulling the strings? Who is manipulating the consciousness and in what direction is it going?

I have many good things to say about Buddhists, Christians, and Hindus. All of them are contributing greatly in a positive way, yet even the best organizations can be infiltrated. Key positions can be penetrated and the influence filters down through the organization. For the most part, they're praying. That is a positive affirmation. If you do Buddhist chants, you're emanating a higher, more positive frequency. There are other energies out there, but the Darkside, like anything else, has learned to mimic the Force. It can adapt to the situation and attempt new ways to overcome it.

So it mimics and does similar things, getting more complicated and challenging. It's trying to achieve its goals just like the Force.

Does the Darkside only affect this physical dimension or can it also affect higher dimensions?

There was a time when it really wasn't able to enter the higher frequencies. It did not have the technology or the ability. So it worked on a more organic level, manipulating politically. Of course, it had its own frequency, but it wasn't in a good enough position to affect the consciousness of the planet. So it worked differently.

In the last two hundred years, the Darkside has adapted and learned enough that it now has a foothold in this higher frequency. There are now beings, in a dark school, which are being educated and becoming skilled enough to be able to reach the higher frequencies. This has created a whole new set of problems. We are living in a key time when something still may or may not go down. This is what makes things critical but, for the most part, the Darkside lacks the ability. Only the very strongest of them are able to really enter a higher frequency.

"They" are finding other ways to integrate, mimic, take the science, and refine it. So there is a very complex integration going on. It's very difficult to see the layers. I always feel like a researcher who has to count all of the little DNA strains to find the differences.

So, at this point we've had to deal with the Darkside on more of a psychic level. In my opinion, the psychic level is still very organic. Telepathy and moving energy fields are not necessarily a higher spiritual frequency. They are still organic like your five senses. It's just the closest bridge to this realm. This is what you are using to develop abilities to advance to that higher level. The Darkside is also working on mastering these abilities. This leads to psychic wars, where they're pitting their mind against yours or pushing certain barriers.

When it comes to moving into this higher frequency, they can't necessarily do it, because that frequency is made of the fabric of God! It is also the material that is inside of us. *We just turn it inside out and pop into this greater place where we like to be.*

The Darkside isn't able to pop into that inner-dimension. If they attempt it, they end up in a Darkside place. It's that other mimicking frequency, but there is nothing there; it's lifeless. They are working very hard to get up into those higher frequencies. These are the things you have to take into consideration, keeping in mind that the Darkside will adapt. They are recruiting White Cells because of our abilities, potential, and the design of our being. If they were to look inside our physical bodies, they would probably not find a difference between us and them but, harmonically, there is a difference. It's like a genetic advancement. It's very complex.

How does the Darkside find us if we don't go out looking for it?

When you come across a darker being, it makes itself present to you for several reasons. You might think that you weren't out looking for it, but you have become a light in the darkness, dimensionally. Imagine a big pool with fish swimming around in it. The pool is made up of an energy field and you're shining like a beacon of light. You appear very different to them because of this sparkling energy radiating from you, so they come over to investigate it. They're either going to manifest into this dimension in an energy form to check you out or remain as a static energy.

So if you feel negative energy, it's not necessarily an evil entity. It's curious about you. When people don't know what the negative energy is the first thing they usually feel is fear. So they react to it in that way. That's probably a good precaution because if it is something bad, it's probably not a good idea to go up to it, pet it, and say, "Nice kitty." So have a little apprehension, but don't let it overwhelm you. Don't let it take control of you. Most of the time, it's not even anything negative. Sometimes, people will tell me that it was a bad spirit and they saw red eyes. There was likely a presence there, but you probably filled in a lot of the details based on your fear.

Remove the Babbler. Remove the fear. Let your mind glide. Make your good presence known to it. Ask it to come to you with what it wants. If you think something negative is looking for you, just think about your heart chakra. It is a pure resounding of the God frequency. It's like a laser beam to a piece of paper. Anything negative is going to move out of there super-fast. Think about moving to that heart chakra spot because the second you think about it, you already did it. You've already changed your frequency just by thinking about it. It's a safety valve. That's how quickly it happens. If you're thinking that I'm telling you all of this to make you feel a little better, go ahead and try it.

You have complete control when it comes to the energy. If a person kicks your door in and you hear them marching up the stairs, go for a weapon or escape out the window instead of going for your heart chakra. That's common sense. There is a difference. You'll know the difference. You'll feel it instantly. It's that fast. You just have to be sensitive enough to get it. Then you can react to whatever your Navigator is telling you. *Don't listen to your brain because it will always screw things up.*

We often have skirmishes when we enter the higher realms. Some of you have already dipped in and are now wondering how you can get back. *Stop thinking about how you got there and you'll get there.* It comes down to a duel of which emotional programming is going to dominate. They're going to put this dark energy around you. It's trying to encompass you, seduce you, and hold you in, hoping you'll eventually give in. Instead, lift this frequency. Think about the most beautiful thing you can imagine in your heart center. Take a breath, and as you breathe, feel you are like a blowfish, and blow out the air. Then come down and breathe again. Light up the whole city! Don't put a limit on it. Say, "Do you really want me? Try this out!" That's it!

The only thing that can defeat you is fear itself – the fear of failure. Never doubt how much light you have in you. There is an *ocean.* It's beyond comprehension! There is a doorway that you're holding right in your chest center. You can feel it! You know it's there: that little minor pressure, that sensory spot. As soon as I talk about it, your inner knowing understands what I am talking about. You will know when the time comes. Your absolute inner truth knows it.

How will we know when to radiate this light energy?

When that moment comes and you really need to call on it, you'll open it. Nothing can stand up to it, except maybe a nuclear blast. Regardless, you'll walk right through it if you have the right frequency. It's as if it doesn't even exist, but if you aren't at the right frequency, you're going to be gone.

When you encounter different levels, there will be negative people. Very quickly, cut the negative energy. It's that simple. If you feel lousy, investigate why you feel that way? Should you be ignoring that? You know that something isn't quite right. Sit down; use your tools; use your sword to cut it away. Or do some breathing and burn it all off like cobwebs being thrown on a fire. Literally, you'll know that it's gone! It's an inner knowing.

If you feel it again the next day, go with a system of super blades. *Program it to spin any time that energy approaches you.* In essence, you're programming your subconscious and setting up an automated defense mechanism. Just like you can program a pillow with bad energy, you can set up your natural sensory with a defense that sets off a red flag. Before you can even think about it, your subconscious blocks it. Like a software program that filters out certain words, it scans for negative energy and filters it out.

You are programming your energy field. The only difference is you're intentionally setting standards. So when you feel the bad energy, mark it. You know the bad energy. You can sense and recognize it. Clear it out whenever it comes in. You have full control of whatever energy comes near you. Nobody can master that energy, not even me. It's a choice you make. Your energy can simply stop it, if you choose.

When you're dealing with negative energy, that's how you do it. You simply set up a program to block it. Acknowledge it; affirm it; feel it for a second. It's almost like picking up a hand grenade. You know what it can do even if the pin is still in it. Don't pick it up; just look at it. Acknowledge it so that when you see it again, you know its destructive potential . If you don't acknowledge it, you're going have a problem.

When most spiritual people have a confrontation, they don't know what it is. Feel it; sense it; it's that weird, achy feeling. Where did it come from and what caused it? A tree has a feeling; water has a feeling. It's a specific frequency. Know that's what it is. It doesn't have to be something; it doesn't have to be a person; it doesn't have to be a structure. Don't worry about it. Analyze it later.

If you think you have to meditate to put a lot of positive energy out because this is a critical time, don't panic. *It will never be the end of the world because we will live forever.* This is just one phase. How many life crises have you thought you were never going to be able to get through? Those are in the past now. You're going to be hit with the next crisis whether you are ready or not. Life is like that. Right now, we are dealing with the moment.

So, when you meditate, go into that zone. Follow your system. Every time you meditate, you're broadcasting a light out. You are going up for a breath of air and coming back down. Whether you realize it or not, my meditation system is multi-faceted. It serves many purposes, and as you start to figure that out, it'll make more sense. *You're putting out a proper frequency and you're donating it to the Gaia consciousness.* You are contributing but you are also receiving. It's very important to receive and give. It's good because it's building you and that means a contribution to itself because of what you can now do with it as you're projecting it back out.

When you enter these higher dimensional frequencies, emanate from your chest center. Think about how much you love God and how much you love the Universe. Think about that absolute undying devotion you have for the Force. It is *profound*; it's deep in you. Let it come forward! At that very moment, express the very thing you feel for God! It will move the world. It really doesn't matter what else is out there.

All I ask is that you express that deep feeling that you have for the Force. Just say, "This is how I feel," and let it out. That's all you have to do. It's that simple. *If your life ever gets so bad that you're in a really dark place, don't think about how the Universe can help you. Think about how you can help the Universe.* Just simply open it and give it! That's it. It's that simple! The rest is in the teachings. The rest is all of these other micro levels, all the training. Work with that, and apply it. That's the bottom line. You feel it so open it! If you ask how the door opens, I just told you. You just felt it. That's how you open it. Sit, go into a meditation and just say, "I'm going to open it. I just need you to know." Then open it.

CONTINUE YOUR JOURNEY

THANK YOU FOR joining me on this journey. My hope is that you take what you have learned, apply it, and watch your life transform as your spirituality flourishes. The light of knowledge is vital on your journey, but you must apply it. That is why I am giving you additional tools, you can download for free, to assist you in putting the methods you have discovered here into practice.

Before you do that, there is one thing I would ask of you: leave a short, honest review at Amazon.com.

Higher Balance is a dedicated, grass-roots organization. We rely on the power of people to help spread this knowledge. Assist others out there searching, like you, find this book.

ADD TO YOUR EXPERIENCE
READERS ONLY FREE MATERIAL

As a reader you receive special reader-only bonus material you can download for free. You will get new tools and knowledge to enhance all the practices found in the book.

Receive:

Babbler Beater: Eliminating 'Brain Babble' is one of the most important aspects of any meditation. It is the deciding factor to whether you experience hyper-dimensional states of consciousness or simply relax. This sound tool was designed to eliminate babble and assist in training the techniques in this book.

Energy Movements: Apply the techniques on energy movements with ease with simple, instructional videos featuring Eric Pepin. There are 3 videos, which show you how to begin enhancing your sensory and amplifying your field of personal energy.

Higher Balance Method: An entire 3 part, 2 hour, special course led by Eric Pepin on beginner and advanced practices for the meditation technique taught in this book. Called the Higher Balance Method, this extra course gives you entirely new information that continues where *Waking the Immortal Within* leaves off.

Go to *www.wakingtheimmortalwithin.com/readers-only*

Other Books by Eric Pepin

Intro: The Handbook of the Navigator: *What is God, the Psychic Connection to Spiritual Awakening, and the Conscious Universe*

1: Meditation within Eternity: *The Modern Mystics Guide to Gaining Unlimited Spiritual Energy, Accessing Higher Consciousness and Meditation Techniques for Spiritual Growth*

2: Igniting the Sixth Sense: *The Lost Human Sensory that Holds the Key to Spiritual Awakening and Unlocking the Power of the Universe*

3: Silent Awakening: *True Telepathy, Effective Energy Healing and the Journey to Infinite Awareness*

4: Waking the Immortal Within: *Develop your Spiritual Presence, Awaken the Inner Master and Explore Hidden Realities*

5: Coming Soon Summer 2014

6: Coming Soon Fall 2014

7: Coming Soon Winter 2014

Books by Higher Balance

Bending God: A Memoir

To discover more techniques and knowledge from Eric Pepin, and to experience awakening yourself beyond what is discussed in this book, visit:

www.higherbalance.com/experience

APPENDIX – GLOSSARY OF TERMS

Akashic Records
The *Akashic Records* is a term for the dimensional data of the Gaia Mind (see *Gaia*). It is an energy vibration that contains a record of any and all planetary events, actions, thoughts, and feelings that have ever occurred or will ever occur in the future. These records can extend beyond the planet into all universal experience since the beginning of time, and are stored permanently in an energy substance named "Akasha."

Astral Projection
An "out-of-body experience" often occurring during sleep or a meditative state during which the ethereal or astral energy field of the body separates from the physical body and travels over great distances to other locations. It is a process that sends conscious energy out from the physical body to collect information to bring back for experience.

Awakening
The phrase used to describe the transformation or process of becoming conscious from a prior state of unconsciousness, or unawareness. A dynamic of discovery during spiritual development. To wake from sleep. (see: *Enlightenment*.)

Babbler, The
A term to define repetitious, involuntary thoughts pervading through the mind. Uncontrolled babbling will naturally occur as a result of never learning how to manage the rational thinking process while growing into adulthood. It is also referred to as "Mind-Chatter."

Biochemistry
A term that summarizes the "chemical" functions of any "biological" organism. For example, this term would include human brain chemicals such as Serotonin, Dopamine, Acetylcholine, Phenylethylamine and others that directly relate to states of awareness.

Calibration
A word to explain the conscious or unconscious adjustments or optimizations that take place in one's energy, mind, or physicality. These different energy calibrations are often very subtle and not noticed; they occur all the time as a person adjusts to experiences in life. They are most often felt during meditation or clear states of consciousness.

Chakra
A name for the intersection areas of energy meridians (or electrical pathways) in the body. There are seven primary chakras along the spine. They extend from the tip of the tailbone to the crown of head. These seven are located (from the bottom up) in the rectal area, near the genitals, behind the navel or solar plexus, at the heart, at the neck, between the eyebrows, and on the crown of the head. Each chakra corresponds to certain states of consciousness, emotions, body organs, nerve networks, colors, and energies. There are over 2000 of these energy centers or intersections of this energy in the human body.

Collective Consciousness

As humans serve as the planet's central nervous system, the collective consciousness is a term for the planet's mind state. It is the planetary energy field of humanity's entire evolutionary experiences and expressions. This mind-field or collective consciousness is enriched as humanity develops, whether the development is in language, art, music, technologies, cities, spiritual awakening, or any other area of endeavor. As this consciousness evolves, each succeeding generation of conscious individuals will inherit and be influenced by this collective consciousness as well as add their own experiences to it.

Crystallize

Although this term is also used in its basic form, crystallizing is when one's modes of thinking are set into somewhat permanent patterns. The calcification of the pineal gland is a major contributor to this event causing spiritual inflexibility. Although the age of this biological and psychological event varies for each person, the average age is said to be twenty eight. During late stages of life, one commonly experiences a relaxing of these modes around the age of the late fifties.

Darkside, The

A term commonly used in the movie trilogy "Star Wars" to describe a destructive energy in the universe that destroys any manifestation or potential of creation.

Dimension

One of the countless realms of reality or space. Alternate dimensions of reality can be experienced in degrees, from subtle to total immersion. There are countless dimensions of reality. These concepts are now being used in modern physics to develop theories of reality, such as String Theory. The term referenced by Eric is usually one of parallel dimensions where entities exist.

Doe (or Do)

'Doe' is the first and lowest tone of the diatonic scale. This term is used to define the primary vibratory state of the planet's consciousness. Spiritual states of existence are much higher in tonal. The "Doe" signifies a vibratory state that is limited to the immediate physical dimension which does not recognize higher energy frequencies. Within the 'Doe' state, immediate desires of the body outweigh the subtle urge for spiritual awakening. It is sometimes termed 'Doe.'

Elongation

When entering deep states of meditation, an individual may feel as if their physical body is expanding upwards or outwards. It is actually an initial spontaneous movement of subtle energies of the body and often leads to "projections" of many types. The most common, Astral Elongation, is a result of specific energy frequencies being stimulated, through practicing non-thought, that link the physical body to its subtle energy bodies.

Empathy

The ability where one can tune into another person's feelings or emotions and then experience them as if they were one's own. This is experienced primarily through the heart chakra, although the understanding of the feeling would be enhanced by bringing the mind chakra into play. Empathy without understanding would be of limited value.

Energy
A term that refers to the simplest essence, condition, or state in all things. A dynamic and flexible word that can be used to express the relativity, vitality, and intensity of anything that exists.

Enlightenment
A higher state of consciousness in which a person transcends beyond his or her ego, and becomes aware of his or her divinity; a state where a person is one, or whose consciousness is existing near or at the frequency of the Multidimensional Universe or God.

Entity
A term that defines any living thing in existence. It is also used to describe a spirit normally assumed (often wrongly) to be that of a dead person. Sometimes in reference to a spirit or a being from another dimension.

E.S.P.
An acronym for Extra Sensory Perception. Not only does it define the state in which all five body senses deliver a greater amount of information for the brain, it also encompasses 'paranormal' or psychic abilities such as: telepathy, precognition, psychometry, photometry, telekinesis, psychokinesis, projections, clairaudience and clairvoyance.

Expansion Modules
In-depth audio courses which offer specialized techniques and advanced information on specific areas of interest not covered in The Foundation Set from Eric Pepin's book "Meditation Within Eternity." If the Foundation Set creates the core of development, Expansion Modules just add onto or expand that core. These can be accessed at: *http://www.higherbalance.com/products/*

Force, The
A term and concept for the positive life enriching conscious energy of the Universe. It is commonly used in the "Star Wars" movies to describe the life energy of the universe which binds any manifestation of matter together.

Frequency
A term used for the property or condition of an occurrence taking place at frequent intervals. Any form of existence has a range of frequency in order for it to exist. Frequency is a form of energy.

Gaia
(Greek - Goddess of the Earth) The Gaia Hypothesis, formulated by James Lovelock, states that all living matter on the Earth contributes to a single living macrocosmic organism. Retrospectively in the system of a living earth, the collective consciousness of humanity would be considered the central nervous system.

Governor
An unconscious pattern and function of the brain that binds a person's awareness to the physical world. It is a specific vibratory state which subsequently contributes to the rejection of all things that are not normal or that have yet to be discovered. (see: *Doe*)

Grid, The
An invisible planetary energy web that interconnects all living things. If one can plug into this grid, they will have access to planetary collective experiences existing in higher dimensional vibrations. (see: *Akashik Records*)

I's, The
The alternate personalities, roles, or egos within a person. A product of unconscious functioning, these I's unconsciously assist a person in coping with the environment.

In-Between, The
To be consciously shifted. There is a place between matter and energy where one can exist and be aware of both simultaneously. Not simply to be aware of yourself but to be in a special state of consciousness.

Innerverse
The inner universe of the human body. Like the world of intelligent life that we experience, there are also intelligent life forms within our bodies; experiencing within their own universe.

Intent
Something that is intended consciously or unconsciously; an aim or purpose. Intent precedes any choice or course of action.

Kirlian Photography
A photographic process using a high voltage, low amperage field of 50,000 volts or more. This process was invented by Semyon and Valentina Kirlian. It captures the radiation around objects and humans which is not visible to the naked eye. It is often used to photograph the energy field (Aura) that surrounds the human body and the energy transmissions when different forms of organic life cross each other.

Kundalini

The elemental energy of the human body which, like a serpent, rests coiled at the base of the spine. Everyone uses Kundalini energy or power to maintain consciousness, but it very seldom rises up the central spinal channel beyond the first chakra center (the groin chakra). The Foundation meditation practice can be used to ascend to and activate the higher chakra centers.

Lotus, Full

This traditional body position provides a solid base for the practice of meditation and Prana breathing exercises. The spine is erect; the legs are crossed over one another; and the flow of blood to the legs is constricted and redirected to the internal organs. Traditionally the posture is a reminder to emulate the lotus plant, with its roots in the earth and its face reaching towards the sunlight. It is also the basis of many other yogic postures.

Lotus, Half

This seated meditation posture is almost identical to the Full Lotus position stated above. However, with the half-lotus, one foot rests on top of the opposite thigh with the sole pointing upwards, while the other foot rests on the floor, as in the common Indian position. (see: *the meditation map provided with the Foundation Set in "Meditation Within Eternity."*)

Matrix

The Matrix is a term or allegory that dramatically conveys the view that ordinary appearances do not depict true reality and that gaining the truth transforms one's life. The Matrix is the sensational world that traps one into believing that nothing outside the five senses even exists. The matrix is also a term for the apparent fabric of the reality in this dimension.

MDC
Multi-Dimensional Consciousness. (see: *Consciousness*)

Metronome
A device used to mark time by using regularly recurring ticking sounds or flashes at adjustable intervals. An effective tool for inducing states of deep trance or hypnosis.

Micro-Macro
A term to reference zooming from micro (the very small) to macro (the very large).

Middle Pillar
A term in reference to the deepest core of one's consciousness that is completely interconnected with the universe and all manifestations of life: It is the ultimate Self without a notion of ego separation.

Mindfulness
Discipline in which the mind reflects is focused on a single point of reference. The state of attention or reflection of the mind's activities. The trait of staying aware. Using desired thought.

Navigator
The subtle urge everyone has in them that drives them to evolve and seek out the experiences of life to the fullest extent. It is an intuitive mechanism of the causal spirit used to perpetuate and direct the will of the Force.

OBE
An acronym for Out-of-Body Experience. An experience (similar to Astral Projection) which occurs when the astral body or etheric body leaves the physical body while the individual is in meditation, at rest, asleep, near death, or temporarily dead.

Paranormal
Beyond normal. Beyond the range of normal experience or scientific explanation. Beyond or above normal human ability or senses. (see *E.S.P.*)

Parapsychology
The study of E.S.P. and any other sort of psychic phenomena. Dates back to the foundation of the English Society of Physical Research in 1882 and continued through laboratory research at Duke University Parapsychology Laboratory, Stanford Research Institute and elsewhere.

Pineal Gland
A small endocrine gland in the brain; situated beneath the back part of the corpus callosum; secretes melatonin; realized by many to be 'the seat of the soul.'

Planes of Light
A blissful vibratory state usually attained after maintaining deep prolonged focus during meditation and consistent Prana circulation. Perceived as an all-encompassing brilliant illumination that internally and externally surrounds the meditator.

Prana
This is originally a yogic term for cosmic energy or the evolving life force of the Universe. Prana is thought to

flow through the body, enriching and aligning health and vitality. It is considered the vital link between spiritual dimensions and material dimensions. Harnessing this energy through meditation enables people to accelerate the development of psychic states and the ability to perform miracles.

Psychokinesis

The power of mind over matter without the use of physical or sensory means. Together with ESP, psychokinesis (PK) includes telekinesis (the paranormal movement of objects); levitation and materialization; mysterious events associated with given people or houses, hauntings, and psychic healing. Since the 1930s, PK has been a major research interest among parapsychologists, especially in the United States and Russia.

Psychometry

The ability to gather information or impressions that are hidden to ordinary sensory perception from a physical object. The vibratory information and impressions could be the history of the object and its history of people and events associated to it. The term was coined in the mid-nineteenth century by an American physiologist named Joseph R. Buchanan.

Red Cell

A person who lives according to the natural purpose of Gaia and the vibration of the 'Doe' and is unconscious of the urge to pursue their full spiritual potential.

Samadhi

Samadhi means being in the state of undifferentiated being. It is a state of consciousness whereby one realizes the oneness of self while other I's are put aside. Eric's reference of Samadhi is one of an ecstatic state of bliss.

Scan
A technique of psychically receiving information from, but not limited to, a person, place, or thing.

Siddhartha
Siddhartha Gautama, known as the Buddha, was born in the sixth century B.C. as a son of a chief in what is now modern Nepal. Siddhartha left a life of wealth and submitted himself to rigorous ascetic practices. Not fully satisfied, he discovered a path of balance rather than extremism. He called this The Middle Way. Buddha attained enlightenment, thus earning the title Buddha, or "Enlightened One." Buddha preached the Dharma in an effort to help others reach enlightenment.

Sixth Sense
The Sixth Sense is the ordinary term for the faculties of Extra Sensory Perception. (see *E.S.P.*) The Sixth Sense is the ability to receive or send information beyond the realm of the five senses of sight, sound, taste, touch, or smell. The term was coined by German researcher Dr. Rudolf Tischner whose book "Telepathy and Clairvoyance" was written in German in 1920 and published in English in 1925. The first serious paranormal research was done by Dr. J.B. Rhine, Professor of Parapsychology at Duke University, North Carolina.

Shangri-La
A mythical country allegedly located in the mountains of Tibet, created by James Hilton in his novel "Lost Horizon," in which he describes the perpetual youth and vigor of its residents.

Sleeper

Someone who lies dormant. One who has yet to awaken their Sixth Sense but can feel the impulses of their Navigator.

Soul

A term for the life energy of an individual; an energy body of the non-physical self. That part of the individual which survives death and lives on into the hereafter, before being reincarnated.

Super Being

A White Cell who has fully awakened and become a Super White Cell. (see: *White Cell.*)

Telekinesis

The ability to move physical objects by force of will or mental energy alone. (see:
Psychokinesis)

Third Eye

The Mind Chakra. The area approximately between the eyebrows, thought to utilize intuitive sense. Also believed to be the center of psychic vision.

Tones, The

The "Voice of God." A high pitched frequency usually heard on one side of the head – either the right or the left. Comes from within your consciousness. Focusing on it allows it to become louder and louder.

Tonal

This term refers to the vibratory degree of frequency that the energy of a
person, place or thing exists at. (see: *Frequency; Vibration*)

Vibration
A particular frequency or resonation of a thing or event in existence. Not necessarily specific to that person or entity. (see: *Frequency; Tonal*)

White Cell
One who lives their life according to the divine will and direction of the Force or Universe.

GET FIRST HAND EXPERIENCE

Higher Balance Institute is dedicated to giving you all the tools and knowledge you need to empower yourself and transform your life. The purpose and mission of the Institute is to awaken the world one mind at a time. Toward fulfilling that goal, we know that the greatest results come when you can experience something for yourself rather than just reading about it.

Visit *www.higherbalance.com/experience*
for retreats and programs.

Higher Balance Institute
515 NW Saltzman Road #726
Portland, OR 97229
+1-503-646-4000

www.higherbalance.com/experience

Sit vis vobiscum.